REAL LIFE Marriage: It's Not About Me

"Tim and Anne have given us a marvelous tool to help each of us in our marriages. Biblically based, frankly stated, and oh so relevant in today's world. It is a must read. Once you have read *REAL LIFE Marriage: It's Not About Me* you will want to share the insights with others."
Josh + Dottie McDowell
Campus Crusade for Christ

"I'm excited about this remarkable study that is destined to transform marriages in a way that glorifies God. *REAL LIFE Marriage: It's Not About Me* is exactly what every couple needs if they want their marriage to thrive and survive!"
Dr. Dick + Dee Eastman
President, Every Home for Christ

"We have always liked to learn from successful people! Our good friends Tim and Anne have produced this practical book out of years of successful marriage, counseling, and teaching. We highly recommend them, their Marriage Advance seminars, and especially this book.
Dr. C. Peter + Doris Wagner
President, Global Harvest Ministries

"Tim and Anne Evans effectively communicate thirty-plus years of real life experience and godly wisdom in their writing. Through a balance of candid observations and humor, *REAL LIFE Marriage: It's Not About Me* helps husbands and wives find a fresh perspective on sensitive topics surrounding marriage and gives hope to couples in crisis. In their honest and direct style the Evanses share practical ways for couples to become one in Spirit, Soul, and Body. They identify the counterfeits and focus on the truth of God's plan for a successful marriage. I'm honored to serve as their pastor, and recommend Tim and Anne Evans and REAL LIFE Ministries to you."
Brady + Pam Boyd
Senior pastor, New Life Church, Colorado Springs, Colorado

"*REAL LIFE Marriage: It's Not About Me* is simply the best book on marriage that we have ever read — period. We highly and enthusiastically endorse it."
Dr. Che + Sue Ahn
President, Harvest International Ministry, Pasadena, California

"Expressing their life work, Tim and Anne have gifted us with a desperately needed power tool for marriage transformation. It is biblical, penetrating, tenderhearted, and rich in real-life illustrations. Thanks for calling us to risk entering the LARGER STORY where God (not 'me') is the main character, empowering change and destiny. 'For such a time as this' cries out for this now book."
Dr. Chester + Betsy Kylstra
Restoring the Foundations Ministries

"By the time you read this book the definition of marriage in America may no longer be only between a man and a woman. The ancient covenant is under siege. Only a mighty return of the church to the glory of Eden's dream and the fulfillment of the book of Revelation can save a nation from a moral slide into the abyss of relational anarchy. Tim and Anne's remarkable lives and teachings could not have arrived at a more prophetic or pregnant moment. Read it, do it, and you will become a sign and a wonder."
Lou + Therese Engle
The Call, Kansas City, Missouri

"*REAL LIFE Marriage: It's Not About Me* has more wisdom and information packed into its pages than any one marriage may ever need. Anyone who knows Tim and Anne knows that this book is the fruit of a long and happy marriage; they are what it says a marriage should be. This book will nourish; use it and be fed."
Ben + Lauretta Patterson
Westmont College, Santa Barbara, California

"*REAL LIFE Marriage* is a must read for those who really want to be and stay married! Tim and Anne Evans are true followers of Jesus, and they have learned how to follow the Beloved in tandem! When the Lord said of Adam, 'It is not good that the man should be alone; I will make a helper fit for him,' I have a serious hunch Tim and Anne were in his mind. Read this book and live it, and your marriage will be better!"
Dr. Timothy + Nancy Brown
President, Western Theological Seminary, Holland, Michigan

"I have known Tim and Anne Evans for more than 25 years. They embody and exemplify what God intended marriage and family to be. The proof is seen in the health, strength, and joy of their relationship and the stability and security of their children. They understand God's truth concerning marriage in profound ways. They speak the truth with heart-piercing relevance under the anointing of the Holy Spirit. This combination of factors makes their content life and marriage altering."

Don Cousins
Author, Teacher, and Consultant

"The Evans have forged *REAL LIFE Marriage: It's Not About Me* not only from a deep commitment to make their own marriage God-honoring but also from years of work with couples. They challenge you to give your marriage a transfusion and allow God to touch you deeply through these pages full of practical and biblical wisdom."

Willy + Joan Wooten
LMFT, LCSW, Marriage and Family Therapist, Colorado Springs, Colorado

REAL LIFE **MARRIAGE**

it's not about me

REAL LIFE MARRIAGE

it's not about me

tim + anne evans

Spirit Oneness

+

Soul Oneness

+

Body Oneness

REAL LIFE
ministries

REAL LIFE Marriage: It's Not About Me
Published by REAL LIFE Ministries
For ordering information visit
www.RealLife.us.com
or e-mail
info@RealLife.us.com

The stories in this book are based on decades of ministry, counseling, and real-life experiences. Names and details regarding some individuals whose stories are told in this book have been changed to protect their privacy. Editorial liberties have been taken to combine certain stories and circumstances for the purpose of clarity and illustration.

ISBN 978-1-60725-306-8

Book design by fuel D   www.fuel-d.com

Printed in the United States of America
2009—First Edition

10 9 8 7 6 5 4 3 2 1

We dedicate this book to God, the Author of marriage

And to four groups of people:

+   To our children, grandchildren, and future generations.
    We pray each one of you is passionate about God and marriage.

+   To our Prayer Shield Team, who faithfully love, encourage, and
    pray for us.

+   To the men and women who have been spiritual fathers and mothers
    to us. Your spiritual DNA and fingerprints are all over this book.

+   To every person who reads this book and humbly puts its truths into
    practice.

ABOUT THE AUTHORS

Life is about story. Take a retired Chicago-suburban fire chief, a nurse, thirty-plus years of marriage, six adult children, four grandkids, one dog, and what do you have? The story of a Real Life marriage and family.

Tim + Anne's story began in the Chicago suburbs, where they were raised in large Irish-Catholic families. They were married at twenty-one and began attending a new church. In the context of a small group they heard a story about Jesus that sounded familiar. However, this time they connected to Jesus and His story in personal and life-giving ways. As newlyweds and new followers of Christ they grew in intimacy with God and in community with others. They joyfully served at Willow Creek Community Church for twenty years.

Since their life-changing encounter with Jesus, Tim + Anne's constant prayer has been to listen to God, reach agreement in unity, and step out in faith. This has resulted in a lifetime of adventures. One major faith step involved giving up the familiarity and comforts of living in their childhood hometown; leaving family, friends, and a great church; taking an early retirement from fire department and nursing professions; and moving to Holland, Michigan, to serve full time in a local church.

After five years in Western Michigan, God's next major invitation included selling their home and moving to an apartment in Pasadena, California, to help birth a leadership school for the emerging generation. God then invited them to move to Colorado Springs to serve alongside passionate followers of Christ. More recently, Tim + Anne quit their paid ministry jobs to follow their vision quest of encouraging men and women full time in all God has designed for marriage.

Viewing themselves as bridge-builders, Tim + Anne have gleaned wisdom from relationships with evangelical, charismatic, Catholic, and home church leaders. They do not focus on the "jots and tittles" of Greek and Hebrew but on biblical principles lived out in real life.

This real-life couple has had their mettle tested. Tim + Anne have experienced the marital hopes and heartaches of "two becoming one." They are parents, grandparents, and ordained ministers. Tim has a degree in fire science, and Anne is a licensed nurse. They both have master and doctor of practical ministry diplomas from Wagner Leadership Institute. They currently live in Colorado near the base of Pikes Peak.

Contents

FOREWORD

Years ago, when this young couple took my two-semester college course on Marriage and Family in the New Testament, I noticed the intensity of their involvement with the material being presented in class. They were visibly discovering biblical truth and internalizing it in ways that were personally meaningful to them and to their own relationship. At that time, I was far from suspecting that this classroom experience would provide the incentive for Tim and Anne to pursue their quest on their own so as to launch a whole ministry, of which this book has become the quintessential expression.

In a time of societal drift, when the validity and the viability of marriage are under cultural attack, this book makes distinctive contributions. Instead of defining marriage as just one of the institutions of society, the authors place it, more fundamentally, within the broad context of the nature of God, who is the original and eternal community of oneness. God, who is triune community, loves community and gives community in the form of His image. He creates two as community of oneness and commands them to fill the earth with more community.

This book vividly describes the shape that marriage takes when it conforms to God's creational intent for it. It is written with authenticity and enthusiasm. While its themes are grounded in Scripture, they are also steeped in the confirming evidence of lived-out experience. When so much confusion surrounds the theories and practices of marriage, even within Christian circles, this book provides an invaluable tool for individuals, couples, and groups to find their Scriptural bearings and receive real-life guidance for the proper conduct of the most fundamental of all relationships entrusted to humankind.

Dr. Gilbert Bilezikian

Cofounder of Willow Creek Community Church
Professor Emeritus, Wheaton College

Life Is About Story

Whether or Not You Realize It, Your Life Tells a Story

Whether or not you realize it, your life tells a story.

Each day your decisions, your encounters with other people, and your response to God help determine the story your life is telling.

Every person faces a daily choice of living in one of two stories: the **Larger Story** or the **smaller story**. In one, God is the main character; in the other, self is the main character. [1] Which story you choose to live in not only determines how you live your day but also how you approach your marriage relationship.

Will your story feature God in the starring role, or will you steal the scene for yourself? Will the next chapter include a love scene with your spouse, or will it reveal some conflict eating away at your intimacy?

Our challenge to you in the pages ahead is to step into the **Larger Story** with God as the main character by choosing this as your personal theme: "It's not about me." When you begin to walk that out, we believe your life and your marriage will advance to new dimensions of excitement, satisfaction, and joy.

Be forewarned: this book is not a fairy-tale fantasy about a never-ending honeymoon. Life is hard, and no marriage is without its challenges. We are living in a season of history where marriage, as God originally designed it, is under unprecedented attack. Men and women are lost in seas of tradition, confusion, secular humanism, and relativity. Open a newspaper, turn on the television, go online, or read a magazine. Examine the ways schools teach about marriage. Study the rulings of judges who attempt to redefine it. Soberly evaluate how Hollywood portrays marriage. Even churches are giving mixed messages. It seems everyone is getting involved in the unfolding marriage drama. It's time to advance and not retreat in reclaiming and living out God's original Plan A design for marriage.

REAL LIFE Marriage: It's Not About Me is biblical, relevant, and real life. It is based on our thirty-plus years of marriage, as well as our extensive experience counseling other couples.

We believe marriage is, as Dr. Bilezikian wrote in the foreword, "the most fundamental of all relationships entrusted to humankind." For this reason, we challenge you to be open to exploring truths about God's original design for marriage and then passionately advance in living them out together in three key areas:

Spirit Oneness — joining together in relationship with God.

Soul Oneness — growing in intimacy by living out God's Plan A for marriage.

Body Oneness — celebrating the one-flesh sexual relationship.

This book will explore four key purposes of marriage: to Reflect and Reveal the plurality and character of God, to Rule together in unity, and to Reproduce, bringing forth new life to advance the kingdom of God. We will offer practical tools and include plenty of real life stories to illustrate how obstacles in marriage can be transformed into opportunities.

Although the insights in this book are geared to married couples, anyone interested in marriage — including those who are engaged or currently single — will also benefit from the principles we highlight. In addition, we've created a Companion Journal for this book with study questions and personal applications for each chapter. To learn how you can get a copy, visit www.RealLife.us.com.

Before we begin this journey together, we'd like to pray a blessing over you:

Father, thank You for creating marriage. Thank You for placing this book in this person's hands. We ask that You open each person's heart and mind as they revisit Your story. We pray that every reader will personally encounter You as they supernaturally live out the principles of REAL LIFE Marriage: It's Not About Me.

1

REAL LIFE MARRIAGE

it's not about me

Spirit Oneness

Chapter 1

The Starting Place

Reflecting and Revealing God in Marriage

A familiar slogan goes something like this: *Where you start determines where you end*. A recent experience confirmed for us the truth of this saying.

We live in Colorado Springs near the base of Pikes Peak, and we decided last spring that we wanted to climb this mountain — all 14,110 elevated feet of her. We knew that to succeed we would have to commit to disciplined training, so we set some goals. According to our calculations, we had five months before the first snow. Since neither of us grew up in the mountains, we had a lot to learn. Web sites provided great photo journals of the trail and stories describing some of the challenges people faced on the mountain. We hoped to learn from the invaluable wisdom of these experienced hikers so that we could avoid some common mistakes.

Over the summer we hiked four or five times a week, gradually increasing our distance. The big day finally arrived, and we rose when the alarm clock went off before sunrise. We had already packed the car with our equipment, so we headed to the trailhead. Since I (Anne) am directionally challenged, Tim and I decided it would be a good idea to build my confidence by having me run point on map reading and directions.

It was pitch dark when we arrived in the parking lot, so I used our flashlight to read the directions I had printed out:

"From the parking lot you will see the beginning of the trailhead. Within a mile you will see a sign marking the 664A trail. Follow the 664A fork and continue up the trail on a gradual ascent. When you come to a log bridge, cross over it and begin an aggressive ascent."

As I looked at the sign at the beginning of the trailhead, I was surprised that it only included a few safety reminders for hikers. I guess I'd been expecting to read something more declarative, like PIKES PEAK DEAD AHEAD! My first reaction was, *That's strange. The trail doesn't seem to be as clearly marked as I'd hoped.* But in the spirit of Sir Edmund Hillary, the first man to conquer Mount Everest, we were full of excitement as we forged ahead. We stepped onto the path and began our journey toward the summit together.

According to my directions, we would reach our first landmark about a mile into our trek. But hiking in the dark, we found it difficult to determine how far we had gone. When we didn't pass the 664A sign, I was mildly concerned. I remember turning to Tim and saying, "We must have missed the sign for the 664 trail, but this looks like the log bridge just ahead of us." Side note: When you are certain that you're on track, you often overlook the obvious. What looked like the log bridge later turned out to be a dead tree that had fallen across a shallow creek.

As the sun began to rise, the scenery surrounding us was beyond description. Our exhilaration level increased as the full mountain range came into view. The sky was clear and the air was cool. It could not have been a more perfect day. I glanced at the directions to make sure we were on the right path. They read:

"Continue up the trail, as you prepare to begin an aggressive ascent above tree line. There is an area marked 'Devil's Playground.' At this point the summit will be in full view. "

I definitely would not have described the next section of the trail as "an aggressive ascent." But instead of stopping to check the map to make sure we were on the right path, I ignored my uncertainty, saying, "Wow, if this is what they consider an aggressive ascent, this climb is going to be a lot easier than I expected. We're in better shape than I thought!" Despite my attempt to keep a positive mindset, as the hours passed I commented every so often, "I wonder why we haven't reached the tree line yet?"

A few miles later I pointed to a mountain parallel to us and said to Tim, "That sure looks a lot like Pikes Peak over there, doesn't it?" Discounting any thought that we could possibly be on the wrong trail, we continued to assure each other that we had started at the trailhead, followed the directions, and we were on the right track. Whenever doubt arose, we seemed to always come up with a logical explanation for why things were not going according to plan.

Finally, as midday approached we could no longer deny that something was wrong. Stopping to assess our situation and review our options, we realized we were lost in the middle of a forest. To complicate matters, we were out of cell phone range and had no GPS system. With the summit nowhere in sight, we agreed it was time to turn around.

Let me just say that climbing a mountain can be exhilarating, but being lost and having to retrace your steps is a total downer.

Thinking we could save time, we decided to take an unknown shortcut. It didn't take long to realize that the shortcut was leading us even farther in the wrong direction. We were now officially lost. Our only hope was to find our way back to where we had stepped off the trail and continue on from there. We eventually found a dirt road and hitched a ride the rest of the way down the mountain.

Completely exhausted and discouraged, we made our way back to the car and reviewed our steps to see what went wrong. We soon discovered that in the early morning darkness "Sir Edmund Hillary and his wife" must have missed a turn. We apparently drove into the wrong parking lot and started our hike a few hundred feet from the correct trailhead. That explained why the original sign at the trailhead was not as clear as I had hoped. We were so close…yet so far. The hike we had prepared for all summer ended up a total disaster.

Driving home together we wondered, *Why didn't we see our mistakes sooner? Why did we wait so long before we turned around? Did we really think we could save time by taking an unknown shortcut?* That familiar slogan came to mind: *Where you start determines where you end*. We had started at the wrong place!

Our mountain misadventure reflects the experience of many couples who set out to enjoy the adventure of marriage. Many take logical steps to prepare themselves — maybe getting premarital counseling, seeking advice from wise and experienced friends, or reading some books in search of a roadmap to success. Others believe they can "take the mountain" without any training or preparation.

When the big day arrives they stand before God, family, and friends to exchange vows and be declared husband and wife before setting forth on their journey. But life rarely looks quite like we expect. It's easy for a couple to lose their way even if they have directions. They may be tempted to ignore the warning signs that caution them to pause and check their location. By the time they realize something is definitely wrong, they may be too proud to ask for help. Reaching a crisis point, they may try to convince themselves they will find their way if they just keep going. They propose logical conclusions for why they are lost. Often they make a bad situation worse by taking a chance on an unknown shortcut that only complicates their problem.

When you're lost, whether on a mountain or in your marriage, the obvious solution is to stop heading the wrong way and locate the starting point that will lead to your destination. We're convinced that the best starting point for every couple, whether newlyweds or veteran travelers, is God. He is the One who designed marriage. He knows the way. So let's see what direction He suggests for your marriage.

IN THE BEGINNING...

At the beginning of every story an author chooses words intended to draw a reader in. God, the supernatural Author of the Bible, chose to begin His story by introducing Himself as the main character. Genesis opens by unveiling aspects of God's identity that provide a model for marriage. Let's go back to the creation account in Genesis and explore God's original design for marriage. We've italicized three words we'd like you to especially note.

"In the beginning *God* created the heavens and the earth. The earth was formless and void, and darkness was over surface of the deep, and the *Spirit* of God was moving over the surface of the waters. Then God *said*..."[1]

Verse 1 introduces the first person of the Trinity, God the Father. However, He is not alone. There are others with Him who are often overlooked. Verse 2 introduces the third person of the Trinity, the Spirit of God. Most people think of the Holy Spirit as a New Testament character who arrives on the scene only after Jesus returns to the Father, but right there in the beginning the Holy Spirit's presence is "hovering over the face of the waters."[2] At the start of verse 3, the second person of the Trinity is introduced. The text reads, "God *said*."

Who does the Bible identify as the spoken Word? The Gospel of John refers to Jesus Christ as the spoken Word and confirms His presence at creation: "In the beginning was the *Word*, and the *Word* was with God, and the *Word* was God. He was in the beginning with God."[3] The Bible continues, "And the *Word* became flesh, and dwelt among us, and we saw His glory, glory as of the only begotten from the Father, full of grace and truth."[4] Looking at the text, it is clear that Jesus Christ is the Word. He was present in the creation account. From what we read in the text all three persons of the Godhead are present and participate in creation: God the Father, God the Son, and God the Holy Spirit.

Why did God begin His story this way? Could He be pointing to something significant about His nature that He wants every person to know? From the beginning God declared His triune plurality; He revealed Himself as a multifaceted, three-in-One, relational being.

Biblical scholars and religious leaders have debated the triune nature, or Trinity, of God for centuries. We will leave the debating to them, but we'd like to offer one imperfect illustration to explain this infinite concept in finite terms. Water is a three-in-one substance; it can take the form of liquid, ice, or steam. Yet regardless of form it remains water, H_2O. The same is true of God in the context of the Trinity. Each of the three persons of the Godhead takes on a different form — God the Father, God the Son, and God the Holy Spirit — yet His substance, His oneness, remains. Thus, both of the following equations are equally true:

One Father + one Son + one Holy Spirit equals three $(1 + 1 + 1 = 3)$

One Father + one Son + one Holy Spirit equals one God $(1 + 1 + 1 = 1)$

REFLECTING AND REVEALING THE IMAGE OF GOD

You're probably wondering what all this has to do with marriage. The answer is, *everything*. Hang in there with us just a bit longer and the connection will be clear.

Just after we meet the triune God in the first verses of Genesis, we witness the miracle of Creation. God called into existence...light and darkness;

the heavens and seas; land, plants, and trees; sun, moon, and stars; birds and fish; and all the animals.

Let's look at the words He spoke next, again noting in particular the italicized words:

"Let *us* make man [humankind] in *our* image, in *our* likeness, and let *them* rule over the fish of the sea and the birds of the air, over the livestock, over all the earth, and over all the creatures that move along the ground."[5]

Do you see how God repeatedly refers to Himself in the plural form with the words *us* and *our*? Jesus referred to this plurality as a mystery. "Don't you believe that I am in the Father, and that the Father is in me? The words I say to you are not just my own. Rather, it is the Father, living in me, who is doing his work. Believe me when I say that I am in the Father and the Father is in me; or at least believe on the evidence of the miracles themselves."[6] This is significant because the plurality in the Trinity of God directly relates to His design and purposes for marriage. Notice that His design and instructions concern both the male and the female:

"God created man *in His own image*, in the image of God He created him; male and female He created *them*. God blessed *them*; and God said to *them*, 'Be fruitful and multiply, and fill the earth, and subdue it; and rule over the fish of the sea and over the birds of the sky and over every living thing that moves on the earth.'"[7]

Being made in the image of God (the *imago Dei*) has far-reaching implications. Every person's God-likeness is the basis for the dignity and value they possess. Being made in the image of God makes humans different from other created beings.

However, since God created man *and* woman in His image, marriage invites a husband and wife to represent His triune nature in a unique and remarkable way. Traditionally people refer to God as "He." However, God is neither male nor female. His very nature includes aspects of both maleness and femaleness. God transcends sexuality. As His image bearers, a husband and wife become God's representatives as they *Reflect and Reveal* His character, as they *Rule* over His creation, and — as we'll see later — as they *Reproduce*, bringing forth new life. In fulfilling these roles together in God's image, a couple is called to live out His intrinsic traits of love, mutual equality, community, reciprocal servanthood, and interdependency.

Why those particular traits? Let's look again at our triune God.

The three persons of the Trinity have distinct roles within the Godhead. Their roles are often revealed by the names they have. God the Father is referred to as the Creator, Almighty One, and the great I AM. God the Son is known as the Savior, the Lamb of God, King of the Jews, the Door, the Way, the Truth, and the Light. God the Holy Spirit is known as the Comforter, the Counselor, the Spirit of life, and the Spirit of wisdom and understanding.

We see no evidence in the Bible of confusion or competition between these roles, nor do we see evidence of a pecking order or hierarchy. We do not see one person of the Trinity dominating or ruling over the others. God cannot be inferior to God; therefore, the triune nature of God is the essence of *oneness*. The three persons of the Trinity model interdependence and mutual equality. So it is in marriage; a husband and wife are called in oneness to mirror the relationship modeled in the Trinity.

Can you imagine what the Trinity would look like if competition, comparison, or conflict was present? Imagine God the Holy Spirit complaining about all His counseling responsibilities as He pleads with God the Father to switch roles with Him? What if God the Son was sick and tired of being the Lamb of God and expressed a desire to do some creating? Can you imagine God the Father filing a complaint about His role as *Abba* and demanding one of the other members of the Trinity walk in His shoes for just one day?

God the Father, God the Son, and God the Holy Spirit are perfectly content in their roles. Their model of oneness within community becomes our model for marriage. Their relationship gives couples a glimpse of what it means to walk together in unity, mutually submitted and interdependent.

SPIRIT ONENESS IN MARRIAGE

So the Trinity is our model for marriage. Two individuals — one man and one woman — miraculously become one as they covenant with God and each other. In this way every married couple is invited to Reflect and Reveal the plurality and nature of the triune God — a God who from the very start has been all about relationship.

As represented by the first triangle below, the three persons of the Trinity exist intimately as one in a relationship of mutual equality and interdependence. The second triangle represents a Judeo-Christian marriage in which one man and one woman enter into a covenant relationship with God and each other. The husband and wife relate equally as one as they submit first to God and then to each other. We call this *spirit oneness*. It is important to note that in this illustration the dotted lines connecting God to a husband and wife signify that man and woman are not equal with the Godhead, although each has an equally intimate relationship with God.

We want to be sure to point out that fulfillment of God's purposes in life is not only available in marriage. "To the contrary, the Bible teaches that believers who can manage singleness find greater fulfillment in lives of celibate service than if they were married."[8] However, for those of us who are married, the privilege and responsibility of living out the miracle and mystery of two becoming one can utterly transform our approach to marriage.

WHAT IS GOD'S DESIGN FOR MARRIAGE?

The two of us were twenty-one years old when we got married. By the time we were twenty-nine, we had four children, a dog, a house, and a growing list of responsibilities. No marriage book or class could possibly have prepared us for the kind of learning curve we were experiencing.

I (Anne) remember walking into bookstores, standing in the family and marriage section, and just staring at literally hundreds of books on every topic imaginable. With four children at my feet, I didn't have the time or the energy to learn all the things I thought I needed to know. As a new believer, I wanted to know what specifically made a Christian marriage different. What I really needed was a large-print, red-letter edition of the Cliffs Notes on marriage.

In the hope of quickly learning something — anything — helpful, I read the titles of books, visually scanned the front and back covers, and flipped through the table of contents, looking for what I called the *good parts*. To me, the good parts of a marriage book provided keys that opened the doors to understanding. The good parts answered questions I found too difficult or too embarrassing to ask, usually related to issues of communication, sex, or the differences between men and women. The good parts revealed the mystery of marriage.

The truth is, whenever I skimmed through a marriage book, I specifically remember skipping over the biblical foundation. In my twenties, I couldn't understand how the Old Testament could possibly contain the kind of life-transforming insight that would relate to my understanding of marriage. To me, the creation account was just a familiar Bible story that lacked the fresh insight I was looking for.

Tim and I continued blundering along until our tenth year of marriage when we were invited to audit a class at Wheaton College on New Testament marriage. I'll never forget when Dr. Bilezikian opened the book of Genesis and began to unwrap God's creation design for marriage. It felt as if we were hearing the account for the very first time. We began to see the Trinity as our model for marriage. We began to understand that God was telling a story about His design for marriage. It was like a veil came down in our hearts.

Learning about God's original design for marriage completely changed the direction of our lives. We discovered that marriage is not a human invention. God created marriage; it is a good thing. After God saw everything He made, He declared it was *very good*.[9] Centuries later, Jesus affirmed God's creational design for marriage:

"And He answered and said, 'Have you not read that He who created them from the beginning made them male and female, and said, "For this reason a man shall leave his father and mother and be joined to his wife, and the two shall become one flesh"? So they are no longer two, but one flesh. What therefore God has joined together, let no man separate.' "[10]

God's "very-good" design for a Judeo-Christian marriage includes these components:

1.   One man and one woman. God created humankind in His image, "*male* and *female* He created them." Therefore, any marital relationship apart from one man and one woman (for example, same-sex couples or polygamy) violates God's design. God's command to the first couple to "be fruitful and multiply" involves one man and one woman becoming one flesh for the continuation of society. To have children — to Reproduce and nurture new life — is one of God's purposes for marriage.

2.   A monogamous relationship. In other words, a husband and wife cannot engage in sexual relations with anyone else. There is permanence and exclusivity in one man and one woman entering into covenant relationship with God and each other. The miracle and mystery of a husband and wife becoming one flesh should be treated as sacred and precious.

3.   Both husband and the wife are in a personal relationship with God. Community with God is a critical aspect in a Judeo-Christian marriage. If either the husband or wife is not in a personal relationship with God, they cannot Reflect and Reveal the plurality in whose image they are created. (For more about the challenges of living with an unbelieving spouse, see page 35.)

YOU CAN'T REFLECT AND REVEAL WHAT YOU DON'T SEE

God has placed within the heart of every person a longing for love and relationship. Every man and woman is created with the ability and freedom to choose relationship with God. Just as earthly parents initiate relationship with their children, God initiates relationship with His children. He reaches out to every person's heart and invites them to experience the spark that ignites a loving relationship.

We'll consider His invitation more thoroughly in the next chapter, but for now we'd like you to pause and consider how well you really know God. Are you truly living in relationship with Him, or are you playing at hide-and-seek?

When our kids were little, I (Tim) would often encourage Anne to get out of the house and try to regain her sanity after she had a busy week. Even a few hours away from four little ones felt like a gift to her. While she was away, we had no problem filling an evening with fun. One of the kids' favorite games was hide-and-seek. It would begin with me shutting my eyes and counting out loud: *One thousand-ONE, one thousand-TWO, one thousand-THREE…* This gave the kids time to find a hiding place somewhere in the house. When I reached SIXTY I would open my eyes and yell out loud, "*Ready or not…here I come.*" The search was on. I walked from room to room looking for them. I would describe each step aloud. "*You are not in the closet…not under the table…not behind the chair.*" The more noise I made, the more excited the kids got.

With four kids at different ages, I never knew exactly how the game was going to play out, but each child had his or her own special way of hiding. Our oldest, Timmy, always found the most ingenious places to hide. He was the only one who actually made the game somewhat of a challenge for me. Once he climbed up to the top shelf in his closet and covered himself with a folded blanket. Amy, our second child, often hid in the kitchen. One time she hid inside a kitchen cabinet. The pots and pans she stacked on the floor were a dead giveaway. Colleen was always creative. I remember one game when she lay on top of her bed, surrounded by a mountain of dolls and stuffed animals. Her eyes were wide open as she tried not to blink. Her camouflage strategy allowed her to blend in with the background.

I can still picture our youngest, Cate-the-Great, standing in her diapers as a toddler. When the counting began she got so excited she could barely stand up. Instead of finding a hiding place, she would just run around in circles, giggling. Too young to understand the strategy of the game, she just loved to be included.

One by one, I would find the older kids, but I always left Cate for last. She would still be in the living room where the game had started. She was usually standing in the center of the room with her eyes tightly closed and her hands over her face. We would all pretend we couldn't see her. "Where is Cate? Where is she hiding?" Opening doors and looking in closets we'd shout, "Cate's not in here…where can she be?" One of the best parts of the game was the fact that Cate actually believed that she was hidden from our sight. Eventually someone would say, "Wait a minute, I think I see Cate. Is that her in the living room?" The purity of a toddler's giggle is beyond description. Finally we'd pull her hands down from her eyes and declare, "We found you, Cate!" Then we'd wrap her in a big group hug.

In many ways, people play hide-and-seek with God, attempting to conceal their hearts as if He can't see right through them. But God is calling their names, eagerly awaiting the moment when they'll be ready for Him to pull aside their hands, look into their eyes, and wrap them up in His love.

The truth is, you can't pass on something you don't have. Only by entering into a relationship with God will you and your spouse be able to Reflect and Reveal His character to each other and to the world.

+ Chapter 2

Just the Three of Us

Responding to God's Invitation to Relationship

The theme of this book, "Marriage is not about me," invites a question: "If marriage is not about me, then who is marriage about?" A Judeo-Christian marriage is about God. Every couple is called to live out the miracle and mystery of marriage in relationship with God the Father, God the Son, and God the Holy Spirit. Relationship is the heart of God and the heart of marriage.

As we saw in chapter 1, God's very essence is relationship. The three persons of the Trinity relate intimately as one. This is our model for intimacy in marriage: a love triangle in which one man and one woman are in a personal relationship with God and each other. A couple cannot Reflect and Reveal the plurality and nature of God if they are not in relationship with Him.

Entering into relationship with God is not defined by a list of things a person does for God. The heart of relationship with God is how a person responds to what God has already done. God is constantly initiating relationship. He initiates relationship twenty-four hours a day, seven days a week, and three hundred sixty-five days a year. Sometimes it is difficult for us to comprehend that God longs to be in relationship and to grow in intimacy with us, but His desire is apparent right from the first lines of His story.

"Then the LORD God formed man of dust from the ground, and breathed into his nostrils the breath of life; and man became a living being."[1] Up to this point in creation God spoke everything into existence. But when God created a being made in His image, He changed His style of creating; He got more intimately involved.

Can you imagine this most intimate encounter? The God of the universe, the great I AM, takes a hands-on approach when creating man. He reaches down and takes dust from the ground and forms man. In an act of unfathomable intimacy, God comes down to earth and actually breathes life into the man with the intimacy of a kiss.

Whenever we officiate at weddings we love to highlight this moment in creation. After a man and woman are declared husband and wife, the groom is invited to kiss his bride. This kiss symbolically seals the marital covenant between God, the husband, and the wife. This kiss is also a symbol of the man breathing life into his bride. New life begins as they enter into covenant with God and each other.

FROM "NOT GOOD" TO "VERY GOOD"

Could life have been any better? Man lived in a sin-free environment. He enjoyed intimacy with God while being surrounded by beauty in the garden. The weather was perfect. He didn't need or wear clothes. Cultivating the garden was a joy for him. Doesn't this sound like a perfect world for man? However, in dramatic fashion God demonstrates an immeasurable depth to His character and humility. For the first time in recorded history God declares that something is not good. God says, "It is not good for the man to be alone."[2]

Why was man's situation "not good"? Because God wanted more for man. God wanted man to identify with the part of His nature that longed to create. God wanted man to be fruitful and multiply, to fill the earth, to take dominion, and Rule together with his wife. God wanted man to experience the plurality of partnership.

How did God respond to man's "not good" situation?

"So the LORD God caused a deep sleep to fall upon the man, and he slept; then He took one of his ribs and closed up the flesh at that place. The LORD God fashioned into a woman the rib which He had taken from the man, and brought her to the man."[3]

God put man to sleep and fashioned one of his ribs into woman. God created woman to rescue man from his "not good" situation.

Notice the Bible says God *formed* man and He *fashioned* woman. *Forming* reminds us of a construction term. Forms are laid when a concrete foundation is poured. *Fashioning* reminds us of an artist creating a beautiful, priceless piece of art. After God had formed man and fashioned woman, He instructed them to be fruitful and multiply and rule over the earth. Then He stepped back and "God saw all that He had made, and behold, it was very good."[4]

Think about this: everything God creates — including day and night, the sun and moon, the seas, the plants, the birds, and animals — He declares "good." Then God creates man in His image from dust of the ground. After man is created, for the first time we hear that something is "not good."

God said, "It is not good for man to be alone." It is not until after God creates woman and the first marriage that God declares all He created "very good."

Remember, community and relationship are essential to God's nature. Man could not fully Reflect and Reveal the plurality of God without the plurality that marriage provides. Just like the animals, man needed to be partnered with someone after his kind. Man needed another human being to become one with. God could have created many different relationships to begin humankind. God did not choose a family, a church, a town, or a village to Reflect and Reveal His image. Instead, God chose a man and a woman. The marriage relationship is sacred. It is "very good."

AN ONGOING LOVE STORY

But the story doesn't end with the creation of humankind. Our God isn't an impersonal deity who sits on a throne plopping created beings on earth and expecting them to obey His laws as they figure life out on their own. From the beginning we see a good Father reaching toward humankind, talking and walking with them.

Tragically, relationship with God changed when man and woman chose to sin. But the heart of a loving Father never gives up on His children. How did God respond to humanity's sin? Again, He initiated relationship by sending God the Son to earth. Jesus took on human flesh and stepped into the role of the Savior, "to seek and to save that which was lost."[5] His life, death, and resurrection enabled men and women to return to relationship with God.

God is love; love invites relationship. He created a longing in every person's heart that can only be satisfied in Him. Think about it: even our ability to love comes from God. The Bible says, "We love, because He first loved us."[6] As simple as it may sound, God loves you. In fact, contrary to many religious beliefs, there is nothing a person can do that could make God love them more. His love is perfect and unconditional. However, relationship with God requires engaging with Him. This starts when a person repents or admits they have sinned.[7] To repent simply means to turn around from sinful behavior. Repenting involves personally asking

God for forgiveness for sins you have committed. It's amazing that even repentance starts with God. The Father heart of God initiates a process of repentance in a person. The Bible says, "The kindness of God leads you to repentance."[8]

Entering into relationship with God includes relationship with all three Persons in the Trinity. However, for the sake of simplicity, we will refer to entering into relationship with God as entering into relationship with Jesus. This relationship can never be reduced to a formula. We are cautious not to describe relationship with Jesus as a number of required steps, reciting a certain prayer, or repeating certain words. You may be surprised to learn that the only individual Jesus personally promised would be with Him in paradise was the thief who hung beside him at Calvary. This criminal did not recite a particular prayer; he never even got a chance to show his faith through service. He was never baptized. He simply admitted he was a sinner and put his trust in Jesus.

Entering into relationship with Jesus is as simple as a person choosing to open their heart and connect with the heart of Jesus. All one needs to do is acknowledge who Jesus is, repent of their sins, and place their trust in the Savior.

I (Anne) was in my early twenties when I began my relationship with Jesus. I was sitting at someone's dining room table when I repented of my sins and invited Jesus to be my Lord and Savior. As a young mom who was just beginning to grow spiritually, the thought of teaching my children biblical principles seemed overwhelming. Spiritually, I felt like a child trying to teach my own children. When my kids brought home their Sunday school lessons, I was learning along with them.

When our oldest child, Timmy, was in third grade, he came bursting through the door for lunch. He related a conversation that he'd had on the playground with his best friend, in which he explained that Jesus lived inside of his heart. His friend responded, "I want Jesus to live inside my heart too." My son wanted to know, "Mom, how can Jesus live inside of Jimmy's heart like He lives inside of mine?"

As a young believer, I remember thinking, "That's a good question!" At that moment, I longed to be one of those spiritually mature moms who could walk her son through the steps of how to share his faith. I knew that being in relationship with Jesus wasn't about saying a certain prayer or repeating a certain Bible verse, but I lacked the confidence to answer Timmy's question.

I said a quick prayer and asked God to help me put words to what was inside my heart. I looked at Timmy and said, "Do you remember those two words from Sunday school: 'sinner' and 'Savior'?" He nodded.

I continued, "When someone disobeys God, it's called sin. The only person who can take our sin away is Jesus. All Jimmy has to do is tell Jesus he is sorry for what he did and ask Him to live in his heart."

As lunch ended and Timmy headed back to school I said, "Just remember those two words: 'sinner' and 'Savior.'"

I spent most of the afternoon praying as I waited for Timmy to return home from school. When he walked in the door, I asked how things went with his friend.

He said, "Me and Jimmy sat by the ballfield backstop. When I asked him if he was a sinner, he said yes. So I told him that Jesus wasn't mad. All he had to do was ask Him to come inside his heart and He would."

I listened quietly as my son illustrated what it means to have the faith of a child. Anxious to hear more details, I said, "Then what happened?"

Timmy said, "Jimmy told Jesus he was sorry and asked Him to come inside His heart to live with him." With that, my little boy started walking toward his room.

"Wait! What happened next?" I asked.

Timmy looked at me as if he was confused. "What do you mean what happened next? We played ball!"

He modeled how simple it can be to step out of our own story and choose to live in the **Larger Story** of God's love!

WHAT'S YOUR RELATIONSHIP WITH GOD?

Entering into relationship with Jesus is an individual decision that must be made in faith.

Our experience is that many people resist being categorized or placed into certain groups, feeling that labels don't adequately represent their individuality and uniqueness. We certainly get that. However, a person's family of origin, the way they live, and the choices they make place them in different groups. A person is born into a male or female group. A person's ethnic and cultural background places them in different groups. There are groups of people who are married or unmarried, who have children or do not have children. A person's career choice can place them in groups, such as tradesmen, emergency workers, or entertainers.

Jesus also grouped people according to their life experiences and choices. He spoke about people who mourned, those who are gentle in spirit, the merciful, the pure in heart, and people who were peacemakers. One time Jesus used figurative language to distinguish people who are like sheep from people who are like wolves.[9]

In one specific instance Jesus boldly placed people into one of two groups: those who acknowledge Him and those who don't. He said, "Therefore everyone who confesses Me before men, I will also confess him before My Father who is in heaven. But whoever denies Me before men, I will also deny him before My Father who is in heaven."[10]

Based on His statement, every person falls into one of two groups:

Group 1 consists of people who know Jesus and are in relationship with Him. This group includes those who try to live in the **Larger Story** with God as the main character.

Group 2 consists of people who are not in relationship with Jesus. While this includes people who have not heard about Him, it also includes people who know at least something about Him and may even understand some of His story. Whatever the case, individuals in this group have never made a personal decision to repent of their sins, accept Jesus as their Lord and Savior, and enter into relationship with Him.

If you belong to the first group, we encourage you to thank God for the relationship you have. Ask Him to help you advance in intimacy. Ask God to give you ways to humbly share Jesus and His story.

If you fall into the second category, we encourage you to put aside religious preconceptions and misperceptions and ask God to open your eyes, your heart, and your mind as you honestly answer Jesus' penetrating question, "But who do you say that I am?"[11] During Jesus' trial He was directly asked, "Are You the Son of God…?" And He said to them, "Yes, I am."[12] How will you respond to that answer?

We challenge you to examine Jesus' life and story. Maybe you have unintentionally confused religion and religious people with a relationship with Jesus. Jesus is not about any religion. In fact, Jesus reserved some of His strongest and most negative words for religious people. Jesus was embraced by salt-of-the-earth fishermen, tax gatherers, prostitutes, and the multitudes. These common men and women experienced Jesus. They saw His love, His heart, His righteous judgment, His death, His resurrection, His real life.

We encourage you to invite the real Jesus to find you. Remember the hide-and-seek story in chapter 1? As a toddler, Cate thought she was hiding from her dad. She had her eyes closed tightly and her hands covering her face. The truth is, your heavenly Dad sees you. In fact, He has never taken His eyes off of you. You may not know and believe in Jesus, but Jesus knows and believes in you.

Re-read Jesus' words: "Therefore everyone who confesses Me before men, I will also confess him before My Father who is in heaven. But whoever denies Me before men, I will also deny him before My Father who is in heaven." Which of these two groups will you choose to be in? This is the most important decision you will ever make. Your marriage, family, and future generations will all benefit from your choice to live in the **Larger Story** with God as the main character.

INVITING OTHERS INTO THE LARGER STORY

Relationship with Jesus is the key to abundant life and a deeply satisfying marriage. Why? Because entering into that relationship moves us from the self-centered **smaller story** where we ask, "What's in it for me?" to the **Larger Story** where we live out the truth, "It's not about me." Such a shift in the way we live can't help but impact our marriage and our interactions at every level. Choosing to follow Jesus' example and die to self brings real life to a couple and to their marriage.

A husband and wife who are passionately in love and in relationship with God and each other have unlimited potential to positively impact our culture and advance the kingdom of God. Couples joined together in spirit oneness through their shared relationship with God are uniquely positioned to Reflect and Reveal His love to each other and to everyone they encounter.

In 1997 our family moved from the Chicago suburbs to Western Michigan to be part of a growing church. After we arrived, one of the first things we did was begin building relationships. For the two of us the best way to do that was by leading a small group Bible study. We wanted the heart of our group to be about relationship with God and each other. Instead of studying the Bible or choosing a specific book, we decided to spend our time just "being" in relationship with one another.

We began by asking the Lord to help us choose which couples He wanted us to invest our lives in. God answered our prayers and brought together four couples. We held an initial meeting at a local restaurant just to get acquainted and map out our plan. After that we gathered twice a month around our dining room table to share a meal and tell stories.

We started things off by sharing our own story. We told them about our families and where we grew up. We told stories about our dating and marriage. We shared with the group how entering into relationship with God literally changed the course of our lives and impacted every story we told.

At the end of our first meeting Tim said, "Now that Anne and I have shared our story, who wants to take a turn the next time we meet?" The group hesitated and looked around the room at each other. No one wanted to go next. One woman said, "I don't really feel like I have a story to tell. I went to church my whole life…stayed out of trouble…went to a college…got married…and had babies. My life really isn't very exciting."

Later I (Anne) invited that woman to meet me for coffee before our next small group gathering. We sat together on a park bench as her kids played on the playground. Through casual conversation I learned so much about her life. She told me about the family she grew up in, how she met her husband, and how God had been part of her life for as long as she could remember. As I listened, I began to hear some of the stories God was telling through her life.

We talked about how God used some of the circumstances in both of our lives to tell a story that points us to Him. Through our conversation, she realized that seeing God as the main character of her story gave her a renewed perspective, a way of looking at life she'd never seen before.

When our group met the following week, my new friend shared some of the stories she had told me on the park bench earlier that week. By the end of the evening we not only felt like we knew her better, we also felt that we'd learned some new things about God through her stories. As each month passed every person had the opportunity to share their story, offering us a window into their lives and their faith. God had gathered this handful of couples together in our home so He could use the power of stories to build intimacy and relationships.

Others in the church began to hear about the power of story. Over time other small groups began to gather together, share meals, and tell stories. It was exciting to see how God used the power of story to draw us closer to Him. In fact, when our small group ended I wrote a workbook called *Sharing Your Faith and Telling Your Story*.[13] God continues to use this tool to help many people connect their story to the story God is telling through their life.

When both you and your spouse are in relationship with Jesus, your marriage has tremendous potential to advance the kingdom of God. Remember, every marriage tells a story. The story God is telling through your marriage builds intimacy with Him, your spouse, and others. Whether you realize it or not, your marriage may be the only Bible some people ever read. A husband and wife who live in the **Larger Story**, guided by the conviction that *marriage is not about me*, will positively impact their family and our culture in ways they cannot imagine. Take a moment to ask yourself this question: "What story is God telling through our marriage?"

YOU DON'T HAVE TO BE AN EVANGELIST TO SHARE GOD'S STORY

Years ago we served together on the premarital ministry team at Willow Creek Community Church. At one point we were counseling a young man we'll call Tony. Tony's fiancée had invited him to Willow Creek, where he heard Jesus' story. Although he'd been raised in a religious home and attended religious schools, he had never made a personal decision to enter into relationship with Jesus. Tony had confused being a member of a religion with being in relationship with Jesus. We shared our story with Tony and found him to be spiritually hungry. After meeting with him several times we sensed he was ready to make a decision to repent and receive Jesus.

Just before our next scheduled appointment, I (Anne) was caught off guard when Tim said, "Hon, I think Tony is ready to give his heart to Jesus. When that time comes up during our counseling session, I want you to handle it. I'm not going to say a word. I want you to be the one who shares the Gospel with Tony."

My stomach dropped. My heart began to race. I thought, *Tim is the one with the gift of evangelism, not me*. I'm a conflict avoider. I don't like to ask spiritual questions that could potentially be answered with "no thanks."

Unfortunately we didn't have time to discuss it because right then Tony walked in the door. I knew Tim well enough to know that he was not going to budge on his challenge.

I began the session by reviewing with Tony our previous discussions. We talked about how religion and relationship often get confused. I took a deep breath and stepped out in faith. I asked, "Tony do you have a personal relationship with Jesus?"

He shook his head and said, "If you mean, have I ever personally asked Jesus to lead my life…to take the steering wheel…to take control…the answer is no."

I asked, "If you died today do you think that you would go to heaven?"

Tony said he wasn't sure. He thought it would depend on what he had done that day. He believed the deciding factor as to where he would spend eternity rested on what he *did* for God. I looked at Tony and said, "Tony, it's not about what you do; it's about what already has been done for you on the cross by Jesus. Are you ready to put a stake in the ground today and ask Jesus to be your Savior and Lord of your life?"

With tears in his eyes, Tony said he wanted to give his heart to Jesus.

All of a sudden, my mind went blank. I forgot every verse I had ever memorized. I didn't know what to say next. I looked at Tim, but he had his eyes closed as if he was praying. (I hoped he was praying for me as well as for Tony.)

There was a long pause. Tony was looking at me, waiting for direction. With my heart racing, I took a deep breath and said, "Tony, let's get on our knees." (I said that because I was so nervous I thought I was going to fall off my chair.) We got on our knees and I told Tony to just open his heart and tell Jesus in simple words that he was a sinner. I told him to ask Jesus to be his Savior. Tony prayed a simple prayer of faith.

Afterward, we told Tony the Bible says all the angels in heaven celebrate when one sinner repents.[14] The angels were rejoicing over Tony's decision, and I believe over my mustard-seed-size faith in sharing Jesus' story.

Sharing Jesus with Tony was not about me. It wasn't about my maturity level, how many verses I had memorized, or whether or not I could accurately articulate the *Sinner's Prayer* or *Romans Road*. Sharing Jesus with Tony was about telling him a story, a story about a Person who loved him and would never fail or forsake him.

+   +   +

Before we move on, we want to mention that we realize some passionate followers of Jesus Christ are married to unbelievers. Our experience is that this situation provides many opportunities for the believing spouse to live life in the **Larger Story**. We encourage the believing spouse to Reflect and Reveal God to their unbelieving husband or wife. The way a believing spouse treats their unbelieving spouse tells a powerful story about the Person they are following. We encourage every believing spouse to continue to pray that their spouse's heart will be open to Jesus and His story. Remember that sharing the life of Jesus is not about convincing or converting anyone. Sharing Jesus is all about sharing His story: His love, birth, life, death, and life-giving resurrection.

Whether or not your spouse shares your faith, the best way to invite others into the **Larger Story** is to live your life the same way Jesus did, in the context of love and relationships.

We encourage you to pause for a moment and ask God, "Is there anything you desire for me?" The Bible says, "You do not have because you do not ask."[15] Now is a great time to ask Jesus to help you…

+ See yourself and others as He does.
+ Avoid any unrighteous judging of others.
+ Resist the temptation to focus on outward appearances.
+ Live your life and marriage in the **Larger Story**.
+ Grow in loving God and loving like God.

Then in humility choose to love God with all your heart, all your soul, all your mind, and all your strength. Choose to love others, starting with your spouse, as you love yourself. Ask the Holy Spirit to continually fill you with the supernatural ability to love and treat others the same way Jesus would.

Relationship with God is at the very heart of spirit oneness.

+ Chapter 3

One Step at a Time

Believing God Is Good When Life Is Hard

Spirit Oneness

Walking out relationship with Jesus is a lifelong journey. We agree with pastor and author Dan Kimball who says, "For far too many, conversion is seen as a birth certificate instead of a driver's license…. Conversion is a marriage rather than the marriage certificate."[1] Just as marriage is a commitment to a lifetime of growing in intimacy, so the person who makes a decision to repent of their sins and begin a relationship with Jesus enters into a lifelong journey of growing in intimacy and relationship with God.

The two of us began our journey together as a married couple in our early twenties, and soon after that we launched into our adventure with God. By the time we celebrated our second anniversary we had moved out of an apartment and into our first home, had a baby, began attending a new church, joined a small group, and made the decision to follow Jesus Christ. As husband and wife our marriage was off to a whirlwind start. Since we've never been the kind of people that wade in the shallow waters, we were ready to jump right into the deep end of a relationship with God.

As new Christians we began by reading the Bible. The story God was telling us through His Word drew us in and taught us more about who He was. But we didn't just want to read stories *about* Him; we wanted to know Him personally. We wanted to experience Jesus the way men and women in the early church experienced Him. We weren't biblical scholars, but the Bible made it sound like that kind of relationship was possible through the Holy Spirit.

As we write this book today, we are looking back over thirty years of growing in intimacy with God. Through all the years neither one of us has ever once regretted our decision to follow Him. We've found out along the way that God's dreams are always bigger than any we can dream for ourselves. But following God and believing in His dreams for us had one catch: *we had to trust Him.*

At the beginning of our relationship with the Lord, trusting Him didn't seem like much of a challenge. But as life began to happen, choosing trust grew much harder. Now we know, at fifty-plus years old, that trusting God is a lifelong journey that a person takes one step at a time. Some days are easier than others, but through it all God never changes. He is good.

DO YOU BELIEVE GOD IS GOOD?

Everything God does originates in His goodness. God provided the Trinity as the model for what marriage should look like. He also gave us the Bible, filled with life-giving principles. God sent Jesus to be the Savior, and the Holy Spirit to be the comforter and counselor. Every time God gives another gift, it confirms that He truly is good. But in the midst of difficult times, we can easily lose sight of that truth.

A key component of REAL LIFE Ministries is the "Marriage Advance" seminar we lead all across the country. The reason we decided to call these gatherings "Marriage Advances" rather than "marriage retreats" is because we believe it is time for Christ followers to *advance* rather than retreat in their relationships with God and their spouse.

At every REAL LIFE Marriage Advance we ask couples to answer this question: *Do you believe God is good*? Without hesitation people answer with an affirmative "yes." However, we have learned that simply knowing the right answer or saying the right words is not enough to carry someone through the difficult times of life. The Bible warns us, "Those who marry will face many troubles in this life."[2] In other words, journeying together as husband and wife leads to a life full of surprises and unexpected challenges. The truth is, having an intellectual understanding of God's goodness will never be enough to get you through the trials and difficulties of life or marriage. This is just one reason why God longs for every person to be in relationship with Him and to embrace His goodness...and to believe that He is really good to you.

God is a God of order. He knows that if men and women are to fully understand who they are, they need to first understand who He is. If they are going to love others, they must first love themselves. If they are going to love themselves, they must first love God. Why would a person choose to love God if they did not believe He was good?

We don't remember anyone ever asking us directly if we believed God was good during the early years of our marriage. If we had been asked that question, we would most likely have responded with an enthusiastic "yes." We have both known God our entire lives, and we believed that He was good because that's what we'd been told.

As I (Anne) look back over my life, I remember being challenged at a young age about the reality of God's goodness. During my early childhood, I'd seen death visit our family frequently. My first experience with loss came when my four-year-old sister suddenly died. My dad tried his best to explain her death by saying, "The angels took Mary Beth to heaven."

My three-year-old mind logically reasoned that my sister must have felt the same way I did. Surely she had no desire to leave our family and go to heaven. That conclusion left me with a visual picture that I held onto for years: I imagined a pack of angels grabbing my sister out of our bed one night and making their escape through our bedroom window. Even at a young age, the enemy planted seeds of fear by convincing me that Mary was kicking and screaming in resistance as the angels began their ascent to heaven. My sister's imagined abduction reminded me of the scene from *The Wizard of Oz*, when the Wicked Witch of the West sent her flying monkeys to carry Dorothy away to her evil castle.

After Mary's death I often fell asleep with a blanket over my head and my leg wrapped around my older sister. It wasn't just a habit; I actually had a strategy in place. In the event this pack of angels returned looking for more little girls to take to heaven, I would be ready. My plan was to hide under the covers so they wouldn't see me. And if their x-ray vision enabled them to spot us beneath the covers, they would be forced to take both my sister and me since our legs were securely locked together. If I had to go to heaven I was not going alone.

For years, I secretly thought God was scary and unpredictable. He took away the people that I loved without asking. For my family, Mary's death marked the beginning of a long season of loss and pain. Her death was followed by the death of a newborn boy named Timothy, who was buried next to Mary under a headstone that reads "Our Children." In the next few years my mom had two pregnancies that ended prematurely. The following year promised new life as we awaited the birth of my younger sister. But the week before she was born, my mom's father died suddenly of a heart attack. His death overshadowed the joy accompanying my sister's arrival. Six months later, we buried my grandma next to my grandpa. This long season of loss seemed to come to a close toward the end of my grammar school years, when my uncle died of a heart attack, leaving behind his pregnant wife with five young children to raise.

Through those years of pain and loss, my parents consistently modeled a marriage marked by a deep love for one another and a strong faith. Their pain never seemed to pull them away from God. Instead, it seemed to have the opposite effect, drawing them closer to Him in search of comfort. I don't remember my dad or mom ever blaming God or expressing anger toward Him, although they must have experienced all those feelings.

As for me, I knew the Bible commanded me to love God *with all my heart, with all my soul, and with all my mind*. Since I was compliant, I did what I was told to do. I loved God, but I never trusted Him. In hindsight, it took years before the knowledge of His goodness penetrated my heart. So you see, knowing God is good (in your head) and experiencing Him as good (in your heart) are two different things.

In contrast to Anne's childhood experience, I (Tim) didn't experience much pain or loss during my growing-up years. The first funeral I ever went to was my grandma's, and that wasn't until I was a teenager. But once I joined the fire department, the reality of life's pain often stirred up doubts that caused me to question God's goodness. Dealing with the devastation of fires, tragic accidents, heart attacks, crib deaths, and vehicle and motorcycle fatalities were all part of the job. For every fireman there are those few calls that are never forgotten. For me, it was two separate fires where I had to place young children in body bags. At times like those, I struggled to understand how a good God could allow such bad things to happen to good people.

WHEN FAITH SMACKS UP AGAINST REAL LIFE

One of the most tragic events in both our lives happened in our eleventh year of marriage. My (Tim's) brother-in-law, a generous and loving man, committed suicide. Tom was only thirty-seven years old when he died. He was so much more than just our brother-in-law. He was a husband, a father, a son, an uncle, a brother, a friend, and a fireman. Tom had his whole life ahead of him. For reasons we will never understand this side of eternity, his life ended way too soon. He not only left my sister with three young children, he left a huge void that still exists today in the lives of many who loved him. Looking back, Tom's death began a season of loss for our family. This tragedy only added to the growing question we both kept locked in our hearts: We know *God is good, but is He really good…to us?*

A few years after Tom died we moved back to Elk Grove Village, the town where Anne and I grew up. We wanted to live closer to our parents. Two months after we moved into our house, I was sitting on the couch in our family room with my son Timmy watching the seventh game of the World Series, the Atlanta Braves vs. the Minnesota Twins at the Metrodome. The phone rang and Timmy picked it up. When he handed the phone to me, I heard my mom say, "Dad collapsed." I hung up the phone and dialed 9-1-1. Anne and I jumped into my fire department car and raced to their house with emergency lights on and sirens blaring. By the time we pulled up, the paramedics had already arrived. They defibrillated my dad as we stood in the kitchen holding Mom. Every effort to save Dad's life was unsuccessful. Only three short years after Tom's death, we lost Dad.

It was during those difficult days, as we gazed honestly into our own hearts, that we realized that at times our theology didn't match our real-life experiences. Although we knew in our heads that God was good, our experiences seemed to block us from personally embracing His goodness. We realized that it wasn't enough for us to just know that God was good. We wanted to truly believe He was good to us. It wasn't enough to know that God is love. We had to come to the place where we truly believed that God loved us. We wanted to know that He saw our pain and cared about the circumstances in our lives. We didn't want our understanding of God's love and goodness to just be intellectual; we wanted it to be real. After a number of years of marriage, we needed to answer a deeper question: *Do we believe that God is good to us?*

GOODNESS AT WORK THROUGH PAIN

While we were still processing the pain of losing Tom and Dad, our friend Barb was diagnosed with terminal cancer. We'd met this young woman when she was just nineteen years old. She was volunteering her time in the Sonlight Express youth group at Willow Creek, where Tim also was a leader. Barb seemed to fall in love with our family, and Tim naturally took her under his wing like a little sister.

One day we were visiting her at the hospital. The cancer had progressed so far that the doctors were giving Barb only a few weeks to live. Afraid to die alone, she asked if we would pray about her moving into our home. I (Anne) will never forget her saying, "I feel so alive when I'm around you and your family. If you just let me move in, I know I'll get stronger."

Well-meaning friends suggested that it might not be healthy for our young children to share their home with someone who was terminally ill. One couple who cared deeply about us said with conviction, "This is too hard. Your kids are all going to end up in counseling one day." In spite of what we were hearing, we really felt like God was in this and we invited Barb to move in.

The months that followed were more difficult than we ever could have ever imagined. But at the same time, we witnessed holy moments during those five months that were also unimaginable. Once again, God was telling us a story through the circumstances of our life. He used cancer to teach us how to live near death while praying for life. God used people we didn't even know to illustrate His goodness.

I'll never forget the day a woman from another church showed up at our door with a guitar and a few other women, asking if they could pray with Barb. God used those women to transform our house into a house of worship. They prayed with a boldness we had never experienced. They read Scriptures and anointed Barb's head with oil. It wasn't what they did that communicated to us so much as what they believed. They believed they were speaking to a good Father and therefore were very comfortable asking Him for good things on Barb's behalf.

God used these women to teach us how to pray for someone who was too weak to pray for herself. I wonder if those women knew that God was telling a story through their lives, a story that modeled an aspect of His character we had never seen before. Listening to them pray and worship gave me permission to ask God for things I didn't realize I could ask Him for. Somehow their faith was being imparted to me. I was beginning to believe that God was not only good…but He was good to *me*. I watched as a good Father surrounded His daughter with family and friends in those last months, ensuring that her fear of dying alone would never be realized. We all experienced God's goodness and love as He prepared

Barb for her heavenly homecoming early one January morning before the sun came up.

During the months Barb lived in our home, Tim's mom also had been battling cancer. Only days after Barb's funeral the doctors were talking about admitting Mom into the hospice program. It didn't take Tim's family long to decide that she needed to come home instead. Since we already had a hospice room set up for Barb, we decided Mom would stay with us. Everyone in the family agreed to take turns helping out, but none of us realized how quickly she would deteriorate. One night Mom was so sick we couldn't leave her side. Tim and I were up all night taking turns caring for her. We lay on the floor next to her hospital bed, trying to get some sleep before the sun came up. We planned to call the family in the morning to tell them we couldn't do it anymore, that we were not equipped to give her the kind of constant care that she needed. We didn't have to make that call. Mom died in our arms before sunrise. It had only been a month since Barb died.

It was during those difficult months that our belief in God's goodness moved from our heads to our hearts. When our faith was challenged, we were positioned to see Him in new ways. In the midst of our trials and difficulties we didn't always have the right answers. In fact, we weren't even sure what the right questions were. But God was inviting us to live in the **Larger Story** where He was the main character. He was birthing within us an unshakable conviction in His goodness.

Are you familiar with the saying, "You can't take your children further than you have already gone"? While God was weaving His story of goodness into our lives, our children were watching. It wasn't until years later, when we moved to Colorado Springs, that we began to see the fruit from that long season of pain and loss. Our daughter Colleen was completing her master's degree in social work at Denver University, where she specialized in family trauma response and recovery. At that time, she was accepted into an internship program at the Air Force Academy. While training as a counselor, she met a woman who had been diagnosed with terminal cancer. This woman lived a very quiet life without family in the area. Although Colleen hadn't known her very long, she found herself sitting at this woman's bedside shortly after she was admitted to the hospice program at the hospital.

Within days the woman slipped into a coma and her body began to fail. Tim and I watched from a distance, moved by Colleen's ability to respond to this woman's needs with wisdom and insight that was far beyond her years. Colleen moved around death with a confidence and grace that only God could have given her. It wasn't until later that I realized the circumstances of our life had equipped Colleen to respond to trauma, death, and the needs of others.

It did not really matter whether or not Colleen knew this woman personally. After all, it wasn't friendship that brought the two of them together; it was God. Colleen had something valuable to offer this woman who was facing death. Colleen had a personal relationship with the only One who could save this woman. So she spent her days telling her about the great Physician, the Healer, and the Comforter. Our daughter did what she'd seen us do, what she'd seen others doing in our home. She sat at the bedside of this comatose woman and loved her like Jesus. She held her hand and whispered stories in her ear. She played worship music in her room and prayed for her. She told her what she imagined heaven to be like. Her quiet presence was saying, *Don't be afraid…I'm right here with you and so is Jesus. You are not alone.*

Observing our daughter, we realized God was turning the pain of the past into hope for the future. God was bringing us full circle. I (Anne) was reminded that throughout my childhood, I was watching…and God was there. Likewise, through the years of death and loss our children were watching us…and God was there. They were listening to the worship music that played softly in our home and they heard our prayers. They were watching as we held Barb's hand and combed Mom's hair. They watched as laughter and tears often broke the grip that death sometimes held. All those years our children were watching…and God was there.

Our oldest child, Tim, has his master's degree in social work from Colorado State. He is a caseworker in Colorado Springs where he transitions youth who have been convicted as felons back into the community. Our daughter Amy and her husband live in Michigan, where Curt is a banker who works with non-profit institutions and Amy is fulfilling the noble call to be a wife and mom. Our daughter Colleen lives in Texas with her husband, Johnny, who is a pastor at a local church. Colleen is a new mom and works part-time as a counselor. Last but not least is

Cate-the-Great, who earned her social work degree at Colorado State University, where she worked with developmentally disabled adults. Cate is currently completing her master's degree at the Jane Addams College of Social Work. Her field placement is at a Chicago County Hospital where she is working on the Pediatric unit as part of the Child Protective Services team. We see in Cate a natural ability to connect emotionally with people. Her insight and perspective are healing to those the Lord brings into her life.

Each of our children has an unbelievable capacity for love and nurture. They have a tenderness that often comes through knowing God and experiencing His faithfulness through difficult life circumstances. Believing God is good changes everything!

SEEING OBSTACLES AS OPPORTUNITIES

As we look back over thirty-plus years of marriage, one thing we've learned is that the reality of God's goodness is not information a person learns in a classroom or finds in a book. Gaining a personal conviction of God's goodness is something that happens only over time through real life experiences.

Through the circumstances of life, God continues to teach us that He is good. If someone were to ask us today if we believed God was good, we would say yes. If someone asked us if we believed God was good to *us*, we again would say yes. We believe with all our hearts that God is good to us. We have personally experienced His goodness. This has positively impacted every area of our lives and marriage.

The Bible does not say, "Consider it all joy *if* you encounter trials"; it says "*when* you encounter various trials."[3] Every marriage faces trials. Every man and woman will have their mettle tested. The foundations of their faith will be shaken. The Bible says that difficulties, pain, and trials make a person complete. There is something about the process of pain that invites a person to trust God and believe in His goodness. Trusting God allows a person to respond with deeper levels of maturity.

We will never fully understand why God allows bad things to happen to good people. Or why He sometimes seems silent when we long for Him to speak. Over the years Job 1:21 has become our family life verse. We've held on to these words during times of death and loss: "The LORD gave and the LORD has taken away. Blessed be the name of the LORD." Job had more than his share of suffering, and he never got the answers to many of his *why* questions. He was unaware of a battle that was going on in the heavens between God and Satan. But despite his wife's urging to curse God and die, Job chose to trust that what was happening to him was part of God's **Larger Story**.

Job's life lesson — and ours as well — is that faith is not about what happens to us but about how we respond to what happens to us. At some point in our own trials, we had to choose. We made a decision to anchor our faith in these bedrock truths: God is love, He is good, He can be trusted. We pray you believe and live out each of these truths.

Remember, while you may not always like the story you are living, the story is not about you! Every challenge you face in your marriage is an opportunity to Reflect and Reveal God's goodness to each other, your families, and the world.

+ Chapter 4

A Three-Way Conversation

Growing in Unity Through Prayer

I (Anne) grew up in a praying family. When my parents took us all to church, I watched them kneel down, fold their hands, and close their eyes to pray. Occasionally I would hear them say to someone, "We're praying for you." When we gathered together for a family meal, my dad would lead us in praying, "Bless us, oh Lord, and these Thy gifts, which we are about to receive from Thy bounty, through Christ our Lord. Amen."

As children we prayed the Lord's Prayer at bedtime. Every night for years I repeated the exact same words to God: "Our Father who art in heaven, hallowed be thy name. Thy kingdom come, Thy will be done on earth as it is in heaven…" Even as a young child I must have had a desire for a more personal connection with God, because at the end of the Lord's Prayer I always added a personal message. "God bless Mom, Dad, Patty, John, Colleen, Skokie Grandma, Skokie Papa, big Gram and big Papa. God bless all my friends and relatives, make me good and keep me healthy. Amen."

My bedtime request for blessings was the closest I ever got to a personal conversation with God. For the first twenty years of my life, my prayers remained virtually the same. I viewed God as a powerful Creator rather than as a loving Father who longed to be in relationship with me.

It never occurred to me to ask my parents why they prayed…or what they prayed…or if God ever answered their prayers. None of those questions seemed to matter. What made the deepest impression on me as a child was the simple knowledge that my dad and mom prayed. Something about their consistent prayers provided a foundation for my understanding that prayer was worthwhile, but it wasn't until I became an adult that I began to experience the intimacy connected with being in relationship with the God who longs to hear from me and respond back.

In a book titled *Prayer*, Richard Foster describes the miracle and mystery that happens every time a person prays. He says coming to prayer is like coming home.

+   "Nothing feels more right, more like what we are created to be and to do. Yet at the same time we are confronted with great mysteries. Who hasn't struggled with the puzzle of unanswered prayer? Who hasn't wondered how a finite person can commune with an infinite Creator of the universe? Who hasn't questioned whether prayer isn't merely psychological manipulation after all? We do our best, of course, to answer these knotty questions but when all is said and done, there is a sense in which these mysteries remain unanswerable.... At such times we must learn to be comfortable with the mystery."[1]   +

Just as the marriage relationship, in which a woman and a man become one, is both a miracle and a mystery, so prayer is a miracle and a mystery. The miracle is being able to communicate with the Creator of the universe. The mystery is God's desire to relate back to us in ways that draw us into deeper intimacy and relationship with Him. One of the ways that happens is through prayer.

Marriage can be described as an ongoing conversation between a husband and wife. Often, a couple can increase their intimacy simply by talking and listening to each other. In a similar way, prayer can be described as an ongoing conversation with God: a person talks and God listens, God communicates and a person listens.

The Bible makes it clear that praying is part of God's will for our lives. Not only do we have numerous examples of Jesus praying to His Father, but He also told us how to pray, reminding us that we should not lose heart.[2] The apostle Paul urges us, "Be anxious for nothing, but in everything by prayer and supplication with thanksgiving let your requests be made known to God."[3]

In his book *Prayer Is Invading the Impossible*, Jack Hayford includes a chapter titled, "If We Don't, He Won't."[4] C. Peter Wagner further expands on this truth:

+   "The sovereign God...has chosen to order His creation in such a way that many of His actions are contingent on the prayers of His people. It is as if God has a Plan A He will implement if believers pray. If they do not, He has a Plan B. Plan A is obviously better for all concerned than Plan B. The choice, according to God's design, is ours."[5]   +

As individuals joined in relationship with God, we pray not only because it's our responsibility to do so, but because it is our delight to engage with the One we love. Prayer is an invitation to deeper intimacy through conversation with God.

For the two of us, prayer is much more than a spiritual discipline. It's an act of intimacy that draws us together as husband and wife. In order to pray, we must first slow our lives down long enough so we each can hear the heart's cry of the other. Prayer represents an invitation to join each other in an intimate dialogue with God. Praying together reconnects us to our life source, thereby helping us refocus.

God uses prayer to knit our hearts together with Him and with each other. Whether we are thanking God for His blessings, asking Him to impart His strength, petitioning Him for things we cannot accomplish on our own, or seeking His direction for our next step — prayer is a constant reminder that *it's not about "us"*.

THE POWER OF PRAYER IN A MARRIAGE

Engaging in prayer not only helps you draw closer to God; it also impacts your relationship with your spouse and those around you.

Throughout our marriage, God has placed prayer mentors in our lives, men and women who have blessed our family through their consistent prayers on our behalf. Dick Swetman, our first small-group leader, is now an eighty-two-year-old spiritual father. Every day for almost thirty years he has prayed on his knees for each member of our family. As our children continue to grow up, get married, and have children of their own, he adds each new family member to his prayers. He has modeled the power of consistent prayer to us. With each passing year, His prayers have protected our family in ways we will never know this side of heaven.

God has also blessed us with other spiritually gifted men and women who have encouraged us to advance in our prayer lives. Because of those who have modeled the way for us, prayer is a top priority in our lives. We believe prayer is a key to successfully living out God's design and purpose for marriage.

One day I (Anne) had the television turned on while I moved from room to room, cleaning up around the house. Even with the vacuum running I recognized the familiar theme song from the *Oprah* show. Then as I began folding laundry, I could hear a muffled version of an interview and the occasional applause from the audience. Something about the interview caught my attention, so I sat down on the couch and tuned into the show. Oprah was interviewing a woman who had written a book about health and fitness. Since I missed the introduction I didn't catch her name or recognize her work, but this guest appeared to be in great physical shape. Her diet sounded unbelievably strict with a narrow focus on whole foods. From what I heard she exercised regularly and her blood levels were exceptional. She was the picture of health.

As an observer and a young mom with four children, the lifestyle this woman was promoting seemed unattainable to me. Instead of feeling motivated by her story, I felt discouraged. I realized that she was giving out a lot of information but failing to give the audience practical steps on how to achieve the lifestyle she was so passionate about. Then just before it was time to cut to commercial, Oprah looked directly into the camera and said something like, "If I were in the audience and I just heard all that, I'd be thinking to myself, 'Well, all that sounds wonderful, but *how* do we do it?'" The talk-show host put into words exactly what millions of her viewers were probably thinking.

No matter what the topic — how to eat right, how to have a great marriage, how to parent your child, live in financial freedom, dress with a sense of style, or communicate effectively — people don't need *more* information as much as they need to apply principles they already know to their life in a way that will empower them to change.

That's exactly why we're not going to spend time in this chapter giving you more information on why you should pray; instead, we want to offer practical steps to encourage you *to* pray. We want you to experience for yourself how praying with your spouse can increase Spirit and Soul Oneness.

NONSTOP CONVERSATION

The Bible says, "Rejoice always; pray without ceasing; in everything give thanks; for this is God's will for you in Christ Jesus."[6] The phrase *without ceasing* means "nonstop, never-ending." That kind of praying may bring to mind a picture of a monastery filled with cloistered monks on their knees constantly crying out to God.

It makes us wonder, Can a person really "pray without ceasing" in the midst of real life?

We believe the answer is yes. Praying without ceasing is not repetitively saying certain prayers out loud. Praying without ceasing refers to living in a constant state of awareness that God is with you. Because of God's total, constant presence, a person can engage in ongoing conversations with Him even while carrying on the activities of daily life.

God created men and women with the ability to multitask. Our minds are capable of doing more than one thing at a time. A person can be busy at home or at work and simultaneously be in tune with God. We call this "dual listening." While having a conversation with a spouse, a person's heart can be listening to the Holy Spirit and seeking His direction. For example, whenever we teach at a Marriage Advance, we are speaking to the audience while we are simultaneously listening to God and each other. We are talking, looking at our notes, preparing ourselves for the next section, and keeping our eyes on the clock all at the same time. As we are doing all these things we are also listening to God as we pray without ceasing.

Phillip Yancey touches on this point when he writes, "Prayer means keeping company with God who is already present."[7] Brother Lawrence also refers to living out a life of prayer in his book, *The Practice of the Presence of God*.[8] This small book is filled with letters and conversations that explain what it means to pray without ceasing. Brother Lawrence describes prayer as an ongoing relationship with God, an intimate interaction flowing out of a deep connection with the lover of his soul.

Prayer is not a religious activity. It is not something a person does for God. Prayer is like breathing. We take God into our heart and soul and release Him back into the atmosphere around us. Prayer needn't involve spoken words; it may be an attitude of praise, worship, or thanksgiving. It may be a wave of grief at the thought of someone who is lost or hurting. In that moment, we turn our hearts to God and silently express our feelings to Him.

PRAYING TOGETHER

This concept of prayer as an ongoing conversation carries over into your prayer life as a married couple. Whenever a husband and wife encourage one another, build each other up, or comfort each other, this is prayer. When a couple shows love and respect to each other, this is prayer. When they Reflect and Reveal the heart of Jesus to each other, this is prayer. When they affirm God's love and celebrate His presence in their lives, this is prayer. When they celebrate sexual intimacy, this is prayer. When they are listening to worship music or celebrating God's majesty, this is prayer. Prayer can be a tender touch or an encouraging look that conveys God's love and care to a spouse.

God lives in every Christ follower. A married couple who is aware of God and has a desire to include Him in every area of their lives understands the essence of what it means to "*pray without ceasing*."

At the same time, incredible closeness and spiritual unity can result from setting aside times to pray aloud together. Such prayer times can take a variety of forms. Some couples lean toward a formal liturgical style, while others like their conversations with God to be spontaneous and very personal. When it comes to prayer and being in relationship with someone you love, there is no right or wrong style of sharing your heart. After all, "Peter knelt, Jeremiah stood, Nehemiah sat down, Abraham prostrated himself, and Elijah put his face between his knees. In Jesus' day most Jews stood, lifting their open eyes to heaven. The Virgin Mary prayed in poetry; Paul interspersed his prayers with singing."[9]

Merging your personal prayer styles, however, can sometimes present a challenge. We've learned that being a good listener is a vital part of a shared prayer life. But listening is a learned skill; it does not come naturally.

When the two of us first started praying together, we often found the experience disappointing and frustrating. I (Tim) particularly tended to be distracted when Anne was praying. Although I started out determined to listen, my mind would start to wander and I became preoccupied with my own thoughts. At times when Anne prayed I got bored with what seemed to be her monologue to God. I felt as if I was listening in on someone else's private conversation. Rather than being a participant in a shared activity, I felt like an observer, watching Anne connect with God.

In spite of the rough start, we were committed to praying together as a couple. We knew there was untapped power in a praying marriage. We just had to figure out a way to make it more relevant and enjoyable. One thing we didn't want to do was turn it into a religious activity. Prayer is supposed to be a living relationship with a good Father, not a duty we're required to perform.

We decided to try a different way of praying together. Since we knew that long dialogues with God didn't work for us as a couple, we agreed to take turns praying in short sentences. We went back and forth, creating a rhythm that kept us flowing together. From the first time we prayed together like this, it has worked for us. It feels like something we are doing together.

Here's how it works. Typically we begin with thanksgiving and praise:

Tim: *"Lord, we are so glad that You are our Father…"*

Anne: *"Yes, Lord, we praise You today for Your love and goodness…"*

Tim: *"We worship You today…"*

We continue going back and forth until one of us feels it is time to shift to another prayer focus. At some point in our time together we pray for our marriage and for each member of our family:

Tim: *"Thank you for our marriage…for our oneness in You…"*

Anne: *"Lord, thanks for Tim…for the way he loves you and reflects Your character…"*

Tim: *"Give us a very long, healthy, and faithful marriage together as one…"*

Anne: *"Let us leave a marital spiritual legacy to our kids and others…"*

Implementing this simple model of short, one-sentence prayers revolutionized our prayer life. The creative options of this style of praying together are limitless. For example, you can rotate through specific prayer topics, like this:

Monday — family prayer
Tuesday — special requests
Wednesday — the local church
Thursday — people who don't know Jesus
Friday — the sick
Saturday — world issues
Sunday — praise and thanksgiving

We encourage you to experiment with different approaches to prayer, some of which we'll detail in the next few pages. Whatever format you choose, remember that praying together in unity is powerful and the enemy knows it. He will do everything he can to discourage a couple from advancing in prayer because he understands the synergistic power that occurs through spiritual encounters with God. This is one reason a couple often finds it difficult to begin to pray together and why it's so important that they grow in their listening skills. A couple needs to learn how to listen to one another and to the Holy Spirit. He is the Comforter and the Counselor. The Holy Spirit loves to give His children wisdom, revelation, and new insights.

Here are some keys we've found to successfully praying together:

+ Invite the Holy Spirit to lead your prayer times.
+ Use short, one-sentence prayers. Long monologues invite distractions.
+ Alternate back and forth to stay focused and hold your attention.
+ Give each other permission to stop and listen to the Holy Spirit.
+ Keep your prayers conversational. Remember prayer is about relationship with God. Prayer is a husband, a wife, and God together celebrating friendship, oneness, and community.
+ Don't get religious; praying isn't about rules but about being in relationship with God.
+ Pray as God leads. Ask Him to give you creative ideas specifically for you and your marriage.

We're convinced that praying together strengthens a couple's unity with God and each other as few other activities can. We challenge you to engage regularly in this life-giving experience, and we'd like to suggest a few other ideas for keeping it fresh.

Prayer Walking

We have always enjoyed walking together outside. When our children were younger we often bundled them into a stroller and headed down the street to the park. Walking gave us a chance to talk to each other while we enjoyed the outdoors.

Shortly after we were challenged to pray together as a couple, our walks became prayer walks. Getting out of the house provided some fitness activity while we prayed for our family and friends. We followed the same approach we described earlier of taking turns in short prayer; we just added walking. This was even more enjoyable than sitting at home praying. Walking increased the length of our prayer times and encouraged us to stay focused.

We found that adding variety and creativity to our prayer walks was also important. We prayed for neighbors as we walked past their homes. If we saw an emergency vehicle or an accident, we prayed for the situation. When we walked past a hospital or nursing home, we prayed for those sick or injured. When we walked by a fire hydrant, we prayed for firemen we knew. If we saw a funeral procession or passed a cemetery we prayed for those grieving the loss of loved ones.

We have prayer walked in specific areas of a city and asked the Holy Spirit to lead us. It is amazing what He brings to mind. Even as beginners we were surprised at how long we were able to pray together as a couple and stay focused on a specific topic. Time passes quickly when you're outside enjoying God's beauty and companionship in the company of your spouse.

Praying Scripture

On many occasions during His time on earth, Jesus quoted from the prophets and other passages in the Bible. He knew the Scriptures and understood their power. Hebrews 4:12 tells us, "The word of God is living and active and sharper than any two-edged sword."

When we were pastors of prayer at a local church we introduced the concept of praying Scriptures at a mid-week prayer gathering. We made a list of our favorite Scriptures and prayed them out loud. We invited those in attendance to open their Bibles, ask the Holy Spirit to lead them, and declare God's Word out loud. Our prayers sounded something like this:

"Lord, your Word says, 'Ask, and it will be given to you; seek, and you will find; knock, and it will be opened to you.'[10] *We are asking for a miracle today. Will you open the hearts of the unbelievers in our city? Lord, your Word says that if we want favor with both God and man and a reputation for good judgment and common sense, then we are to trust you completely and not ourselves. In everything we do we are to put you first and You will direct us and crown our efforts with success.*[11] *We trust You, Lord, and we want to put You first in everything. Give us strength to let go of our desires. Lord, give us Your desires."*

Over the years we've received very positive feedback from couples who pray together using Scripture. They tell us that doing so helps them focus on the promises of God rather than on their prayer request. This seems to bolster their confidence as they lean on God's Word, fully expecting Him to answer.

One particular time we challenged couples to focus on the promises in 2 Peter 3:9 as they prayed for friends and loved ones who were not in a relationship with the Lord. Their prayer may have sounded something like this: *"Lord, Your Word says that You are not slow about Your promise, as some count slowness, but patient, not wishing for any to perish but for all to come to repentance. Based on the promises of Your Word, I pray for _____ ."* Reading through the Word reminded couples of God's promises and faithfulness.

When husbands and wives discipline themselves to pray and begin seeing their prayers answered, their faith is built up as they advance in intimacy. You can only imagine how motivated they are to continue praying together. This is just one example of the power available in praying the Bible.

God's Word says if we pray then He will act: "If My people who are called by My name will humble themselves, and pray and seek My face, and turn from their wicked ways, then I will hear from heaven, and will forgive their sin and heal their land."[12]

We challenge you to invite the Holy Spirit to lead you in this exercise: Open your Bible, locate a portion of Scripture that speaks to your heart, then pray it out loud. Stand firmly on God's promises.

Praying Scripture not only helps you align your requests with God's purposes, but it is also a good way to put His Word in your heart. You can use your Bible or invest in tools to help. Early in our marriage we purchased prayer books that highlight specific Scriptures to help us pray. We regularly declare these Scriptures over each other and over our family.

Praying as Spiritual Warfare

Years ago I (Tim) had a desire to pray more specifically for our marriage and family. I had been reading some books on spiritual warfare and learned that prayer is an offensive weapon that provides protection against the attacks of the enemy.

As the servant leader of our home, I made a commitment to cover our family in prayer on a daily basis. I developed the following spiritual warfare prayer that I pray out loud during my personal prayer time over our family.

Spiritual Warfare Prayer

I declare to all powers and principalities, to all demons and enemy forces that God has given me authority in my household. May nothing interfere with my prayer life for my marriage and family.

I love, care for, honor, respect, and want to sacrifice for Anne, the kids, and grandkids. Therefore, in the name of Christ Jesus, I forbid the enemy and any evil spirits to attack or scheme against my wife, children, grandchildren, or me.

In Christ Jesus' name and Truth...in the Sacred Blood of the Lamb...I specifically address any schemes of the enemy: you have no power, authority, or legal rights in my marriage, family, or home. Any and all schemes, curses, footholds, strongholds, generational sins and iniquities, these are all cancelled and returned with blessings. Any ground previously gained by the evil one is taken back in the power of God and the Holy Spirit. You will have to go through God the Father, God the Son, and God the Holy Spirit to get to me and my family.

Lord, please daily fill me, my wife, kids, and grandkids with your Holy Spirit.

I humbly pray this prayer in the name, power, and authority of God the Father, God the Son, and God the Holy Spirit. I also pray this prayer in the authority you give me as servant leader in my marriage, family, and home.

While a written prayer does not contain any special power, it is one way to train yourself to cover specific areas that need to be prayed for. At the beginning of this chapter we emphasized that it is not *what* you pray or *how* you pray…but *that* you pray. If you believe that marriages and families are under attack, you may want to write a spiritual warfare prayer of your own. People who implement spiritual warfare prayers tell us they are more aware of the spiritual battle in their home and feel the protection that prayer provides.

Whether you do it in writing or simply commit to verbally covering your family in prayer, we challenge husbands and wives to prayerfully implement a plan to pray for their marriage and family.

Creating a Prayer Shield for Others

The Bible says, "Where there is no vision, the people are unrestrained."[13] When we consider the power available to husbands and wives through prayer, we envision the church playing a larger role in strengthening today's family. Just imagine churches scheduling specific times to gather together to pray for marriages and families. What if husbands, wives, and children, as well as singles, divorced, and widowed, were invited to gather together to pray? These diverse and intergenerational gatherings could be a tool to facilitate intercession and prayer specifically for marriages and families.

We encourage you to pray about whether God is calling you to launch such a ministry at your church. However He leads, we believe that part of your role in Reflecting and Revealing the character of God involves caring deeply about other people — caring so deeply that you commit to supporting them in prayer. One way to do this is to create a prayer shield.

We first heard about the concept of prayer shields when we met Dr. C. Peter Wagner and his wife, Doris. For years, the Wagners mentored us by modeling the importance of prayer. After reading Dr. Wagner's book

Prayer Shield,[14] we were more convinced than ever of the power of prayer. Dr. Wagner describes a prayer shield team as any number of people who are intentional about their commitment to pray for an individual, a family, church, organization, or nation. We decided we wanted to increase our spiritual protection by forming a prayer shield team for our family and REAL LIFE Ministries. Since this team has been in place, we have felt the protection that our prayer shield provides.

We believe there is a positive synergistic effect when people agree and strategically pray together. We encourage you and your spouse to consider forming a prayer shield team to target the specific prayer needs of your family and marriage. We also encourage you to return the blessing by being a part of someone else's prayer shield team.

We are very serious about the importance of a prayer shield. In fact, every time we go to local churches to minister we have two non-negotiable requirements:

1.   The authority of church leadership is extended to us, and;

2.   A prayer shield team is in place before, during, and after each Marriage Advance or REAL LIFE Ministries gathering. Our experience has convinced us that prayer shields provide a powerful defense against the enemy.

While creating a prayer shield involves praying for a specific person or group on a regular basis, periods of crisis call for a different kind of intercession.

During my (Tim's) years as a firefighter, I knew that for every major fire and emergency incident an officer and a team of firefighters would be assigned as a Rapid Intervention Team (RIT). The RIT team was not responsible for any of the immediate tasks required in handling the emergency; they were assigned to the incident commander and required to remain at the command post. The team members were in full turnout gear and had all their firefighting tools and equipment. They were available at a moment's notice should anything occur to place firefighters in danger. If the RIT team was called upon, it meant something bad had happened to their brothers and sisters fighting the fire. In any sudden emergency, such as a flashover, backdraft, or collapse, the incident commander would immediately direct the RIT team to handle it.

Imagine what it would be like if local churches developed marriage Rapid Intervention Teams. This could include teams of couples who have a heart for God, are trained in marriage and prayer, and are standing by in the event of an unexpected marital emergency. The marriage RIT team would be available in situations where a couple is confronting abuse, adultery, addiction, or some other threat. The RIT team would be notified and could step in with help and support at critical times. Just like in the fire service, marriage RIT prayer teams could be used by God to save marriages. They would hold up the arms of those too weak to pray for themselves.[15]

POWER UP!

We believe prayer is the most untapped source of power on the planet. We urge you to make the choice to develop and implement a prayer strategy for your life and for your marriage.

Be forewarned, if you make this decision, you will get resistance from the enemy. Stand strong, put on the full armor of God, and clothe yourself with God's mantle of humility. Although we've tried in this chapter to equip you with several ideas for increasing your unity through prayer, the best strategy for taking your prayer life to the next level is to stop reading this book and pray! Ask God what next steps He has for you in your prayer journey as a couple.

Review Part 1

In Part 1 we looked at God's original design for marriage (**Spirit Oneness**), established at Creation. We looked in detail at how He intended for man and woman *together* to Reflect and Reveal His character. We also noted His instruction for them to Rule over Creation (the creation mandate) and to Reproduce (the procreation mandate), and in the chapters to come we'll look at each of those responsibilities more closely.

As we conclude Part 1, we encourage you to take a closer look at your marriage and review your life story, asking yourself the following questions:

+ Am I in a personal relationship with God?
+ Is my spouse in a personal relationship with God?
+ Am I Reflecting and Revealing the unity and community of the Trinity?
+ Am I living in the **Larger Story** with God as the main character?
+ Am I growing in intimacy with God and my spouse through prayer?

REAL LIFE *Companion Journal* is available for study questions and personal applications for each chapter.

2

REAL LIFE MARRIAGE
it's not about me

Soul Oneness

+ Chapter 5

Rulership Lost

How Sin Distorted God's Design for Marriage

Beeeeeeeeeeeeeep...

The speaker crackled and the piercing alarm tone activated.

"Request for the fire department, 1880 Bonnie Brae Lane...woman with a gunshot wound to the head..."

Adrenalin pumped into my system and sent my heart racing as our team hustled into action. "Ambulance 8, Squad 1, and Battalion 1 responding."

As we headed to the location, we got an update from dispatch: "Ambulance 8, be advised the gunshot victim's husband is in the apartment building. He is armed and dangerous! There are small children in the apartment... Stand by for police and proceed with extreme caution."

Upon arriving at the scene we were escorted into the apartment building by a police officer. We took the elevator to the third floor, then hurried down a long hallway behind the officer, who had his .357 Magnum drawn. When we kicked in the apartment door, what we saw was beyond description.

There was blood everywhere. Three young children were running around the apartment screaming, "Daddy shot Mommy! Daddy shot Mommy!" As a rookie fireman who had been on the job for only a few months, I didn't know what to do. I felt as if the scene was racing past me at fast-frame speed while simultaneously unfolding in slow motion. Our portable radios were blaring. The police officer rushed through the apartment with his gun held high, screaming for the husband. The kids were hysterical. The sights, smells, and sounds of death assaulted me.

But we had a job to do. Kneeling in the large pool of blood next to this beautiful young wife and mom, we started checking her ABCs (airway, breathing, circulation). We held our personal emotions at bay and focused on what little we could do at this point. We quickly realized there would be no good end to this tragic situation.

Later, in the calm of my own home, I couldn't help but wonder how things had gone so wrong for this couple. I imagine their marriage started out like most marriages. Surely at one time this husband and wife had felt the kind of love that motivated them to choose each other for a lifetime. At some point they both stood together before God, family, and friends vowing to love, honor, and cherish each other all the days of their lives.

For better, for worse,
For richer, for poorer,
In good times and in bad,
In sickness and in health,
To love and to cherish,
Until death do us part.

Surely on that day no one could have predicted such a tragic end to this marriage. So at what point after this couple was pronounced husband and wife did their hopes and dreams begin to die? When did they lose sight of God's purposes for marriage?

While most couples will never experience this level of violence, the reality is that countless husbands and wives are guilty of murder — maybe not with a gunshot wound to the head but with lethal blows to their spouse's heart. Negative words and cruel actions can do more damage than bullets. While they may not lead to physical death, they contribute to the death of a spouse's spirit and soul. They nurture doubts that cause couples to ask themselves "Why isn't our marriage as fulfilling as I had hoped? What happened to our dreams of unity and oneness? How can we experience the relationship that God promised to the first couple in their paradise home?"

IMAGINE THE POSSIBILITIES

As we saw in the Creation story, God's primary purpose for marriage is for a man and a woman to Reflect and Reveal the plurality and character of God through their relationship with Him, with each other, and with all whose lives they touch. We also saw that God appointed man and woman together to Rule (to take dominion) over the earth. He declared this purpose first in Genesis 1:26, then reaffirmed it directly to the man and woman in verse 28:

"God blessed them; and God said to them, 'Be fruitful and multiply, and fill the earth, and subdue it; and *rule* over the fish of the sea and over the birds of the sky, and over every living thing that moves on the earth.'" *(emphasis added)*

What does it mean for a man and a woman to Rule? The term Rule can be used interchangeably with the phrases *take dominion* and *subdue the earth*. The same concept can be expressed as *taking authority, taking care of*, and *bringing under godly control*.

In the beginning God instituted the following authority structure:

God

Man and Woman

Nature

To understand God's intent for Rulership you need to know that all authority comes from God. He is the ultimate authority. But He does not wield His authority like a power-obsessed control-freak. Instead, He is the author of free will and the original servant leader who is committed to relationships. Jesus not only understood this, He demonstrated that true authority comes through submission. Standing at the cross, the cosmic crossroads for all of human history, Jesus had a choice. He could have chosen to live in the **smaller story** by asking "What's in this for me?" He could have taken a pass on suffering and death and made self the main character in His story. But Jesus understood the importance of relationship. He knew sin had caused relational brokenness. He also knew the price required to restore relationship between humanity and God.

Jesus did not want to endure unspeakable suffering. Shortly before His betrayal He cried out in anguish, pleading, "Father, if You are willing, remove this cup from Me." Then He made the unselfish choice to step into the **Larger Story**, saying, "Yet not My will but Yours be done."[1] Jesus modeled and declared for all humanity, "It's not about me!"

In marriage, taking authority in Rulership requires a couple to submit to God and to one another. Each spouse chooses to die to their own selfishness as they try to out-serve each other. Through Rulership a husband and wife step into the **Larger Story** with God as the main character. Couples who understand Rulership understand the incredible possibilities for kingdom advancement that come from living out "marriage — it's not about me."

God's vision for a loving marriage is much bigger than any man or woman. He designed this relationship to positively influence and impact the world unlike anything else. Notice that the text reads, "Be fruitful and multiply, and *fill the earth, and subdue it.*" God commanded couples to extend their Rulership into the world.

Rulership flows out from a husband and wife's oneness and extends to the next generation as couples raise God-centered families. But when a couple extends their God-given rule and subdues the earth, it is not just about their children and future generations. From the family it extends outward to the church, communities, cultures, and nations. Rulership includes caring for the lost, homeless and hungry, widows and orphans, those physically and socially oppressed, as well as next-door neighbors.

Rulership influences every area in a couple's life: how they act, what they say, how they parent their kids, how they relate as lovers, and how they care for others. To accomplish all that God intends for a marriage, to truly take dominion over their world, a couple must rule together in unity by loving, honoring, and respecting each other.

The Trinity provides the blueprint for a couple's unity. God the Father, God the Son, and God the Holy Spirit relate intimately as one. They each have authority, Rulership, and dominion. They mutually submit to one another in equality as reciprocal servants. And since man and woman were created to Reflect and Reveal the nature of the triune God, the same mutual interdependence should mark the marriage relationship.

But unity and interdependence are all too rare in most marriages. So what happened to God's original design?

A SNAKE IN THE GARDEN

At creation the man and woman were mutually dependent on God and each other within their community of oneness. God assigned the authority

Soul Oneness

to Rule over the earth to both the man and the woman. He did not designate any hierarchy within the first marriage. The couple enjoyed mutual equality. Their identity was established through their relationship with God and affirmed by each other. They Reflected and Revealed the plurality of the Trinity. They were naked and not ashamed. Pure, innocent, and without sin they celebrated the one-flesh relationship that is exclusive to marriage.

But the man and woman were not alone...

Satan had entered the garden in the form of a serpent. We don't have a lot of information about Satan, but the Bible describes a point in time before creation when Satan and a third of heaven's angels rebelled against divine authority and became fierce enemies of God. Since that time, Satan's mission has been to steal, kill, and destroy.[2]

The enemy must have been present during creation and watched the story unfold. He watched God form man out of dust from the ground and breathe life into him. He watched as God took a rib from the man and fashioned the woman. He was there when God gave to the man and woman dominion and authority over the earth — the very sort of power he wanted for himself.

Satan is notorious for wanting what is not his. First he wanted to be God, but that position was already taken. So he turned his efforts to stealing Rulership, dominion, and authority from the man and the woman. Satan must have heard God give man this command: "From any tree of the garden you may eat freely; but from the tree of the knowledge of good and evil you shall not eat, for in the day that you eat from it you will surely die."[3]

Dr. Gilbert Bilezikian, in his book *Beyond Sex Roles*, writes:

+ "Quite often, the tree is viewed as a means for testing Adam's obedience, as a malevolent device to make him trip, as a trick perpetrated by God on humans for some mysterious motive hidden within the inscrutable ways of divinity. Such a view demeans the character of God. The definition of the tree shows that it was provided by God to fulfill a positive function. It was the visible reminder to Adam of his humanity and therefore of the necessity for him to remain subservient to God as his creator."[4]   +

In other words the tree was God's reminder to the man and woman that

"I am God; you are not!" Satan knew that if he could get humans to eat from this one tree, he could take over Rulership. Perhaps remembering his own frustration at being denied the role of God, Satan decided to appeal to the humans' longing for power by twisting God's words.

He strategically approached the woman rather than the man. Maybe he knew that the woman was at a disadvantage, having not yet been created when God gave man the command not to eat from the tree of knowledge of good and evil. She did not have the benefit of receiving the prohibition directly from God, although she must have heard about it from her husband.

Knowing this, the enemy asked the woman, "Indeed, has God *said*, 'You shall not eat from *any* tree of the garden'?"[5] This question was carefully designed to deceive.

First, he deliberately minimized the seriousness of God's command by misquoting one word. Satan suggested to the woman that God had *said*, but the text tells us that God had *commanded*.

Second, he purposefully misquoted God's command, asking if "you shall not eat from *any tree* of the garden?" But God's command clearly stated, "From any tree of the garden you may eat freely," except from the tree of the knowledge of good and evil.

The woman responded to the enemy's lies by repeating what she had probably heard from the man: "From the fruit of the trees of the garden we may eat." This is correct — God had said they could eat freely.

She continued, "But from the fruit of the tree which is in the middle of the garden, God *has said*, 'You shall not eat from it or touch it, or you will die.'"[6] This is incorrect — God did not *say*, He *commanded*. The woman had picked up Satan's wording. Not only that, she added to God's command; He never said anything about touching the tree.

Seizing his opportunity, the serpent told the woman another lie: "You surely will not die! For God knows that in the day you eat from it your eyes will be opened, and you will be like God, knowing good and evil."[7]

The enemy introduced suspicion by questioning God's goodness. He suggested that God was holding out on the woman. As is observed in a quote often attributed to Oswald Chambers, "The root of all sin is the suspicion that God is not good."

The woman's response to the serpent's lies may be the most tragic scene in the entire Bible. She rebelled against God and His authority, stepping into the **smaller story** with self as the main character. The text reads, "When the woman saw that the tree was good for food, and that it was a delight to the eyes, and that the tree was desirable to make one wise, she took from its fruit and ate; and she gave also to her husband with her, and he ate."[8] *Her husband with her* implies that the man had watched in silence as this encounter unfolded.

THE SHAME-FEAR-CONTROL CYCLE

Despite Satan's assurance that "You surely will not die," that first bite of forbidden fruit ushered death into the garden, destroying first the couple's intimacy with God and then their intimacy with each other.

"The LORD God called to the man, 'Where are you?'"[9] Now, God is omniscient — He knows everything. He asked Adam a question He already knew the answer to.

Adam's response revealed the devastation already inflicted by sin: "I heard the sound of You in the garden, and I was afraid because I was naked; so I hid myself."[10] Sin opened the door to shame, fear, and a desperate desire for control. *What if our nakedness is exposed? What if our actions are found out? Our only hope is to control the situation by hiding.* This would be the first of countless hide-and-seek games men and women have played with God and with each other throughout history.

Adam and Eve first experienced the shame-fear-control cycle when they disobeyed God. The same response to the consequences of sin is still seen today. Shame, fear, and control work together to form a cycle that can have a negative synergistic effect.[11]

Soul Oneness

We often use the words *shame* and *guilt* interchangeably, but they really are two different things. Guilt is connected to a person's behavior. A person may experience feelings of guilt when they *do* something wrong. Shame, however, runs much deeper. It is the awful sense of "feeling uniquely and hopelessly flawed."[12]

Shame convinces a person they are a mistake, bad, even defective. "Shame sucks the very life out of a person as it causes him (or her) to live continually on guard, always afraid that someone is about to discover and expose their 'flaw.' The lie is that, 'I am different.' Of course, this is being 'different' in a bad way."[13]

Sin is at the root of shame. Shame opens the door for fear. Fear says, *What if I'm found out? What if they reject me?* Fear opens the door to control. Control says, *I will handle this. I will cover my sin (shame) so no one will discover the truth. I will control this situation in an attempt to avoid pain and rejection.* People try to exert control in many ways, including withdrawal, emotional or physical separation, blame shifting, perfectionism, aggressive behavior, criticism, judging, being prideful, passivity, etc.

A person may use the shame-fear-control cycle to self-protect in an attempt to avoid being exposed or rejected, but in reality this cycle entraps its victims, distorting the way people see themselves and how they relate to others. Specifically in marriage, the shame-fear-control cycle can cause disunity and isolate a husband and wife from God and each other, much as it did when sin first entered the world.

Sue made an appointment with me (Anne) to discuss some areas of concern in her marriage. One particular issue was her nearly nonexistent sex life with her husband.

As we talked about her family of origin, Sue admitted that she experienced intense feelings of rejection throughout her growing-up years. The pain from childhood had never been resolved. Now it was affecting her marriage because she interpreted her husband's passive style of relating as another form of rejection.

Soul Oneness

To complicate matters, Sue's history included sexually promiscuous behavior from an early age. By the time she was sixteen she had gotten pregnant and had an abortion. Sue's sexual past was such a deep source of shame that she had never revealed it to anyone, not even her husband.

As the years passed, one of the ways she learned to control her pain was through avoidance. She was a master at redirecting conversations whenever they stirred up any unresolved pain from her past. Controlling conversations allowed her to cover her shame by hiding the emotions she kept locked inside.

She began to recognize that the consequences of sin were affecting the sexual areas of her marriage. Sue was punishing herself. Deep down she didn't think she deserved to enjoy sex with her husband. So many times she wanted to talk to him about it, but she was gripped with fear. A record played over and over in her mind: *What if he can't forgive me? What if he judges me? What if my vulnerability only leads to more shame?* Her questions only escalated her fear, which led to more feelings of shame about her past. Once again, she tried to control her fear and hide her shame by withdrawing from her husband and isolating emotionally.

I explained to Sue how the shame-fear-control cycle works and challenged her to consider the many ways it was causing division in her marriage. Sue was perceptive and teachable. She immediately began to see some of the consequences of the enemy's lies and of her own decision to protect herself. Over time she began to make some connections between her sexual promiscuity and issues with her family of origin, specifically tied to her relationship with her father. The shame, fear, and control she experienced as a young girl continued to play out in her marriage. She controlled through denial, manipulating conversations, lying, and rebelling sexually. From a spiritual perspective, Sue knew God forgave her, but she had never forgiven herself.

Sue opened her heart to God and asked Him for healing. For the first time, she forgave herself and was willing to receive God's forgiveness. As we continued to meet she addressed many of her fears and began to explore her control issues. God was beginning to remove the lies that Sue had believed for so long and replace them with His truth. She began to see herself as God saw her.

Understanding how the enemy used the shame-fear-control cycle in her life freed her to process her sexual history. Eventually she invited her husband to join her in counseling. They began to learn about God's design for marriage and they started working through many difficult and painful issues, replacing shame, fear, and control with intimacy, unity, and Rulership.

It was exciting to watch Sue and her husband advance in their marriage relationship, but her experience reinforces the truth that so many challenges in marriages today can be traced back to the Fall.

THE DEVASTATING CONSEQUENCES OF SIN

As we return to the biblical story, we read God's response to the man's words of shame, fear, and control:

"And He said, 'Who told you that you were naked? Have you eaten from the tree of which I commanded you not to eat?' The man said, 'The woman whom You gave to be with me, she gave me from the tree, and I ate.' Then the LORD God said to the woman, 'What is this you have done?' And the woman said, 'The serpent deceived me, and I ate.'"[14]

It is interesting to note the man and woman's different responses when they were confronted by God. The man blamed his wife and then blamed God. However, the woman responded with integrity; "The serpent deceived me, and I ate."

With the situation out in the open, God then spelled out specific consequences to sin, all of which have a direct impact on marriage.

For the Serpent...

First, God cursed the serpent for his deception and declared enmity between the serpent and the woman. Enmity is defined as "mutual hatred or ill will."[15] It is interesting to us that God specifically placed enmity between the serpent and the woman. Have you ever wondered why enmity was not placed between the serpent and the man? Could God be telling us something significant about the discerning heart of a woman? Perhaps the woman's response to God — "The enemy deceived me and I ate" —

Soul Oneness

represents something significant. The woman recognized the serpent as the deceiver.

After cursing the serpent and before God addressed the man or woman, His love and Father's heart offered a glimmer of hope for humankind. God foreshadowed His redemptive plan by declaring that hope would come forth from the seed of a woman.[16] Eve's descendants would bring forth the person of Jesus Christ. A Savior would come to earth, deal with Satan, take back Rulership (dominion), and reclaim God's original design for marriage.

But in the meantime, more consequences were to come.

For the Woman...

God said to the woman,

"I will greatly multiply your pain in childbirth, In pain you will bring forth children; Yet your desire will be for your husband, And he will rule over you."[17]

Originally, the woman was created to have her primary needs met through her relationship with God while celebrating equality and oneness with her husband. When sin entered, her desire shifted. She would now look to her husband to meet her primary needs for significance and security.

We see this dynamic playing out in marriages today. A woman may look to her husband, rather than to God, to meet her needs for security and significance. This is just one indication that she is living under the consequences of the Fall instead of living out God's original purposes for marriage: Reflecting, Revealing, and Ruling together in unity.

Another consequence of sin for the woman was that her husband would now rule over her. In the beginning, hierarchy was never part of God's original design for marriage, but sin distorted God's Plan A. After sin entered, man now ruled over the woman. "The woman wants a mate and she gets a master; she wants a lover and gets a lord; she wants a husband and gets a hierarch."[18] Their shared Rulership turned into domination. Domination is "supremacy or preeminence over another; exercise of mastery or ruling power."[19] Such dominance contradicts the relationship modeled in the Trinity and undermines the one-flesh relationship.

Reviewing the woman's behavior, it makes us wonder, did she show a propensity toward independence when she responded to the serpent without including her husband, "who was with her"? What if the woman was given a do-over? What if she resisted her propensity toward independence and exercised Rulership in unity by inviting her husband into the decision-making process? What if she had said, "Honey, I was not created when God told you which trees we could eat from. The serpent is telling me that it's okay to eat from this particular tree. Is that what God told you?"

Exercising Rulership together in unity would have provided protection for the man, the woman, and their marriage. Unfortunately, the woman acted independently. She chose not to include her husband…and the rest (as they say) is history.

How does this play out in real life? How do the consequences of the Fall affect a wife's ability to Rule together in unity with her husband? We frequently hear husbands express concern over what they see as their wife's misplaced priorities. A man may feel like the children take precedence over their marriage. In her own defense, the wife may justify her relationship with the children by accusing her husband of being passive, disinterested, or failing to engage. She may argue, "What do you expect me to do? I feel like a single parent most of the time. Besides, you are never here for me or the kids anyway!"

This form of processing leads to disunity and only contributes to what husbands describe as their wife's tendency to "fly solo." This scenario plays out in many ways. A wife may intentionally withhold information from her husband in regard to the children, relationships, purchases, or finances. She may control the situation by deciding what her husband needs to know and what he doesn't need to know. The wife may justify her independence by convincing herself that in excluding her husband she is "only trying to keep the peace and avoid marital chaos."

This form of independence is self-protective and may be an attempt to control. Perhaps the wife feels rejected by her husband's passivity.

Soul Oneness

Instead of processing her pain with him, she takes control by leaving him out of her decision-making process. In an attempt to avoid conflict, her response fosters an illegitimate form of independence.

A wife living independently may seem admirable at first glance. However, this behavior can cause division. Recently, a woman approached us at a Marriage Advance and admitted tearfully, "I stopped including my husband years ago. Eventually, I guess I just fired him. His passivity and failure to engage has been such a source of pain for me. I thought if I acted independently...if I learned to depend on myself and not need him, I thought I could avoid the pain." Breaking down, she continued, "But it doesn't work...the more independent I become, the more alone I feel."

This wife realized she had been deceived. Just like the woman, she believed that independence was better than interdependence. But this style of relating directly opposes the shared Rulership that God intended for a husband and wife. It leads a wife to step into the smaller story, where she is the main character and marriage is all about her.

Do you see how these tendencies toward independence can lead to misplaced priorities that can be traced back to the Fall?

For the Man...

God set forth the consequences for the man's disobedience:

"Because you have listened to the voice of your wife, and have eaten from the tree about which I commanded you, saying, 'You shall not eat from it';
Cursed is the ground because of you;
In toil you will eat of it
All the days of your life.
Both thorns and thistles it will grow for you;
And you will eat the plants of the field;
By the sweat of your face
You will eat bread,
Till you return to the ground,
Because from it you were taken;
For you are dust,
And to dust you shall return."[20]

Soul Oneness

Just like the woman, the man was created to have his primary needs for security and significance met through his relationship with God while celebrating equality and oneness with his wife. When the first couple sinned, the man's desire shifted. One of the consequences of the Fall was that the man would suffer pain as he tried to make a living (from the ground), just as the woman would suffer pain in bearing children.

"The ground once ruled by man now ruled him and eventually absorbed his being. His domain became his cemetery; his throne became his grave."[21] Reviewing the hierarchy established after sin, it is interesting to note that the man became subject to the ground (his work), which was where he came from. The woman became subject to the man, which is where she came from.

We see men living out the consequences of the Fall today as their wives accuse them of giving their careers precedence over marriage and family. In self-defense, the man may justify his focus on work by blaming his wife. "Someone has to pay the bills. You complain that I work too much, but it sure didn't seem to be a problem when we bought the larger home or purchased the new car you thought we had to have. Which way do you want it? You'd better decide because I'd love to work fewer hours!"

Does that retort remind you of Adam's defensive response when God questioned him about events in the garden? First the man blamed his wife, then God, and then he again blamed his wife: "The woman whom You gave to be with me, she gave me from the tree, and I ate."[22] He responded as a victim. Unfortunately, standing up for his wife or taking personal responsibility was not his first response. It was all about him.

Today we still see men playing the blame game. Their shame opens the door to fear, so they control by blaming. This response communicates, "Life is all about me." Men try to cover their shame by blaming their spouse, kids, boss, in-laws, friends, neighbors, life circumstances, and even God. Reviewing the man's behavior, could a man's propensity toward blaming be traced back to the Fall?

In addition to blaming, another behavior we see in the man before the Fall was his failure to engage. Could the man have had a propensity toward passivity? The text reads that after woman ate the fruit, "she gave also to her husband with her, and he ate.[23] The serpent was trying to deceive his wife and Adam failed to engage — he remained passive. Adam knew God's prohibition about not eating from the tree of the knowledge of good and evil. But he did nothing. He failed to engage with the serpent or with his wife.

Today we still see husbands choosing passivity as a form of self-protection. This style of relating goes against the shared Rulership God intended for marriage.

What if Adam was given a do-over? What if he engaged with his wife and the serpent, rescuing his bride by declaring, "God commanded us not to eat from that tree! Do not believe the serpent. He is lying and trying to deceive. Serpent, in the authority God has given me, I command you to leave us alone."

Exercising Rulership by taking dominion in unity and authority could have prevented the Fall. But unfortunately Adam did not engage with the serpent or his wife…and the rest (as they say) is history.

RULERSHIP LOST

When the man and woman disobeyed God, their sin brought many consequences. Death became a reality. Sin opened their eyes; they were no longer "naked and not ashamed." For the first time, man and woman experienced negative feelings of shame, fear, and control. Their relationship to God and to one another was altered dramatically, and the marriage structure shifted radically. The mutual equality the first couple enjoyed pre-Fall was now fractured and fragmented. The unity and shared Rulership they enjoyed as husband and wife gave way to the husband's Ruling over his wife. As a final consequence the man and woman were removed from the garden.

Through lies and deceit the enemy had achieved victory on the level of a cosmic Super Bowl. He stole the Rulership and dominion that God had given to the man and woman and to future generations.

Sin changed God's original authority structure.

Before Sin	After Sin
God	God
Man and Woman	Nature
Nature	Adam
	Eve

After the Fall, the story takes a tragic turn. Having stolen dominion for himself, the enemy quickly leads humankind into all sorts of evil and abominations: murder, death, multiple marriage partners, incest, adultery, rape, divorce, prostitution, slavery, homosexual acts, bestiality, and other perversions of God's original design and purposes for man, woman, and humankind. Under Satan's Rulership humankind became increasingly depraved. In the span of a handful of generations we read, "The LORD saw how great man's wickedness on the earth had become, and that every inclination of the thoughts of his heart was only evil all the time. The LORD was grieved that he had made man on the earth, and his heart was filled with pain."[24]

We still see the consequences of sin playing out today. Many Christian couples settle for a counterfeit form of oneness rooted in the Fall. Couples share the same last name, parent their children, serve at church, enjoy friends, and even share a bed. But too often they are self-focused. They've set aside the protection and strength that comes from marital unity and instead are focused on getting their own needs met. Over time their hearts grow cold toward each other. The mutual equality and reciprocal servanthood they were designed to celebrate is fractured and fragmented. This is not what God designed for marriage.

Surely the Fall of humankind is the most tragic scene in the Bible. But the love of God is without measure and this is not the end of the story.

Although Satan still acts as if he has Rulership and dominion, the truth is that God intervened. In the fullness of time He sent a Savior — and nothing will ever be the same again.

Soul Oneness

+ Chapter 6

Rulership Regained

How Jesus Restored the "Very Good" to Marriage

Genesis 1 and 2 are our favorite chapters in the entire Bible. Immersing ourselves in the story of creation, we can imagine God reviewing all He created and taking a deep sigh of satisfaction as we read, "God saw all that He had made, and behold, it was very good."[1] We find it interesting that God's "not good" was replaced by "very good" after He created marriage.

Before sin entered the story, the man and the woman walked together with God and each other, naked and not ashamed. They had no reason to hide or cover themselves with fig leaves of shame, fear, or control. God had given both of them Rulership and dominion. This "very good marriage" was based on a relationship of oneness, mutual equality, and reciprocal servanthood.

We believe God is on the verge of beginning a Reformation in marriage. This will occur as couples advance and return to God's creational design, what we refer to as Plan A. This plan calls for a husband and wife to be one in spirit, soul, and body. Couples who live out this creational design will Reflect and Reveal God's plurality and goodness. This will open the door for husbands and wives to step into the dominion and authority God has given them as they exercise Rulership together in unity.

The original model for Plan A was God Himself in all His glory: God the Father, God the Son, and God the Holy Spirit. The oneness within the Trinity provides the model for a marriage relationship of mutual equality. *Mutuality* refers to sharing something in common.[2] *Equality* refers to the state of being equal, one to another.[3] Mutual equality describes a relationship between two people not differentiated by a hierarchy of rank or seniority level. Obviously, a hierarchy of authority is important in certain relationships, such as between a parent and child or between a boss and employee. However, God's original design for marriage does not include a hierarchy. One person never rules over the other. Husbands and wives who desire to exercise Rulership in unity work together to make decisions. These decisions can include matters related to caring for their family, managing their home, and engaging with the world around them. In order to do this a couple must understand the importance of mutual equality and reciprocal servanthood. Being one in spirit, soul, and body involves being mutually dependent on God and each other.

Many people who come to our conferences have trouble meshing this perspective with what they've been taught elsewhere. For example, during a question-and-answer session at a recent Marriage Advance I (Tim) was asked a number of questions by a man I'll call Hank. He asked if I considered myself to be an egalitarian or a feminist. I responded by saying, "The problem with terms like these is that the definition can mean different things to different people." The dictionary defines *egalitarian* as "believing in equality: maintaining, relating to, or based on a belief that all people are, in principle, equal and should enjoy equal social, political, and economic rights and opportunities."[4] Personally I don't have any problem with that definition. I certainly believe Anne and I are equal in value and significance as image bearers of God.

On the other hand, *feminism* is defined as "belief in women's rights: belief in the need to secure rights and opportunities for women equal to those of men."[5] Anne and I totally support fair treatment of women. However, unlike some feminists, our primary focus is not on getting individual rights met or protecting power. Instead we focus on reciprocal servanthood because that's what we see modeled in the Trinity.

However, I explained to Hank that even though we might agree with parts of those definitions, neither of the terms egalitarian or feminist are found in the Bible. Personally, Anne and I resist labels because they often lead to confusion and misunderstanding. We simply view ourselves as followers of Jesus Christ who are trying to walk out God's Plan A for marriage. Our model is the first marriage before sin entered the story. Our desire is to walk with God, loving and serving each other as equals created in His image.

GOD PROVIDES THE WAY

Some people find it difficult to grab hold of the concept of mutual equality because they get stuck in Genesis 3 where, as we saw in the previous chapter, Rulership was lost at the Fall. There, the couple's relationship with God and unity with each other was fractured, and the enemy seized dominion in marriage and other areas of life for thousands of years to follow.

Soul Oneness

But God is always in control. His very essence is love and goodness. His nature is such that He refuses to abandon us even when we sin and rebel. From the moment the man and woman sinned, God had a plan to provide humankind with a way to regain His original design for marriage and how life should be for men and women made in His image.

God's plan involved a Savior, Jesus Christ, coming forth from the life-giving seed of a woman to become the Way, the Truth, and the Life. In agreement with God the Father, God the Son came to earth to make the necessary payment for the sins of humankind. Jesus came not only to suffer and die on a cross but also to battle Satan and take back the Rulership, dominion, and authority the enemy had stolen.

Let's revisit the story.

Taking on human form, Jesus was miraculously conceived and born to a pure young girl named Mary. As a boy and young man He grew in stature and favor with God and man. Then at thirty years of age He was baptized in the Jordan River.

At this inauguration of His earthly ministry, we find God the Father, God the Son, and God the Holy Spirit — all together just as when they first set the world spinning. When the Son walked into the water to be baptized, the Holy Spirit made His appearance in the form of a dove and descended upon Jesus. At the same time God the Father declared His presence and confirmed His love for the Son: "This is My beloved Son, in whom I am well pleased."[6] This declaration came before Jesus began His earthly ministry, which means the Father was pleased with His Son before He did anything.

This assurance of the Father's pleasure even before He did anything must have given the Son encouragement for the difficult time He was about to face. Following His baptism, Jesus was led by the Holy Spirit into the desert for a divine appointment with Satan. Jesus spent forty days praying and fasting in preparation for this power encounter between good and evil; then the battle began.

The enemy fired his first missile: "If you are the Son of God, tell these stones to become bread."[7] The devil launched a direct attack on Jesus' identity with this challenge, "*If* you are the Son of God…" Jesus responded by quoting Scripture: "It is written: 'Man does not live on bread alone, but on every word that comes from the mouth of God.'"[8] Jesus knew who He was. In the strength of His identity, He stood on the Word of God.

The second attack also was aimed at Jesus' identity. The devil took Him into Jerusalem and had Him stand on the pinnacle of the temple. "If you are the Son of God," he said, "throw yourself down. For it is written: 'He will command his angels concerning you, and they will lift you up in their hands, so that you will not strike your foot against a stone.'"[9] Again Jesus responded by quoting Scripture: "It is also written: 'Do not put the Lord your God to the test.'"[10]

The enemy is not very creative. He still uses the same strategy, trying to get us to question our identity, our connection with God. He knows the insidious danger that comes in focusing on ourselves, whether we are standing on a mountaintop where everything is going great or wandering alone in the desert.

Jesus understood the truth all of us need to remember: "It's not about me." Every aspect of life, including marriage, is about God. He invites you to live in the **Larger Story** where He is the main character. Most people tend to live in the **smaller story** where self takes center stage as the main character. And selfishness lies at the core of every sin.

+   "In every sin we can see 'self' at work. Although people today classify sins into an untold number of categories, yet inductively speaking there is but one basic sin: all the thoughts and deeds which are sins are related to 'self.'… All sins are committed for the sake of the self. If the element of self is missing, there will be no sin…. Wherever sin is, there is the activity of self." [11]   +

Jesus chose not to make self the main character in His story, even in the face of the devil's determined attacks. For his third attempt, Satan took Jesus to a very high mountain and showed Him all the kingdoms of the world and their splendor. He said, "All this I will give you, if you will bow down and worship me."[12] How did Jesus respond? Yet again He quoted Scripture and pointed out that the story is about God, not self: "Away from me, Satan! For it is written: 'Worship the Lord your God, and serve him

Soul Oneness

only.'"[13] What was the result? "When the devil had finished every temptation, he left Him until an opportune time."[14]

It is significant to note that Jesus never questioned the devil's claim to deliver all the kingdoms of the world. Why? Because He knew Satan had stolen Rulership and dominion from Adam and Eve in the garden. In the garden the woman faced three temptations and was offered three promises. The enemy told her that if she ate the fruit her eyes would be opened, she would be like God, and she would know good and evil. The woman made herself the center of reference — it was all about her. As a result, Satan had authority to offer Jesus the kingdoms; otherwise, it would not have been a true temptation.

Thankfully, Jesus took on human form and came to earth to reclaim Rulership, dominion, and authority for the rightful owners. In the desert He faced three temptations. The enemy tempted Jesus to satisfy His hunger by turning stones to bread. He tempted Jesus to exchange His humanity for power to overcome death. Lastly, he tempted Jesus by offering Him authority over "all the kingdoms of the world and their glory." Unlike Adam and Eve, Jesus made God and His Word the center of reference — it was *not* all about Him. He knew that through His coming death and resurrection, the enemy would be defeated and his Rulership revoked.

While the desert encounter offered a preview of things to come, the ultimate power showdown between good and evil occurred at the cross, where the blood of Jesus paid for the sins of humankind. Then His resurrection confirmed His identity as the Son of God and sealed the effect of His earthly works. After His resurrection Jesus returned to heaven. Then God sent the Holy Spirit, the third person of the Trinity, to indwell every believer and provide us with power.

Although Satan was mortally wounded in these New Testament power encounters, he has not given up the fight. The battle between good and evil continues. Just as he did with the woman, the enemy continues to lie and distort God's truths. Just as he did to Jesus, the enemy questions a person's identity as a man or woman made in the image of God. He tries to convince us that he still has Rulership, dominion, and authority to rule the earth. However, the enemy's roars are from a toothless lion because

Jesus Christ, the Lion of Judah, defeated Satan. Among countless other good things, this means we can return to God's Plan A for marriage.

With Rulership regained, men and women have the ability to resist the devil. "For sin shall not have dominion over you, for you are not under law but under grace."[15] As Jesus demonstrated, we can stand on the Word of God and command the enemy to leave. It is written, "Submit therefore to God. Resist the devil and he will flee from you. Draw near to God and He will draw near to you."[16] Rulership regained enables men and women to defeat the god of this world. "Greater is He who is in you than he who is in the world."[17]

THE STRENGTH AND PROTECTION OF COVENANT

In order for a couple to fulfill God's purpose to Rule in marriage they must be in covenant. A covenant is far more binding than a contract or commitment. In the Bible a covenant with God involves death. "For where a covenant is, there must of necessity be the death of the one who made it."[18] A marriage covenant includes three parties: God, a man, and a woman. So the marriage covenant involves the husband and wife each dying to themselves as they choose to live for God and their spouse.

This idea of death can sound scary unless you recognize that covenant between a husband, a wife, and God provides strength and protection. The book of Ecclesiastes says, "Though one may be overpowered, two can defend themselves. A cord of three strands is not quickly broken."[19] Like a cord with three strands, covenant provides strength in marriage because each partner is in relationship with God and each other. This enables them to give themselves fully to the purposes of God, to their spouse, and to others. Through living out covenant and exercising Rulership in unity, a husband and wife are able to Reflect and Reveal the plurality and character of God.

Looking back over many years of marriage, I (Tim) can see that living in covenant and unity is not primarily about what I do for Anne or what she does for me. It's about who we are in God and how we Reflect and Reveal His character to each other. My treating Anne as a priceless treasure has freed her to live more fully in the ways God has created and gifted her.

Soul Oneness

For example, Anne is spiritually gifted with wisdom and discernment unlike any other person I've ever met. In addition, her personality dovetails well with these gifts, as she is a perceptive observer. When we approach life together as a team, her gifts complement mine. The power of that kind of unity empowers us as a couple and protects our marriage. As her husband, I find joy and satisfaction in seeing Anne grow as we do life together as one.

HOW CAN A COUPLE LIVE OUT ONENESS AND UNITY IN REAL LIFE?

At a recent REAL LIFE Marriage Advance a middle-aged man approached us. "Mike" appeared very sincere and said, "The way you describe marriage sounds so right to me. But I have been going to church my entire life, and I have been taught the husband is the head of the home. I believe that in a Christian home the husband is in charge and the wife is to submit to him and to his leadership." Mike continued, clearly wanting us to understand that he was no bully, "I love my wife and in our marriage I use this word picture to describe how we relate: I am the pilot and she is my copilot. Certainly we are flying together. I may even let her take the controls once in a while. But I am the one that decides our direction, speed, and when and where we take off and land. I don't consider myself a bossy pilot. In fact I make it a point to regularly check in with her. But I am the pilot, I am the head, I am in charge of our journey together."

Mike continued, "It's been really difficult for me to process what you're saying about God's original design for marriage. Can you make His Plan A and the concept of oneness in marriage any easier for me to understand?"

We thanked Mike for his question and the spirit in which he asked it. We appreciated his desire to revisit God's design for marriage and his openness to consider something other than what he had been taught. And we assured him that he wasn't the first person to wrestle with these questions. Over the years our ministry has given us opportunities to travel and teach men and women from all different church backgrounds, and we frequently field similar questions from some of the people we meet.

We explained to Mike that in our marriage we try to live out God's original, Plan A design. Therefore, we have decided to camp in Genesis chapters 1 and 2. These two chapters provide a glimpse of what life looked like *before* sin. Marriage before sin tells the story of a man and woman made in the image of God. It is the story of God creating woman to rescue man from his "not good" situation. It is a story of God giving the creation mandate of Rulership and the procreation mandate to be fruitful and multiply to *both* the husband and wife. It is a story of reciprocal servants who celebrate being naked and not ashamed. God's Plan A is a love story of a husband and wife becoming one.

However, some people choose other ways to walk out marriage. For example, a man approached us during a break at a conference and confidently declared, "I believe God has made the roles for men and women in marriage clear. In the book of Genesis, God speaks directly to the woman and tells her in no uncertain terms, '…Your desire will be for your husband, and he will rule over you.'"[20] This man had cut-and-pasted a specific verse to back up his theology. He tried to convince us how well this worked in his marriage. Unfortunately, we were not able to confirm this with his wife. As we recall, she was getting him coffee.

On other occasions couples — okay, usually just the husbands — approach us to quote other Bible passages that they believe support their position. One husband reminded us that Paul said in Ephesians 5:22-23, "Wives, be subject to your own husbands, as to the Lord. For the husband is the head of the wife." He used this verse to explain that he believed God created a marital hierarchy where the husband's role is to be the head. He told us being the head meant being in charge. At some point he tried to soften his explanation by adding, "Don't get me wrong…I'm open to my wife's input, but in the end, I call the shots."

In trying to explain hierarchy in marriage some husbands have told us that they have a 51 percent vote in making decisions and the wife has 49 percent. As we listen to these men explain their model, we can't help but wonder, *How is a 51/49 control split any different from a husband who has 99 percent control and a wife who has 1 percent?* Either way, the husband has final authority to make decisions.

Other husbands describe their leadership role in marriage as "the first among equals." This interpretation of God's design for marriage seems confusing to us. Our initial question to couples who live marriage in this model is, "What does 'first among equals' mean?" We wonder, *Why is the husband "first"? Is he first because he was created first? Is the husband first in having authority? Is he first in making decisions?* It seems to us that if a husband is first, that means his wife is second. The words "first" and "second" denote a hierarchy; they do not describe the oneness and mutual equality we believe God has designed for marriage. There is no "first among equals" within the Trinity.

After listening carefully to all of this, Mike asked, "But did Jesus Himself teach anything about marriage?" What a great question! What *was* Jesus' view on marriage? Some Pharisees wanted to know the same thing. They came to test Jesus with questions about marriage and divorce. How did He respond? He did not cite the model of male rulership that was the result of the Fall: "...your desire shall be for your husband, and he will rule over you."[21] Nor did His words reflect the perspective of later New Testament writers addressing specific marriage issues, in specific places, at specific times in history. Where did Jesus go for His model for marriage? He went back to the beginning, to Genesis before sin entered the picture. He quoted God's creational design for marriage: "Have you not read, that He who created them from the beginning made them male and female, and said, 'For this reason a man shall leave his father and mother, and be joined to his wife, and the two shall become one flesh'? So they are no longer two, but one flesh. What therefore God has joined together, let no man separate."[22] Jesus described marriage as leaving, cleaving, and becoming one as husband and wife. He reaffirmed Plan A.

BUT WHAT ABOUT SUBMISSION?

Mike then asked us, "When you talk about a hierarchical marriage model, doesn't the Bible command a wife to submit to her husband?"

I (Tim) said to Mike, "You must be referring to Ephesians 5:22, "Wives *be subject* to your own husbands, as to the Lord..." Mike nodded. "First let me say, theologians have been studying and debating this controversial verse for years. Since we are not theologians, our desire is to bring our simple understanding of the Bible and a lifetime of real life experiences to add perspective for you to prayerfully process. That said, before I try to answer your question, let's put this passage into proper context."

I explained to Mike, "When a single verse is separated from the rest of the text, it can be easily taken out of context. It's important to take into account what is written before and after the verse. In addition it's also important to compare a passage with other places throughout the Bible where the same topic is addressed. With that in mind, instead of isolating Ephesians 5:22, let's start with verse 21 and take an overview of what the apostle Paul wrote from a prison cell to a church in Ephesus."

Here's what I laid out for Mike: There are two marriage-related concepts to explore in Ephesians 5 — submission and headship. Let's begin with submission. In Ephesians 5:21 Paul commands everyone to "be subject to *one another* in the fear of Christ" (*emphasis added*). The phrase *one another* directs both men and women to mutually submit with no evidence of any hierarchy or pecking order. The phrase *to one another* denotes a mutual (two-way) process, a relationship between equals.

To illustrate this point, let's look at other places in Scripture where the same phrase is used. Jesus, in the gospel of John, addresses both men and women in 13:34 with a new command, "that you also love *one another.*" Galatians 5:13 says, "Through love serve *one another.*" Ephesians 4:32 says, "Be kind to *one another.*" Romans 12:10 says, "Be devoted to *one another*; …give preference to *one another.*" Philippians 2:3 says, "Do nothing from selfishness or empty conceit, but with humility of mind regard *one another* as more important than yourselves." From these examples, it is clear that the phrase *one another* applies to both men and women. Why would the command "be subject to *one another*" in Ephesians 5:21 be any different? God's overall theme for marriage is mutual submission. This opens the door to live in the **Larger Story** with God as the main character.

The text goes on to read in verse 22, "Wives *be subject* to your own husbands, as to the Lord" The italics here appear in the text from the New American Standard Bible, which provides the most accurate translation of the original text. It is important to note the words "be subject" are written in italics, indicating they are not found in the original text. Literally verse 22 reads, "Wives to their own husbands as to the Lord." Unfortunately, the New International Version and other translations don't make note of this.

Soul Oneness

In both verse 21 and 22 the command to submit directs both genders back to their relationship with the Lord. Verse 21 says, "in the fear of Christ" and verse 22 says, "as to the Lord." Theologian Dr. Gilbert Bilezikian writes:

+ " '[A]s to the Lord' means that a wife submits to her husband in the same kind of loving service that she renders to the Savior. She submits to the Lord not in servility but in servanthood. Likewise, a wife submits to her husband not in servility but in servanthood. Wives submit not because they have to (obedience) but because they want to (servanthood). They submit not because they knuckle down under authority but because they respond to love with love." [23]   +

People often mistakenly use the words *submission* and *authority* interchangeably. Submission in marriage is not about authority. The New Testament requires a wife to submit to her *husband*, not to the *authority* of her husband. This difference is crucial for the proper understanding of oneness in marriage. Mutual equality and mutual authority go hand in hand.

In the book *Beyond Sex Roles* we read, "Husbands are never instructed to exercise authority over their wives. Wives are never commanded to obey their husbands or to submit to the authority of their husbands, and no threat ever accompanies the injunction for wives to submit to their husbands." [24] The only place the Bible mentions authority between a husband and wife is in 1 Corinthians 7:4, which we will look at in a moment.

Personally, when I (Anne) read Ephesians 5, I see submission not as an obstacle but an opportunity for me to love and serve Tim *as to the Lord*. It flows out of my desire to Reflect and Reveal the heart of God to him. Submission isn't dependent on how I feel or whether or not I think Tim deserves to be submitted to. It's not about gender differences or being right or wrong. Submission is not about me; it must begin and end with God.

Likewise, I (Tim) submit to Anne as I submit to God. This opens the door for me to die to selfishness and Reflect and Reveal God to my bride. If husbands and wives spent more time focusing on their relationship with God and less time focusing on who's the boss or who gets their own way, submission wouldn't even be an issue. What wife would have a problem submitting to a husband who loves her as Christ loves the Church? What wife wouldn't want to submit to a man who would die for her...honor her...

regard her as more important than himself? What husband wouldn't be willing to take a bullet for a wife who Reflects and Reveals God's heart to him?

God is so good; He never asks men and women to do something He hasn't already done. Looking to the Trinity as our model for marriage, we see God the Father, God the Son, and God the Holy Spirit mutually submitted to one another in unity and community. When couples humbly follow this model, it opens doors to show the world what it means as "two become one" in marriage. Reviewing submission, both husbands and wives are to submit to *one another*, wives to their own husbands as the Lord.[25]

BUT WHAT ABOUT HEADSHIP?

Mike then asked, "Doesn't the Bible say the husband is the head of his wife?"

I (Tim) responded, "Funny you should bring that up. This is one of the few verses most men have memorized. First let me say, we wholeheartedly agree with the Scripture that says the husband is head of his wife. The key is how people define the word *head*. For many, the word head is code for a hierarchical form of headship where the husband is considered the boss and has authority to rule over his wife. Biblically, however, the word head means exactly the opposite. *Head* is not defined as boss; it describes the husband as a servant provider who "nourishes and cherishes" his wife.[26]

In addition, the word *head* does not mean that a husband has authority over his wife. If the writer wanted to describe a role of male *authority*, other words would have been used. Let me illustrate by referring to the only time in Scripture when *authority* is addressed between husbands and wives. In 1 Corinthians 7:4 the text reads, "The wife does not have *authority* over her own body, but the husband does." But interestingly the text goes on to say; "and likewise also the husband does not have *authority* over his own body, but the wife does" (*emphasis added*). In other words, in the most intimate act in marriage, sexual intercourse, both the husband and wife are given *mutual authority* over each other's body. Stop and think about it: the only time *authority* between a husband and wife is addressed in the New Testament it is *mutual authority*, clearly given to both the

Soul Oneness

husband and wife. Does it make any sense for God to give husbands and wives mutual authority in body oneness and not in soul oneness? Just like submission, headship in marriage is not about authority.

We often hear husbands explain headship like this, "As the man, my wife submits to my headship, I have the authority to make all the *major* decisions in our home." They usually finish by joking, "but in the last thirty years we've never had one *major* decision!" This position seems to point either to a husband abdicating his responsibility to exercise his perceived authority or to a husband who does not acknowledge his wife as having mutual authority.

No matter what your current thoughts on these issues, we encourage you to prayerfully process the biblical meaning of authority and headship. Our experience is that most couples reach the conclusion that being the head does not mean being the boss. The heart of headship involves mutual authority with a husband being the servant provider to his wife.

For me, (Tim) how does headship play out in our marriage? It's the desire of my heart to love my bride the way Christ loves His bride, the Church, which He died for. The Bible tells me how to do this. "So husbands ought also to love their own wives as their own bodies. He who loves his own wife loves himself; for no one ever hated his own flesh, but nourishes and cherishes it, just as Christ also does the church."[27] So how does Christ model headship to the Church? By nourishing and cherishing it. Therefore, how should I model headship to my bride? By nourishing and cherishing her. To me the heart of headship is being the servant provider as I choose to die to selfishness and, by God's grace, nourish and cherish my bride.

As we concluded our talk, I thanked Mike and reminded him that it's important to remember that these issues do not involve salvation or eternal life. God created men and women as volitional beings with the ability to make choices. Therefore, couples are free to choose from among any number of ways to live out their marriage. Couples can choose to live their marriage in a rulership model — "…your desire shall be for your husband, and he shall rule over you"[28] — or in a hierarchical model where the husband is the boss, or in God's creational marriage design —

what we refer to as God's Plan A. In this model the husband and wife are equal, reciprocal servants.

For our marriage, we have found God's Plan A to be the closest reflection to the relationships within the Trinity. We're convinced that because Jesus took back dominion and Rulership from the enemy, by God's grace it is now possible for husbands and wives to reclaim and return to God's Plan A for marriage.

Before we ended our discussion with Mike, we commented on his illustration of marriage where he was the pilot and his wife the co-pilot. We said, "In our marriage God is the pilot and we are His co-pilots. This has resulted in God taking us on adventures in oneness that we could not imagine in our wildest dreams."

Mike shook his head, took a deep breath, and asked, "But…how do you do that?"

We paused before simultaneously answering, "By living out 'Marriage is not about me'!"

WALKING IT OUT DAY BY DAY

Walking out God's original Plan A for marriage is an ongoing process of growing in intimacy with God and each other. In our marriage, a key to intimacy has been understanding how God has individually wired and gifted us. Even after thirty plus years of marriage, we are still learning, but we have studied ourselves and each other to help discern our passions, temperaments, love languages, and spiritual gifts, which we will talk about in upcoming chapters.

We believe marriage is an invitation for couples to celebrate and step into the unique blessings and benefits of two becoming one. "Equality exists among persons who make decisions conjointly and who apportion tasks among themselves on the basis of gifts and qualification rather than rank or gender."[29]

In all sincerity, our experience suggests that God's Plan A for marriage is

Soul Oneness

much more difficult to live out than other models we have observed. This is because waiting on God for unity and agreement often opens the door to selfishness, control, and manipulation. Frankly many times it would be easier if I (Tim) just took charge. With my personality, temperament, and leadership gifts, it would be easy for me to step into the role of the boss. With this model of headship I could even quote a few Scriptures and self-righteously demand that Anne submit to me and my decisions.

However, our marriage works best when we focus on submitting to God and to each other. We try to make decisions based on gifts and experience rather than on the basis of which of us is male and which is female. For us, living a hierarchical marriage model with me as the boss would negatively impact the Rulership, dominion, and authority that walking together in oneness and unity provides.

For me (Anne) a recent experience in our marriage provides a great illustration of how we live out Rulership in unity. The two of us have worked together in marriage ministry for over twenty years. All along we thought that leading our own marriage ministry full-time was a strong probability…someday.

Eleven years ago, we took a leap of faith when Tim resigned from his twenty-plus-year fire department career. We left the Chicago suburbs — saying goodbye to family, friends, a great church, the security and benefits of a successful career, and a lifetime of relationships — in response to God's invitation to serve at a church in Holland, Michigan. After five years there, God invited us to move our family to California. This involved selling almost everything we owned so we could move into an apartment in Pasadena. From California God invited us to move to Colorado Springs, where we currently live.

Then about three years ago, Tim felt God was calling us to begin REAL LIFE Ministries full-time. On the wall of his office hangs a quote that reads, *Leap and the net will appear!* Tim is a natural-born risk-taker whose deep trust frees him to joyfully follow wherever God leads. He was ready to take the plunge.

On the other hand, I am not a risk-taker. I prefer to see the net appear *before* I leap. I'm not sure whether this is a lack of faith or a sign of stability. In any case, leaving our full-time jobs to begin our own ministry — giving up the security of two salaries and the benefits of an insurance and retirement plan — felt to me less like a step of faith and more like free-falling off a cliff. Although I shared Tim's dream of ministering to marriages full-time, I struggled with fear. Many nights I lay awake wondering, *Is this faith or foolishness? What if our ministry doesn't flourish and we lose everything? What if we get in over our heads and the work consumes us? What if…?*

Tim was ready to move forward, convinced the timing was God's. But over the years we've agreed never to make decisions until we are both in agreement. This is one practical way we live out our commitment to Rule together in unity, and it provides our marriage with power and protection.

So Tim agreed to wait on me, and we continued to process together. While we were not in agreement on when to leave our jobs, we did agree on a number of other things. We agreed we definitely needed to downsize in order to adjust to not having regular paychecks. As a first step, we agreed to put our house up for sale. Then we found a smaller home and took another step of faith by putting money down on it. It seemed as if God was opening one door at a time as we walked in agreement with Him and one another. We were scheduled to close on the house in the spring, giving us plenty of time to sell our home. But months passed without a single offer. In March we became owners of two homes and two mortgage payments. This made it impossible for us to quit our jobs and go into full-time marriage ministry. Our frustration and stress levels were high, but Tim still believed this was God's timing. My fears and *what if* questions continued as we waited for the house to sell. We committed to pray and fast and wait on God.

One night I awoke from a deep sleep in which I had a vivid dream that I knew was from God. It wasn't the kind of dream with a story line but one that spoke directly to my heart. I heard two words in my dream: *wiggle room*. When I woke up I knew exactly what those two words meant. Wiggle room refers to having just enough space to "wiggle out" of something. It's like having a safety net or an emergency escape exit…*just in case*. For a person who is not a risk-taker, having wiggle room is very important.

The next morning as Tim and I drove together to work, I told him about my dream and what I thought it meant. "The words 'wiggle room' represent my fears. Fear and indecision provide a safety net for me so I won't have to step out in faith. When I woke up last night I realized that indecision is a subtle form of control. I think God wants me to address my fears instead of letting them control me. I need to focus on God and His power instead of focusing on fear."

When we got to work, Tim stopped the car. I looked over at him and said, "I'm finally ready for both of us to quit our jobs and begin REAL LIFE Ministries full-time. God has been preparing us for this next step of faith. It's time... If you're still up for it, I'm ready to take this leap of faith with you."

Knowing we were both in agreement provided Tim and me with the strength and protection we needed to move forward in unity. We prayed, "Lord, You know we are carrying two house payments. We have lowered our price three times and have not gotten one offer. How can we leave our jobs and lose our salaries and benefits? Should we put both houses up for sale? Is this Your timing for us? We are trusting that this leading is from You, and that You will provide a way."

In our decision-making process, Tim and I include not only God and each other but also a trusted group of friends. When we both decided to quit our jobs, Tim and I joined friends and family in praying together. We found it encouraging that, after praying, every person we included affirmed our direction: "As crazy as it sounds I think you are supposed to take this leap of faith!"

One night neither of us slept a wink. We tossed and turned, seeking God's direction. In the morning Tim said he sensed our resignation date should be effective June 5. That was only two months away. Tim made it crystal clear that we would only do this if we both felt certain it was God's desire — with no wiggle room. I again faced my fears about giving up our financial security net. I poured my heart out to the Lord and sensed His confirmation. The next day we met with our bosses, explained our process, and handed in our letters of resignation.

On June 5 we drove home from our last day at work — no jobs, no income, no benefits, and two mortgage payments. My wiggle room was like an old friend who left town.

The very next day, after over six months without one single offer on our home, our realtor called to schedule an appointment for a couple to walk through. They were pre-approved and had nothing to sell. A few days later this couple made an offer on our house. They made only one stipulation: they needed to move in immediately! God was affirming our adventure.

Looking back now, we see that God was teaching us about the power in agreement and the protection that comes with Ruling together in unity. Over the years waiting for this unity has saved us from making countless unwise decisions.

When a couple processes a decision until they are united, they guard their marriage against the consequences of disunity and division. In the book *Marriage Spirituality*, Paul Stevens captures the essence of unity in marriage with these words:

+ "Sometimes I wonder if God is interested in anything but unity. For husbands and wives to talk, pray, listen, and wait until they have a common mind is not only a good marital strategy. It is the only biblical way for couples to make decisions. God is apparently more interested in husband-wife unity than he is interested in getting his job done. I repeat that if it's not God's will for both, it is probably not God's will, no matter how much one spouse believes he or she has God's guidance."[30]   +

AN EXPERIMENT IN UNITY

God created every person with the freedom to choose. You are free to choose whom you will serve, and whose authority you will submit to. You can choose to submit to God, the enemy, others, or yourself.

In a similar way every married couple has a choice of how they walk out marriage. Because Jesus took back dominion and authority from Satan, husbands and wives are free to return to the Rulership God originally intended for them to have. The life-giving message of the New Testament reminds every couple that "sin shall not have dominion over you, for you are not under law but under grace."[31] With this in mind we encourage couples to prayerfully revisit God's Plan A design for marriage. Your

Soul Oneness

choice to live in marital unity will impact not only your marriage but also your children and future generations.

I (Tim) would particularly like to challenge husbands to prayerfully revisit God's Plan A design. Process it together with your bride and give it a try. Agree with your spouse that, at least for a few months, the two of you will only make decisions in unity, then record what happens. We believe you will be surprised by how Ruling in unity provides protection and power for both of you. We're also convinced that your marital intimacy and oneness will advance to deeper levels as you walk together as one.

Soul Oneness

Chapter 7

From "Me" to "We"

God Designed a Marriage to Be Greater
Than the Sum of Its Parts

Together, the two of us have experienced many miraculous moments, but nothing compares to the birth of our first child. Holding our son for the first time was one of those moments that will be locked in my (Anne's) heart forever. When they placed him in my arms, Tim and I just stared at him for the longest time. We scanned every inch of his perfect little body. We were overwhelmed with the gift that God had entrusted to us. As we looked into the eyes of this new life, there was a moment when it actually felt as if the three of us were one.

During those first days our hospital room was flooded with visitors, flowers, and cards. Everyone was celebrating Timmy's arrival. My family would hold him and say, "He looks just like your baby pictures." Tim's family held him and said, "He is definitely an Evans." Each family saw in our son something familiar — similarities inherited from both of us. Yet, as we stared into his eyes we knew that he was much more than a reflection of his mom and dad. Although Timmy represented each of us in different ways, although his genes come directly from the two of us, he is miraculously more than a simple equation of Tim plus Anne equals Timmy. God carefully crafted him as a whole new creation, full of amazing wonders that we could never have predicted.

Just as a baby is more than the sum of his parents' contributed parts, so a marriage can be much greater than just the two people involved — when God is included in the relationship.

THE BIRTH OF A MARITAL "WE"

Two becoming one in marriage is not about a loss of personal identity but a process where both partners' identity is enhanced. Marriage is about more than "you" plus "me." When a husband and wife become one, a spiritual transaction takes place. "You" and "me" becomes "**We.**"

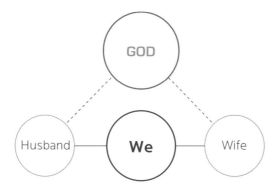

When two people enter covenant with God and each other, a new life — a "**We**" life — is created. Such unity is critical to living out marriage as God designed, because being mutually submitted to God and one another and exercising reciprocal servanthood is the wisest way for a couple to Rule together.

A husband and wife are to Rule in unity over their home, finances, emotions, and sexual relationship. They exercise Rulership by raising children and passing on godly values to future generations. One spouse does not Rule over the other or selfishly push an agenda that says, "It's all about me." Instead, when a husband and wife Rule, they exchange a "me" perspective for a "**We**" perspective, enjoying mutual equality and celebrating each other's differences.

But it's difficult to achieve genuine unity without really knowing someone, without growing in intimacy. Marriage is designed to be an exclusive relationship in which a husband and wife continually draw closer to God and each other. Dr. Gilbert Bilezikian, our professor in that marriage and family class we audited over twenty years ago, defined intimacy as "*to know and be fully known*."[1] As a person grows in *knowing* and *being fully known* by God and their spouse, they grow in intimacy and relationship. The "**We**" perspective that results from such intimacy and friendship can also be called *soul oneness*.

INTIMACY HAS AN ENEMY

But the enemy has been trying from the very beginning to distort the unity God intended for every husband and wife. Satan knows the power of

Soul Oneness

intimacy. He recognizes the strength and protection a couple enjoys when they Rule together in unity. So he continues to rely on many of the same tactics he used in the garden with Adam and Eve.

Remember the immediate consequences of the Fall? Once sin entered the picture, it destroyed the man and woman's unity with each other and with God. When Adam and Eve sinned, they experienced shame for the first time. No longer were the man and woman "naked and not ashamed."[2] Covering themselves with fig leaves symbolized their loss of innocence and the fear that grew out of their shame. What if God found out about their sin? Filled with fear, they tried to control the situation by hiding.

Unfortunately the effects of sin continue today. Satan perpetuates the shame-fear-control cycle that divides so many couples. I (Tim) met with a man I'll call Patrick. Patrick had a history of moving frequently from one job to another. However, he enjoyed his current position, was a well-liked employee, and consistently received excellent performance evaluations. So when he saw a posting for a position that represented a promotion, Patrick put in for it, convinced he was a strong leader who was qualified for the job. In addition, his family could really use the extra income that it provided.

After an extensive application, interview, and evaluation process a woman with less seniority got the promotion. Patrick wondered, *What's wrong with me? Why didn't I get the job? Doesn't the boss like me?* He felt a sense of defeat when he considered the missed opportunity and the loss of potential income. He envied his coworker's success and tried to minimize his pain by cutting her down in his mind. *She doesn't have half the experience I do. Her work ethic isn't even close to mine.*

The enemy tightened his grip on Patrick the next day when his coworkers teased him about a woman getting the job he'd wanted, further prompting him to question his identity as a successful man.

That night he talked to his wife. She responded by asking, "Was there anything more you could have done to prepare? We sure could have used the raise." His failed promotion and his wife's disappointed response triggered familiar feelings of shame and rejection. *My own wife doesn't even believe in me. She thinks I'm a failure. There must be something wrong with me.* Shame opened the door to fear. *Maybe I'll never get promoted. I'll never be the kind of man she can respect and be proud of.*

Patrick's fears opened the door to control. He vowed to never expose himself to this kind of rejection again. Patrick was beginning to give up on himself. He thought, *If this is what happens when a person tries to get ahead, I might as well just cash it in. I'm never going to apply for a promotion again. Why should I work as hard as I do when others who don't work as hard as me get promoted?*

Without processing his disappointment with anyone else, including his wife, Patrick considered quitting his job. He thought he could control his pain by just leaving and starting over somewhere else. Patrick was about to continue a career cycle driven by shame, fear, and control.

As we met together over time, he began to understand that shame is not from God but originates with the enemy. He started to recognize how Satan was using shame to convince him that he was flawed in some irreparable way. This deep-seated belief caused him pain, which he attempted to control by isolating himself, managing his own feelings, and making his own decisions. This resulted in a spiral affect in his life, creating division between Patrick and others along with deeply affecting the intimacy level between him and his wife.

Part of Patrick's healing process was to embrace and believe that what God says about him is true. Patrick is a child of the King who is fearfully and wonderfully made. As he advanced in understanding his identity in Christ, he was able to invite his wife into his process. Growing closer to God gave this man the freedom to move closer to his wife.

Patrick's story highlights how the enemy continues to use shame to block intimacy in a marriage. Afraid of being exposed, a person often conceals his or her vulnerability behind emotional fig leaves. Hiding creates emotional distance that blocks intimacy and leads to a breakdown of soul oneness. Choosing to be emotionally naked with a spouse enables a couple to advance in intimacy, but it also involves vulnerability and risk. In marriage, being part of an intimate relationship brings great joy, but it also exposes a spouse to the possibility of pain and rejection.

Soul Oneness

God's design for marriage requires a husband and wife to place their trust in Him. This begins with a decision to look to God — not to a spouse, or anyone or anything else — for security and significance. God invites and empowers a person to resist fear, give up control, remove fig leaves, and come out of hiding.

After Adam and Eve sinned, God called out, "Where are you?" Adam responded, "I was afraid because I was naked; so I hid myself."[3] We love God's response; it is one of our favorite passages in the Bible: "Who told you that you were naked?"[4] Did you ever wonder why God asked this question when He already knew the answer? We believe God wanted to remind His children that shame does not come from Him. As we saw earlier, unlike genuine guilt that is prompted by a sinful choice, shame is connected to one's identity. It distorts one's perception of who they are rather than addressing what they have done, not done, or what has been done to them.

The Father heart of God never shames His children. Why? Because every person is made in His image and can find their identity in Him. Therefore, God does not shame His children, even when they make mistakes. At times His voice is convicting, but it is never condemning.

Are you ashamed of anything in your life? Does your shame cause fear? Do you ever wonder, *What if someone found out…? If they only knew…?* Do you ever try to control the situation by hiding your true feelings from God, your spouse, or others?

We urge you to avoid this destructive cycle and to trust God by moving toward Him. When you begin to experience deeper intimacy with God you will begin to further discover how He feels about you. Our sense is He will ask you, "Who told you that you were naked?"

LISTENING FOR GOD'S VOICE

God longs for relationship and intimacy with every man and woman. He created each of us with a need for relationship, with a longing to love and be loved. In a book titled *Soul Cravings*, Erwin McManus wrote,

+ "You were created for relationship. This is and always will be at the core of your being.

"All of us have an intrinsic need to belong, and all of us are on a search for intimacy. No matter how many things about us are different, in this we are all the same—we all crave love. It is as if we are searching for a love we have lost. Or perhaps more strangely we are searching for a love we have never known but somehow sense it awaits us.

"The most powerful evidence that our souls crave God is that within us there is a longing for love. We are all connected by a thin red line."[5]   +

The two of us both grew up attending church and believing in God. For the first twenty-two years of our lives we each were connected with a traditional church that emphasized relationship with God the Father. Then as young adults, we fell in love with God the Son. We repented of our sins and entered into relationship with Jesus, purposefully growing in intimacy with Him. In recent years, we've had the joy of becoming more intimately acquainted with God the Holy Spirit, witnessing and personally experiencing His power in our lives.

Along the way we've learned that growing in intimacy and relationship with God is a lifelong process. It seems as if God just keeps getting bigger and bigger, although it's really our understanding of Him that has grown as we have taken deliberate steps to know God better.

In my late twenties I (Anne) began to actively seek God's heart. I studied my Bible and bought books on spiritual disciplines. These encouraged me to pursue a two-way relationship with God. I began to realize that not only could I talk with God but He wanted to talk with me. I was delighted to realize that God wanted to be in an intimate relationship with me.

With a growing family, I needed to start by finding a quiet place. I didn't want anything to distract me. I would pray and wait for God to respond. Sometimes while I was waiting a spontaneous thought would come to my mind. I would write it in my journal.

As my relationship with God deepened, I began to talk with Him

Soul Oneness

throughout my day. We talked about everything. Over time He became my best friend.

However, learning to hear God's voice created more questions for me. At times I wondered, *What if I am listening to my own voice? What if I think God is speaking, but it is really the voice of others in my head? What if I am hearing the voice of the enemy? How can I ever be certain that I am hearing from God? Can I know for sure?*

These are all normal questions for anyone who desires to grow in relationship with God. The truth is, a person can hear a number of different voices. They can hear their own voice, the voice of others, the voice of God, or the enemy's voice. In answer to my concerns, spiritual parents encouraged me to grow in intimacy with God and learn how to discern His voice. I continued to pray, listen, journal, and read God's Word. I noticed that when I spent more time just *being* with God, it became easier for me to recognize His voice.

Let me illustrate this. My sister-in-law, Caryl, has two sisters, Lezlie and Jodi. When she and my brother John first began dating, he would often call her at home, but he found it difficult to distinguish Caryl's voice from that of her sisters and her mom, Vera. Since all the female voices sounded the same, John was never quite sure who he was speaking to. He began every conversation by asking the person on the other end of the phone, "Caryl…is that you?" Inevitably the voice on the other end of the phone would reply, "No… it's Lezlie. I'll get Caryl for you."

But as John and Caryl spent more time together, their intimacy grew. Over time John found it easy to distinguish Caryl's voice from her sisters' and her mom's. In fact, eventually he found it hard to believe there was ever a time he did not easily recognize her voice.

So too, as we advance in intimacy with God we begin to know Him and recognize His voice. The Bible says that a sheep knows its shepherd's voice. God is the Good Shepherd. He wants us to know Him so intimately that we immediately recognize His voice and distinguish it from the voice of the enemy. The Bible says, "See to it that you do not refuse Him who is speaking."[6]

Distinguishing God's voice from that of others involves an ongoing commitment to growing in intimacy with Him and discerning His heart. There is power and protection in marital unity, in a couple's "**We**." Therefore, when either one of us senses God's voice, before acting on it, we make sure that we are both in agreement with what we are hearing. Since we are in a one-flesh relationship, we believe that God will not speak to us in different voices or direct us in opposing ways. When there are differences, we take time to continue processing together until we are both on the same page.

We also make sure that what we are hearing is in agreement with the Bible. We do this because we believe that God's voice will never contradict the principles revealed in His Word. Not only do we rely on each other and on God's Word for wisdom and direction but we also involve other people, those who are more mature in the Lord and can affirm that what we are hearing is in alignment with God's principles.

Knowing God Through His Word

The Bible is the most widely read book in all of history. For some, it is their first introduction to God. The pages of the Bible are filled with powerful stories that God uses to draw men and women into relationship with Him, stories that reveal different parts of His nature and character. The Bible not only introduces us to God the Father, God the Son, and God the Holy Spirit, but we get a chance to meet ordinary men and women like us who were invited to live extraordinary lives through their relationship with God.

Reading the Bible with an open heart can be a spiritual experience. Spending time in God's Word is one way to grow in relationship and intimacy with God.

When I (Anne) first became a Christian I watched other godly women for clues about how to grow in knowing God. The ones I deeply respected seemed to know their Bible inside and out. So I decided to sign up for a Bible study on Tuesday mornings. One of the first things I noticed when I sat down with this group of women was their Bibles. I realized I was the only woman with a paperback version of the *Living Bible*. Everyone else seemed to have thick leather Bibles with complex translations and lots of footnotes. I also noticed that the pages of their Bibles were highlighted

Soul Oneness

with colored markers and their margins were filled with handwritten notes. Some even carried around 3x5 cards to help them memorize specific Scriptures.

As a new Christian I began to assess a person's spiritual maturity by the size and translation of their Bible and the quantity of notes handwritten in the margins. Determined to know God through His Word, I headed to a Christian bookstore. The first thing I did was purchase a cover for my *Living Bible*. Since I wasn't ready to trade in my beginner's version, I thought I could at least hide it under a quilted book cover. This also gave my Bible the appearance of being "thicker." Then I purchased a package of multicolored highlighters and spent the next few months marking every passage that seemed significant. I also scribbled lots of notes in my margins. It wasn't long before my attempt to know God through studying His Word began to feel more like work than joy. I felt as if I were cramming for a test instead of growing in relationship.

Eventually I realized that God never asks me to study His Word as if I were being tested or graded. I didn't want to gather facts about Jesus. I wanted to *know* Him the way the psalmist knew Him. "Oh, how I love your law! I meditate on it all day long."[7] God's Word invites me into relationship with Him — to be still, listen, and meditate on what He may be saying to me.

God's Word is an invitation to deeper intimacy, not a book to be memorized. God doesn't want me to know *about* Him; He longs for me to know and walk together *with* Him.

Spending Time with God

There are many ways to deepen your intimacy with God. In addition to listening to God and meditating on His Word, many other spiritual disciplines provide ways to grow in knowing God more intimately. Richard J. Foster, in his book *Celebration of Discipline*, places spiritual disciplines into three categories.[8] He describes the inward disciplines as meditation, prayer, fasting, and study. He refers to the outward disciplines as simplicity, solitude, submission, and service. Finally, he describes the corporate disciplines as confession, worship, guidance, and celebration. These spiritual disciplines will never take the place of a personal relationship with God, but they represent a doorway that invites a person into deeper levels of intimacy with God.

The two of us have been in personal relationship with God for almost thirty years. For many of those years if someone asked us if we knew God, we would have confidently answered yes. If we were asked to describe our relationship with God, we would have responded with a list of things we were *doing* for Him. We went to church, we prayed, we gave our time, talents, and treasures. We tried to do what we thought we were supposed to do in order to show God we loved Him. The problem was, we never knew if we were doing enough so we kept doing more.

Religion often equates doing things for God with being in relationship with Him. When a person focuses on serving God it can inhibit their ability to *know* Him. When *doing* things for God becomes the priority, God can feel more like a boss than a loving Father.

God enjoys *being* with a person much more than having them *do* things for Him.

When I (Tim) retired from the fire department, we moved from the suburbs of Chicago to Holland, Michigan, where I accepted a full-time pastor's position at a local church. Adjusting to a new home and a new job took time. A seemingly never-ending list of pastoral needs consumed my energy, along with the responsibility of leading our family through major life changes.

It quickly became apparent that serving God could become the biggest obstacle to my *knowing* Him. During my years as a fireman I could easily plan time to *be* with the Lord, but as the needs of our faith community continued to increase, my regular times of just *being* with the Lord were slowly being replaced with *doing* lots of good things for Him. I began to feel more like God's employee than His son. As my joy was drained away, I determined to find a way to just *be* with the Lord.

Down the road from our home on the shores of Lake Michigan was a Christian youth camp that offered area pastors a room for prayer and study at a special daily rate. I decided to rent a room once a month for my DAWG—Day Alone With God. (Yes, I have a thing for acronyms.)

Early one morning I headed downstairs to set out on my first official DAWG day. I was all set: in one hand I carried my backpack, cassette player, and cell phone. In the other I gripped my Bible, two books, a notebook, and my daily planner. Anne met me at the door, and as I leaned over to kiss her good-bye, I couldn't help but notice the confused look on her face. "What?" I asked.

"Honey," she said, "where are you going with all of that stuff?"

"Today's my DAWG day," I reminded her. "I'm going to Camp Geneva. Why?"

She replied, "Well, what if I told you that I really missed you and wanted to spend time with you? What if I rented a room at a camp on the shores of Lake Michigan for an entire day just to *be* with you?"

In a hurry to kick off my DAWG day, I snapped, "What's your point?"

"Well, if I walked into the room and you had your music playing and your Day-Timer out and your books opened and you were busy with a backpack full of work…well…I guess I'd wonder how much you really wanted to *be* with me."

I looked at Anne, then I looked at all my stuff. Then my wife put her arms around me and said, "Hon, why don't you leave all your stuff at home and just *be* with the Lord?"

As Anne helped me realize that day, *being* with God is not about making appointments with Him, although that's not a bad way to get started. Being with God is about spending time in His company, talking with Him, listening to Him, learning to see yourself through His loving eyes.

RACING TOWARD GOD

A while back we attended a wedding in Pasadena. The ceremony was such a life-giving celebration of a man and woman becoming one.

I (Tim) have many great memories of that day. But one particular conversation keeps coming back to me. We were talking with a friend, a wonderful woman with such a heart for God and people. She and her husband have seven children and dozens of spiritual sons and daughters. Both of them are passionate followers of Christ.

Since we were at a wedding, the conversation naturally turned to the topic of marriage. I told our friend we were writing a marriage book and asked if she had any wisdom to share. After thinking for just a moment, she said, "I view marriage as a race to see who can get to the cross first."

This is a woman who understands what it means to live in the **Larger Story** with God as the main character. She passionately lives out "marriage is not about me."

Racing to the cross means recognizing that both partners in a marriage desperately need the grace of God. As the two of you draw closer to Him, you will inevitably draw closer to each other. What's more, when a husband and wife are committed to knowing God and being known by Him, they are better equipped to be in an intimate relationship with each other.

We do not have a specific formula or a detailed step-by-step procedure for couples to know God, themselves, and their spouse. But we encourage every person to start with God. Begin by asking God to show you His ways. From there a husband and wife can take practical steps, such as learning and understanding each other's temperaments, styles of relating, spiritual gifts, and love languages. In the next few chapters we will explore these and other ways to increase intimacy as you move together toward soul oneness by knowing and being fully known.

Soul Oneness

+ Chapter 8

Different Is Good

Learning to Delight in God's Design

When we counsel dating or engaged couples, we remind them that they are intoxicated with love. This is a good thing. There is something wonderful about romantic love. It covers a multitude of sins. Intoxicated, passionate lovers are able to look at each other's differences and only see the best.

We, too, enjoyed this intoxicated state early in our relationship. During our dating season I (Anne) could make an endless list of all the things that attracted me to Tim. I loved everything about him. I loved that he was decisive. I was attracted to his strength and leadership. He was directed, focused, and sure of himself. The way he processed life distinguished him from every other person I had ever met.

However, marriage and real life have a way of moving a couple out of the intoxicated phase of their relationship and sobering them up. After being married a year, I remember looking at Tim and saying, "I don't understand the way you process life. Are you always so strong, so sure of yourself, and so decisive?" The differences that I once thought were so wonderful suddenly bothered me. I often thought to myself, *What is his problem? Why can't he be more like me? Why can't he think more like me? Why can't he respond to life more like I do?* Apparently I thought I was the prototype for perfection. The answer to every problem seemed to rest on Tim being more like me.

The differences I had initially loved about Tim, I was now allowing to divide us. I knew that in order for our marriage to grow in unity and intimacy, I needed to relearn how to celebrate those differences.

Husbands and wives who understand the value of the way God uniquely created them experience a deep level of intimacy with their spouse. They enjoy soul oneness — the relational component that enables them to walk out their love in tangible ways on a day-to-day basis. They understand the importance of celebrating their differences, because they recognize that by joining together they can more fully Reflect and Reveal the nature of God to each other and to the world. Couples soon discover that when they begin to appreciate each other's differences they are better equipped to exercise Rulership in unity, impacting their world and advancing the Kingdom of God.

By contrast, couples who interpret their differences as a negative issue experience varying levels of disunity, which not only affects their intimacy but also inhibits their ability to Rule together as husband and wife.

In their book *Intimate Allies* counselor Dan Allender and theologian Tremper Longman III challenge married couples to take a new look at the differences that are evident between a man and a woman, stating, "We have a choice: We can either delight in diversity or destroy distinctions."[1] Advancing in intimacy, communication, and healthy conflict management is a lifelong process. However, growing in soul oneness is much easier when a couple has the right tools to help them recognize the strength that comes from their differences.

UNDERSTANDING GOD'S VISION FOR WIVES AND HUSBANDS

Jesus reminded His followers of the two most important commandments: "'You shall love the Lord your God with all your heart, and with all your soul, and with all your mind.' This is the great and foremost commandment. And the second is like it, 'You shall love your neighbor as yourself.'" Jesus went on to say, "On these two commandments depend the whole Law and the Prophets."[2]

For every husband and wife, your closest neighbor is your spouse. But how can you love your spouse if you do not first love yourself? A person will grow in loving themselves as they grow in knowing and understanding their identity as a child who is loved and has been made in the image of God.

The Bible says, "Pay close attention to yourself…"[3] This verse is not encouraging us to live self-centered lives. It is not suggesting that anyone spend time navel-gazing or being selfishly preoccupied. This verse is a command to study ourselves for the purpose of seeing ourselves as God sees us. To know who you are in Christ means to embrace your identity in Him.

As a husband and wife grow in their knowledge and love of God, they will learn to know and love themselves. As they better know and love themselves they will advance in knowing and loving their spouse. Celebrating the wonder and uniqueness of the Trinity invites a couple to

Soul Oneness

celebrate the wonder and uniqueness in each other. This is all part of the miracle and mystery of two becoming one.

Another key text in the Bible to help husbands and wives fulfill their need to know and be fully known is in 1 Peter 3:1-6 (NIV). This portion of Scripture instructs men and women in how to relate to each other in light of God's relationship with them.

God's Vision for Wives

The text begins,

"Wives, in the same way be submissive to your husbands so that, if any of them do not believe the word, they may be won over without words by the behavior of their wives, when they see the purity and reverence of your lives."

Whenever I (Anne) teach this section at a Marriage Advance, I ask the women this question: "What comes to mind when you read the words 'Wives, be submissive to your husbands…'"? The response is never positive when it comes to the "S" word. Why? I believe the enemy has distorted God's definition of submission. Women often admit, "I have no problem submitting to Christ, but there are times when I really struggle with submitting to my husband." This kind of response is an indication that something is off. Either the husband, the wife, or both partners are operating from a distorted view of what God intended.

Whenever there is misunderstanding or confusion about submission, we encourage couples to invite the Holy Spirit to give them wisdom, revelation, and understanding. Submission is God's idea, which by definition means it's a good thing. The command in 1 Peter to "be submissive" is meant to bring freedom, not bondage. As a woman submits to her husband, their marriage is protected. A mutually submitted marriage not only mirrors the Trinity but also paints a biblical picture of the cord of three strands that is not easily broken.[4] Submission strengthens a marriage and brings freedom that ultimately advances the relationship.

God never intended for submission to be defined as forced compliance. God intended marital submission to flow out of a willingness to die to selfishness in order to give a spouse life. Looking at our model for marriage, we see God the Son take on human form and willingly submit Himself to God the Father. His death provided life for each and every one of us. As a woman, I need to continually ask myself, *Am I willing to die to my own agenda? Am I willing to choose God as the main character in my story?*

I once heard submission defined as "the courage to allow something to go someone else's way." Submission is an invitation for me to Reflect and Reveal the character of God to Tim. In addition, submitting invites me to step out of the **smaller story** where I am the main character and choose to live in the **Larger Story** with God as the main character. A women's decision to submit is never contingent on her husband's behavior or whether or not she thinks he deserves to be submitted to. The decision to submit is not about a wife, or her husband; it's about God. When I submit to Tim as to the Lord, it's a reminder that *Marriage is not about me.*

Our encouragement to husbands and wives is to reclaim Jesus' life-transforming message on marriage when He reinstated God's original design in Matthew 19. The good news of the gospel includes an invitation to return to God's Plan A for marriage.

The writer of 1 Peter continues talking to wives:

"Your beauty should not come from outward adornment, such as braided hair and the wearing of gold jewelry and fine clothes. Instead, it should be that of your inner self, the unfading beauty of a gentle and quiet spirit, which is of great worth in God's sight."

A woman who knows and loves her husband is a woman who knows and loves herself. These verses emphasize the untapped power of a woman's inner beauty. They remind women of the war taking place between the voice of the world and the voice of God. The world continually encourages women to focus on superficial things, to spend their time, energy, and finances on outward appearances. God is not opposed to a woman spending time on her outward appearance. In fact the Scriptures remind us that the body is the temple of the Holy Spirit. A woman should do whatever she can to be physically fit, to make healthy lifestyle choices, and to make herself attractive.

The aim of this passage is to remind wives to place a greater emphasis on inner beauty, the unfading beauty that is found within a woman's spirit. It challenges women to live a balanced life. In other words, don't spend more time on your outside (physical appearance) than on your inside (nurturing your spirit and soul).

I (Anne) would like to challenge women to reflect on a few questions:

+ Does your life reflect a healthy balance between how much time you spend on your outer beauty and how much time you spend on your inner beauty?
+ Do you regularly nurture your spirit by spending time with God?
+ Would you describe your spirit as gentle and quiet?
+ Do you see yourself as a woman of great worth in God's sight?

I encourage you to consider your answers in light of the next verses:

"For this is the way the holy women of the past who put their hope in God used to make themselves beautiful. They were submissive to their own husbands, like Sarah, who obeyed Abraham and called him her master. You are her daughters if you do what is right and do not give way to fear."

I continue to be uplifted and redirected whenever I read about the holy women of the past who put their hope in God. These women were spiritual mothers who have gone before us. They remind us that our worth as women comes from God and not from our husbands or from the world. Our unfading beauty comes from within. This all begins with intimately knowing God and yourself. It includes refusing to give way to fear, because you confidently find your identity in Christ rather than in anyone or anything else. When your identity comes from God, intimacy with your husband naturally flows out of the security you have in Christ.

God's Vision for Husbands

This next verse (1 Peter 3:7, NASB 1977) directly addresses husbands, and it's packed with pure gold. My (Tim's) spiritual dad, Dick Swetman, required me to memorize and internalize this passage decades ago. The truths in this text have served me well over the years.

"You husbands likewise, live with your wives in an understanding way, as with a weaker vessel, since she is a woman; and grant her honor as a fellow heir of the grace of life, so that your prayers may not be hindered."

The verse starts out telling husbands to do *likewise*. This means "in the same way." So husbands are *likewise* to be submissive to their wives, just as wives are commanded to be submissive to their husbands.

Husbands also are instructed to "live with your wives in an understanding way." For years I thought this meant I had to *understand* Anne. After many years of unsuccessfully trying to understand her, I received additional revelation on this verse. A light went on. This verse does not command me to understand Anne. I've known her for forty-five years. We grew up in the same town and attended kindergarten together. We love each other and are best friends. But after all our time and life together, at times I still don't understand her. You see, Anne speaks woman and I speak man. This Scripture frees me up as a husband. It commands me to dwell with Anne in an *understanding way*. While I will never totally understand her, I will never stop trying to live with her in an understanding way.

What about that phrase "as with a weaker vessel"? Does that suggest that women are inferior to men? No, this is not a justification for taking a "me-Tarzan, you-Jane" approach to marriage. Instead, it simply highlights that wives are different from husbands. We can think of it as comparing the husband to a milk bottle and the wife to a precious vase. The verse reminds us of what we saw in Genesis, that God *formed* Adam and *fashioned* Eve.

This passage also reaffirms that marriage is a relationship meant solely for one man and one woman. A husband and wife are to do life *with* each other, together in unity. The instruction to "grant her honor as a fellow heir of the grace of life" points to the oneness, unity, reciprocity, and mutuality in a Christ-centered marriage.

Husbands are to do all this "so that your prayers may not be hindered." When I (Tim) lead REAL LIFE Men's Advances, I'm often asked to teach

Soul Oneness

about prayer. Most men understand the importance and power of prayer. I teach from this passage to encourage men to live with their wife in an understanding way so that their prayer life won't be hindered. This includes valuing her as a priceless treasure and honoring her as a fellow heir. My experience is that often men who struggle with their prayer life also struggle with honoring and valuing their wife.

I would like to offer husbands a few things to think about:

+ In reviewing this passage, would you describe yourself as a husband who lives with his wife in an understanding way? Would your wife agree with your response?
+ Do you treasure your wife as a precious vase fashioned by God?
+ Would you describe yourself as a husband who honors his wife?

As you prayerfully consider your answers, I encourage you to invite the Holy Spirit to help you develop a plan to strategically advance in these areas.

UNDERSTANDING A WIFE'S WAYS

Did you ever read that poster that states, "All I really need to know I learned in kindergarten"? I (Tim) have another poster I want to market: "All I really need to know I learned in marriage."

One thing I've learned in marriage is that when Anne is talking about something that is important to her, most of the time I just need to listen. Unless she specifically asks, I try not to give my opinions, offer solutions, or direct her. As simple as this sounds, when I focus on listening in *an understanding way* Anne feels loved.

Anne came into my office one day and slammed the door behind her. She was obviously upset. When I asked what was wrong, she started to give me a detailed account of a misunderstanding she'd just had with a coworker. Sensing she was ready to burst into tears, I leaned forward in my chair and looked directly into her eyes. I said, "Hon, do you want my opinion on what happened or do you just want me to listen?"

She replied, "I just want you to listen."

So I sat back in my chair as she relayed the story. Anne just wanted to vent. I could have easily chimed in and even added to her complaint. I could have said, "She said what? Oh really…do you know what she said to me earlier this morning?" Or I could have picked up her offense and declared, "Nobody puts baby in the corner!" But this conversation was not about me. It was about Anne, so I just let her talk it out. I know my wife well enough to know that once she actually hears herself say something out loud, she quickly gains perspective.

When she finished, she got up and left my office. Later on the way home from work she said to me, "I felt so much better after we talked today."

I thought to myself, *We didn't talk today…in fact, I didn't say a word.*

I'm a problem solver. I can usually offer several potential solutions to any given problem. In fact, for me solving problems is as natural as putting out fires. However, after being married to Anne for a number of years, I discovered that she is not a fire I need to put out.

I'm beginning to understand what the Bible means when husbands are commanded to live with their wives *in an understanding way, since she is a woman.* Honestly, I don't think I will ever totally understand her. Anne speaks woman, I speak man. But even if I never totally understand her I will never stop *trying* to understand her. Just as Christ pursues me, I will continue to pursue my bride.

My advice to husbands who want to better understand their wives is this:

First, don't try to fix your wife or treat her like a fire that needs to be put out. It will only complicate things.

Second, grow in your listening skills. Often your wife isn't looking for you to agree or disagree with her but simply wants you to listen with a desire to understand her. Listening well is a primary way to honor your wife.

Soul Oneness

LOVE AND RESPECT

God's unique vision for husbands and wives is wrapped up in His unique design of men and women.

When God created man, He placed him in paradise, gave him a job, and made sure the food was plentiful. Still, something was missing. In order to Reflect and Reveal the plurality of the Trinity, man needed someone who was created *after his kind*. It was not good for man to be alone, so God created woman out of man to rescue him from his "not-good" situation.

Both man and woman were created in the image of God, but their maleness and femaleness reveal different parts of God's nature. He designed marriage so that a husband and wife together would model the plurality in the Trinity. Although the three persons of the Trinity share mutual equality, each is distinctly different, just as men and women are distinctly different.

Have you noticed that the Bible gives husbands and wives specific yet different commands? In Ephesians 5:33 we're told, "Each one of you also must love his wife as he loves himself, and the wife must respect her husband."[5] Why do you suppose husbands and wives are commanded to relate to each other in different ways? Could it be that men and women have different relational needs? Yes, both were created to be loved. In fact, the Bible instructs older women to teach younger women to love their husbands.[6] Love is important. However, it's our experience that a man receives love through the filter of respect.

In his book *Love and Respect*, Dr. Emerson Eggerichs writes,

+ "As a pastor, I counseled married couples and could not solve their problems. The major problem I heard from wives was, "He doesn't love me." Wives are made to love, want to love, and expect to love. Many husbands fail to deliver. But as I kept studying Scripture and counseling couples, I finally saw the other half of the equation. Husbands weren't saying it much, but they were thinking, *She doesn't respect me*. Husbands are made to be respected, want respect, and expect respect. Many wives fail to deliver. The result is that five out of ten marriages land in divorce court."[7] +

Everyone is familiar with a woman's longings for emotional intimacy. However, few people have been taught about a man's desire for respect. When a woman shows respect to her husband, it can be compared to high octane fuel that fills a man up. As a wife's respectful behavior refuels her husband, he advances in understanding what it means to be a man made in the image of God. On the other hand, if a husband interprets his wife's behavior as disrespectful, he often receives this message as contempt for him as a man, which makes it difficult for him to emotionally connect.

A man who feels disrespected by his wife may power up and dominate the situation by coming on strong, being authoritative, or giving high direction. A woman may hear his response as, "Me Tarzan, you Jane! I am the head of this house! I am the man in this family! It's my way or the highway!" Another typical response of a man who senses disrespect from his wife is to desert or abandon her, perhaps by emotionally shutting down or physically removing himself from the disrespectful atmosphere.

One of the best parts of our relationship has always been our friendship. I (Anne) not only love my husband, I really like him. Even after thirty-plus years of marriage, there is no one I would rather spend time with than Tim. He's my best friend. Whenever we're apart I genuinely miss his company. Even so, at times I've said things that left him feeling disrespected. I remember one time years ago, soon after we first started leading a small group for several couples. One member of the group was a new believer who had some reservations about being in a small group. Whenever we met together, she seemed guarded and difficult to engage in conversation.

One night after everyone had gone home and Tim and I were cleaning up before bed, I began making some observations about the evening. I said, "Sometimes I feel intimidated when you ask me direct questions. I think other people are intimidated too. Instead of calling on people to answer, why don't you just wait for them to respond? I don't like when you put people on the spot. It makes me very uncomfortable."

Even before he responded, I could see that Tim was frustrated by my comments. I thought to myself, *Why is he offended? Why doesn't he just lead the group the same way I would?*

Interrupting my armchair analysis, Tim said, "Anne, I am not intimidating anyone. I am leading the group. You were the one who wanted me to take charge of the question and answers. I'm sorry I'm not doing it your way. At our first meeting, every person agreed to answer the questions and participate in the discussion. I am not asking them to do anything they didn't already agree to do" — his voice got louder — "and furthermore, no one is putting anyone on the spot, so *you* don't need to feel uncomfortable!"

When I realized that he was not understanding what I was trying to say, I tried to come at it from a different angle: "Tim, I don't think that you are trying to be intimidating, but…"

He interrupted with a firm voice that he rarely uses, saying, "Why do you always assume that everyone feels the way you feel?" Before I could answer, he added, "I have to wake up early for work, so if we're done here I'm going to bed." Shaking his head, he walked away.

Tim's response to what he interpreted as my disrespect was typical of husbands caught in similar situations. They may leave the room, leave the house, or over time leave the marriage. Many husbands abandon their wives in all sorts of socially acceptable ways without ever packing their bags. Some emotionally desert by spending long hours at work or at church. Others choose to be overly involved in outside hobbies, spending time with friends, joining multiple sports teams, sitting in front of the television, or just emotionally checking out. Wives tend to interpret these behaviors as abandonment. They hear the message, "I don't love you! I don't need you! I'm out of here!"

Respect is a core need in the heart of every man. A respect deficit in a marriage often leads a husband to look for other ways to get his respect tank refilled. Similarly, a love deficit in a marriage often leads a wife to look for other ways to get her core need for love met. During the love and respect section of our Marriage Advance we challenge women to ask their husbands, "Do you feel respected by me?" We challenge men to ask their wives, "Do you feel loved by me?" When a husband or wife gives their spouse an opportunity to share their heart, it becomes an invitation to advance in intimacy with each other. When a woman is loved by a man, her spirit opens up to receive him. When a man is respected by a woman, his spirit opens up and he moves toward her.

JUST A LITTLE R-E-S-P-E-C-T

Early in our marriage I (Anne) became aware of my need to make some changes in my communication style. God began showing me how my words to Tim were often disrespectful. The problem wasn't so much *what* I said to Tim but the *way* I said it.

While raising our family, we always made it a priority to go out twice a month on a date to spend some time away from the kids and focus on the "**We**" of our marriage. Since I'm a conflict avoider by nature, it's easy for me to dismiss potentially difficult conversations that may turn into disagreements. But we both agreed to stay current with any conflict so that things didn't pile up.

I remember one particular date night when I needed to talk with Tim about some marriage concerns, but I wanted to do it while showing him respect. I set the atmosphere by getting a babysitter and making reservations at one of Tim's favorite restaurants. We enjoyed our meal together while I waited for the right time to address my concern. Sensing that I had something on my heart, Tim said, "Is everything okay? What's up?"

I smiled, "Well, I did want to talk to you about some things. But before I do I want to apologize." Tim looked surprised, obviously wondering what was coming next.

I continued, "Lately I've become more aware of my communication style. I've noticed there are times when I'm talking that you seem to shut down. It's usually because I'm being overly dramatic, thinking you'll be more apt to listen. So I tend to make generalizations and exaggerate your flaws. I've realized that at times I sound more like your parent instead of your wife."

I paused for a moment before continuing. "I just want to tell you that I'm sorry for being so disrespectful. Even though that's not my intention, I know it can come across that way. Tim, I respect you more than anyone I know and I really want to be your encourager. I want you to know that I'm becoming more aware of how I communicate and I'm working on showing you more respect. Will you forgive me?"

Soul Oneness

I don't think Tim was expecting the conversation to go this way. My apology seemed to open his heart to me. He dropped his defenses and was hanging on my every word. After a long pause, he responded, "Well, I'm not sure what to say…but thank you. We have had some pretty tough conversations lately. I know you love me and your apology means a lot. It's not just you; I need to work on things too. I need to become a better listener. Is there anything else you want to talk about?"

I reached for the pepper shaker and sprinkled a few grains of black pepper on the center of the white linen tablecloth. He smiled and nodded, a little suspicious of my next move.

Then I said "I want to talk to you about a few things that are bothering me. But they are very, very small. In fact, the only reason I'm bringing them up is because I don't want to be a conflict avoider. So this is the new and improved version of me. I want to find ways to communicate with respect so that my delivery doesn't detract from what I'm trying to say."

After pausing to make sure Tim was with me, I continued with an illustration. "This white tablecloth represents our life together. These few grains of black pepper represent the size of the things I want to talk to you about. In fact, they seem so small compared to all the things you are doing right."

Tim started laughing and said, "Okay, that was a great start. Now, what did I do?" We both laughed. That evening we were able to work through some potentially explosive topics, because our defenses were down and our hearts were open. It wasn't my words as much as the respectful attitude I conveyed to Tim that allowed us to communicate more effectively. The difference in Tim's response was amazing. Looking back, I see that meeting Tim's need for respect was the key that opened his heart and spirit.

Even as I write this, I can't help but think of the TV infomercials that give testimony of miraculous results. Just like the steak knife that can cut through aluminum siding on your house, showing respect cuts through the protective walls of a man's heart and emotions and provides an opening for a couple to advance in intimacy and soul oneness.

AN UNCONDITIONAL COMMAND

We need to remember that God's instruction in Ephesians 5:33 is unconditional. God commands wives to respect their husbands with no strings attached. Likewise, He commands husbands to love their wives with no strings attached. There are no *ifs* in these commands.

Although our culture has, for the most part, embraced the concept of unconditional love, we still tend to make respect contingent on someone's behavior. A wife often places conditions on respect. She may think her husband does not deserve her respect and may withhold it until he behaves or responds in a certain way.

When we counsel couples, we often meet with each spouse individually. In talking with one woman who had been married for more than ten years, we asked her to tell us about her husband. She willingly offered a list of his positive traits: "He is such a good man. He's a great dad. He loves our kids. He coaches our daughter's softball team. He volunteers at school. He helps me around the house. He gets along with both our families. I really love him!"

After listening to her response, we asked a more specific question: "Tell us what you respect about your husband?"

She stopped and thought for a moment. After a long pause, she repeated the word out loud almost as if it were an unfamiliar term. "Respect…" she said. "That is not a word I usually think of when I think of my husband." Tears welled up in her eyes as she continued, "I love him, but if I were being totally honest…there are times I don't really respect him."

We asked her to tell us more. "I guess I don't respect his walk with the Lord, or the way He leads us spiritually," she explained. "I would have to say that I don't respect financial decisions he has made." She seemed surprised by her own admissions. We began to discuss how the disrespect she had for her husband was causing division and disunity. Her attitude was subtle and unspoken, but it had a negative impact on their intimacy and oneness.

Ephesians 5:33 commands a wife to show her husband respect, whether or not he deserves it, just as a husband is commanded to love his wife regardless of whether or not she's being particularly loveable at the moment.

No matter how long a couple has been married, encouragement and affirmation never get old. Your spouse never gets tired of receiving love and respect.

We challenge you to test God's Word on these specific commands. What would your marriage look like if you focused on this principle? Take some time to ask the Lord how you could advance in showing love or respect to your spouse. This takes faith. Living by faith does not come easily. The Bible says faith is "the substance of things hoped for, the evidence of things not seen."[8] In marriage, stepping out in faith with love and respect when you don't "feel" it is not hypocritical; it's an act of obedience.

Husbands who show unconditional love to their wives and wives who show unconditional respect to their husbands declare through their behavior, "Marriage is not about me."

+ Chapter 9

What's It Like to Be You?

Celebrating Your Spouse's Uniqueness

Equality within marriage doesn't mean that men and women are the same. In fact, every marriage could attest to the many ways that a man and a woman are different. But remember, different is good! And differences best reflect God's creative design when they are celebrated.

God is neither male nor female; He transcends gender. Therefore, when He was looking for someone to Reflect His image, He needed more than one gender could provide. The text reads, "God created man [humankind] in His own image' in the image of God He created him; male and female He created *them*. God blessed *them*; and God said to *them*, 'Be fruitful and multiply, and fill the earth, and subdue it; and rule over the fish of the sea and over the birds of the sky and over every living thing that moves on the earth.'"[1]

Something miraculous happens when a man is paired with a woman. Together, their marital "**We**" is a Reflection of the plurality and oneness within the Trinity. When you think about it, life is full of times where two individual things are better when they're paired together. Cookies are better *with* milk, a movie is better *with* popcorn, a hug is always better *with* a kiss...you get the idea.

A husband and wife who are able to recognize and value the many ways their differences complement each other experience a new level of strength in their relationship. The strength that comes from their unity allows them to Rule together. This strong bond protects their marriage as their relationship becomes an illustration to the world of what it means for two to become one.

Here's the million-dollar question: How do couples learn to celebrate each other's differences instead of comparing or competing with one another? One way is by understanding each other's spiritual gifts, temperaments, and personal styles of relating. This will help launch a couple toward deeper intimacy and soul oneness.

SPIRITUAL GIFTS

One of the blessings of receiving much of our spiritual formation at Willow Creek was learning about spiritual gifts. This teaching continues to positively impact our marriage in so many ways.

God gives spiritual gifts to every follower of Christ. They play an important role in how a person functions in life and marriage. As Christians, it is our responsibility to nurture, grow, and steward the spiritual gifts God has given us.

The Bible uses the human body to illustrate this principle. Each part of a person's physical body was created by God with a specific purpose and function. In a healthy body, the individual parts work together effectively. It is the same with spiritual gifts. Every person is given specific gifts that have a specific purpose and function in advancing the kingdom of God. Dr. C. Peter Wagner highlights the importance of identifying spiritual gifts: "I do not think I am amiss in stating that one of the primary spiritual exercises for any Christian person is to discover, develop, and use his or her spiritual gift."[2]

God gives spiritual gifts to help the church function in healthy ways, but spiritual gifts are also important in marriage. God's design for marriage includes a husband and wife who have identified their gifts and celebrate them in unity, without competition or comparison.

When the two of us decided to leave our jobs and step into REAL LIFE Ministries full-time, God used our spiritual gifts to help us reach unity in the decision-making process. We described some of this process in chapter 6, including the complications surrounding the sale of our home and relocating to a smaller house, as well as the timing of leaving our jobs.

This was a busy season for us for other reasons as well. Our daughter Amy was pregnant and awaiting the arrival of our first grandchild. Our daughter Colleen got engaged and was planning an out-of-state wedding in Chicago. Our son, Tim, was completing his master's degree in social work. Our youngest daughter Cate was a full-time college student. Obviously, we had a lot going on in our family.

Soul Oneness

Our spiritual gifts became invaluable as we processed family decisions together. Tim's gift of leadership provided the direction we needed, while his gifts of encouragement, faith, and prayer kept us steady and provided protection during many difficult days.

While Tim is a big-picture thinker who provides direction and vision, God used Anne's gifts of wisdom and discernment to evaluate specific situations and see truths that others might overlook.

As we work together in unity, our spiritual gifts complement each other and enable us to Reflect and Reveal the diversity of roles within the Trinity. Our gifts provide us with strength and protection to Rule in soul oneness. When a person uses the gifts God has given and encourages their spouse to do the same, together they will advance in intimacy and in deeper understanding of their marital "**We**."

TEMPERAMENTS AND STYLES OF RELATING

It is amazing to see lights go on for couples as they gain a greater understanding of how God has wired them. Understanding each other's temperaments increases a couple's emotional intimacy and ability to Rule in unity.

People are born with different personalities and temperaments. These include a person's nature, outlook on life, and disposition. If you don't already know your temperament, a number of tools are available to help you identify and understand how your approach to life may be different from your spouse's. For example, the DISC model for evaluating behavioral styles and preferences describes the four basic temperament types: Choleric (D-type), Sanguine (I-type), Phlegmatic (S-type) and Melancholy (C-type).[3] Another tool is the Taylor-Johnson Temperament Analysis, which measures nine personality traits and their opposites.[4]

I (Tim) have grown to appreciate our marriage even more through understanding how our temperaments affect our interactions with each other and with other people. We've learned that Anne is melancholy. She is quieter, content to listen, analytical, and much more introspective than I am. She is an observer of life. Spending time alone recharges her.

Socially, she prefers a few deep relationships rather than large groups of people.

By contrast, I am sanguine and choleric. I love people — lots of people. Relating with others energizes me. At the same time, I have a serious side. I'm a pragmatic leader who tends to focus on facts and results.

Over the years, God has used Anne to model different aspects of His nature to me. Her lifestyle has taught me how to be still and enjoy solitude. Being still before God allows me to see Him, myself, and others in new ways.

At the same time, Anne's world has expanded by being with me. She tells me that my outlook on life, love for people, and outgoing nature has encouraged her to embrace each moment and be more adventuresome.

Our different temperaments and styles of relating allow us to Reflect and Reveal a clearer image of God than either one of us could do alone.

SPEAKING YOUR SPOUSE'S LANGUAGE

Closely connected to the topic of individual temperaments and relational styles is the idea that everyone has their own love language. In other words, certain things make them feel more loved than others. Dr. Gary Chapman's book *The Five Love Languages* suggests specific ways we give and receive love: words of affirmation, quality time, gifts, acts of service, and physical touch.[5] Readers are challenged to identify their primary love languages — the ways they feel most loved — and to learn how to speak the love language of the people they value most.

A few years ago, we counseled a newly married couple that we will refer to as Roger and Sally. When we first began to see them, they had never heard about love languages. Roger grew up in a very proper family that was uncomfortable with displays of affection. In fact, Roger could not remember his parents ever holding hands or putting their arms around each other. However, some of his warmest memories of growing up centered on his parents bringing him gifts. These gifts were not extravagant, but they reminded Roger that he was loved.

When Roger married Sally he just assumed that buying her gifts would communicate that same message of love to her. He regularly brought home something special and presented it to her as a token of his love. He never understood why she seemed less than enthusiastic about his desire to lavish her with affection through gift-giving.

Sally was raised in a family that openly demonstrated affection. She grew up feeling most loved when someone touched her or communicated verbal words of affection. After she married Roger, she would ask him to hold her hand and put his arm around her. She wanted him to tell her how much he loved her. But Roger was disinterested in nonsexual touch and found it difficult to express himself verbally. Over time, Sally began to pull away from Roger.

Can you see how this couple could feel disconnected? Roger gave Sally gifts, which was what he longed to receive. Sally attempted to show love to Roger through talk and nonsexual touch, which was what she longed to receive. They were using the wrong love languages to communicate with each other. This left them feeling misunderstood and isolated. As Roger and Sally learned to speak each other's love language, their marital intimacy dramatically increased.

Identifying the way your spouse receives love provides a key that opens the door to deeper intimacy. Jesus said, "A new commandment I give to you, that you love one another, even as I have loved you, that you also love one another. By this all men will know that you are My disciples, if you have love for one another."[6] The quality of a person's love for God, themselves, and their spouse is what distinguishes them from the world. Using the love language that best speaks to your spouse cannot fail to increase intimacy and soul oneness.

In our own marriage, learning how to give and receive love completely transformed the way we related to each other. Early in our marriage we wondered why our attempts to communicate love to each other often failed. I (Anne) remember one spectacular failure in vivid detail.

It had been a really long week. I knew Tim would be on duty at the firehouse over the weekend, so I was looking forward to being home with the kids. But first I needed to do some grocery shopping and run a few errands. My sister came over to watch the kids, which allowed me to complete my to-do list in half the time.

As I finally headed for home, my mind began to drift. I imagined myself soaking in a hot bath, getting into my pajamas, and relaxing on the couch with the kids. I had even picked up a movie that we could enjoy watching together. As I pulled into the driveway, I should have guessed something was up when I saw the kids rushing out of the house. They seemed unusually excited to see me.

My sister met me at the car and told me that a big surprise was waiting for me in the house. I'm not a person who really enjoys surprises, but I obediently shut my eyes as the kids instructed and allowed my giggling brood to lead me back to the bedroom.

"Okay, Mommy. Open your eyes!" they shouted. On the bed was an envelope with a single red rose lying next to it. I looked at my sister, confused and hoping for more information or some kind of explanation. The kids were shouting, "Read it, Mom, read it." As I slowly opened the envelope, I recognized Tim's handwriting:

Surprise!
This red rose is just the beginning of a romantic weekend for two.
Don't worry about a thing…The kids are in good hands.
Don't worry about your clothes. I have a suitcase packed for you.
Just kiss everyone good-bye and head back to the car.
Once you get inside, look in the glove compartment.

The kids were jumping up and down, clapping their hands and giggling. I know they expected me to share in their excitement, but I was too tired to feel their joy. My dreams of taking a hot bath and curling up on the couch were slipping away. I started firing off questions at my sister: "What is going on? I thought Tim was on duty at the firehouse. What is he up to? Where is he taking me? When did he write this note? What clothes did he pack? How long will we be gone?" None of my questions were answered. It soon became obvious that no amount of begging would persuade my sister or children to turn informant.

In that moment, I was reminded of why I don't like surprises. I'm one of

Soul Oneness

those people who looks around the house for my presents *before* Christmas. I have even been known to take a quick peek and rewrap them. When it's my birthday, I would prefer a gift certificate. That way I can pick out exactly what I want rather than being *surprised* with things that I don't really need. I began to think about the note Tim had written me — specifically the line that announced, "Don't worry about your clothes. I have a suitcase packed for you!"

How could Tim possibly know what clothes to pack for me? Did he throw in my favorite jeans? Did he remember my makeup and blow dryer? A low-level panic began to set in as I remembered the last time Tim picked out an outfit for me, back when we were dating. He had wanted to surprise me for our first Christmas together. We were sitting with his family as I opened up the first box and pulled out a pair of size 6 pants. I wore a size 10. Tim assured me they would fit because the material was "stretchy"! The next box contained a matching poncho featuring a very distinct design. It looked a lot like a rug, which is fine if you are going for an Aztec look. The third box held the finale — something Tim assured me was a very special accessory to go with the Aztec rug-poncho and skin-tight pants. I was afraid to open it. I finally looked inside the box and found a burnt orange suede Ringo cap!

As you can see, my apprehension about Tim packing my clothes was rooted in painful experience. I checked my closet to see what was missing. My favorite pants were still on a hanger. As I took further inventory, I noticed the blouse that was missing was the one I could barely button since I started breastfeeding. Staring at an empty hanger, I realized the pants he had chosen were the ones I kept in my closet to remind me of my "goal weight."

However, since I really wanted to be a more fun person, I needed to fight my natural tendency to default to party pooper mode. Determined to play along, I followed Tim's instructions and headed back to the car. Sure enough, envelope number 2 was inside the glove compartment. It read:

Let the games begin…it's time to party!
Back out of the driveway and head to Schaumburg Fire Station #1.
When you arrive, park in the side lot and walk inside.
Have fun….

The thought of walking into an unknown situation at the firehouse was a bit unnerving. But I remember thinking that the faster I cooperated, the sooner this game would be over.

When I walked into the firehouse, the firemen began teasing me about "the great adventure" Tim had planned. I tried to get some information from them, but no one was talking. They told me if I wanted the next envelope I would have to slide down the fire pole!

I know from experience that if a person shows any weakness to a fireman, it only adds to the teasing. So I pretended to laugh and enjoy the process as I climbed the staircase to the second floor. Did I mention that I'm afraid of heights? Nevertheless, I wrapped my arms and legs around the pole and slid down. I hit the ground a lot harder than I expected. They said, "Nice job, Annie," and handed me envelope number 3. It read:

Way to go! Mission accomplished.
Let's see, what's next?
Drive east on Schaumburg Road. Head north on Meacham Road.
East on Golf Road. Pull into Houlihan's parking lot.
Walk up to the bar and ask to talk to Tommy the bartender.
He will give you envelope #4.

After my little trip down the fire pole in front of Tim's coworkers, I was not in the mood for any more "fun"! I could feel the blood rushing through my veins as my blood pressure shot up. At this point I was so angry I just wanted to go home. But I pressed on, determined to be a good sport. I walked into the restaurant, asked for Tommy the bartender, who was more than willing to give me the envelope — but only after I sang a little Irish song.

Once I actually got the envelope, I noticed it had some coins taped inside to a note that read:

You are getting closer.
There is a pay phone outside. Use this change to dial the number below.

I walked outside, located the pay phone, inserted the coins, and dialed the number. Tim picked up on the first ring and greeted me in his *romantic*

Soul Oneness

voice. He told me to look across the parking lot toward the hotel on the other side of the road. As I looked in that direction, I saw Tim in the window of a hotel room. He was dancing, waving enthusiastically, and blowing me kisses. He was having a wonderful time! Before I could blurt out a word, he said, "Head up to room 444...I'll be waiting for you. We have the honeymoon suite for the entire weekend. Let the love-fest begin!"

I was so angry I don't even remember driving across the street. I vaguely recall parking the car and taking the elevator upstairs. I stomped down the hallway toward our room. Surely my footsteps were shaking the very foundations of the building. I scanned the room numbers and saw the door to room 444 ajar. I pushed it open. The room was dark, and soft music was playing in the background. A path of rose petals covered the floor. (A side note: I later found out that Tim had stopped by the funeral home down the street to pick up a few dozen "used roses" from the last visitation!) Following the flowery pathway into a candlelit bathroom, I found Tim soaking in a tub full of bubbles. He looked sooo relaxed. His eyes were closed and he had a huge smile on his face.

All I could think of was that I wanted to drown him.

Somehow our marriage survived this weekend from hell, but we obviously had no idea how to speak each other's love language. Unlike me, Tim loves surprises. What would have been a great adventure for him was a disaster for me. I would have loved to have known about our getaway weeks in advance. With four small kids at home I would have enjoyed anticipating and planning for our romantic getaway. I would have gotten some rest and packed my own clothes. But to go from grocery shopping after a long, stressful day...to visiting the firehouse...to sliding down a fire pole...to visiting a bar...to singing a song for a total stranger...then walking into a hotel room and seeing Tim all revved up for a romantic weekend... well, let's just say it was more than I could handle.

This was an invitation early in our marriage to grow in intimacy, in knowing and being fully known. Back then we couldn't even define intimacy, let alone understand how two people could maintain their identities as individuals and still celebrate each other's differences. We needed to learn how to negotiate a weekend that we could both enjoy.

CAN YOU HEAR ME NOW?

In marriage, learning and understanding a spouse's gifts, temperaments, love languages, and styles of relating takes time. And as the story of our unromantic weekend shows, differences often lead to conflict. People who are conflict avoiders may not be comfortable verbally responding to a situation immediately. They may need more time to process. Days later they may think to themselves, *I should have said this or I should have said that.* Others who lean toward a more aggressive style of relating may view conflict and confrontation as opportunities to gain clarity on a subject.

Knowing both the positive and negative aspects of how you and your spouse are wired is vital to moving toward intimacy.

Over the years the two of us have become all too familiar with the good and bad parts of each other's style of relating. One of the negative things about my (Tim's) personality and temperament is I can tend to be controlling. I like to be in charge. This plays out in many ways. For example, when we were leading a REAL LIFE Marriage Advance in New York, the couple running point for the Advance offered to purchase donuts for the set-up team. On the way to the church we pulled in to a drive-thru lane, and the driver casually ordered "a dozen assorted donuts." Sitting in the back of the van, I grew tense as I thought, *Doesn't she know that ordering "assorted donuts" is code for the person to give you the donuts no one else wants, the stale ones that have been on the shelf two days, and the ones they dropped on the floor?* I believe that when a person orders donuts, they must be in total control and select each of the twelve donuts by name.

In years past when Anne tried to point out some area where I was being too controlling, it never seemed to be the right time for me to hear her. I often felt attacked, disrespected, or misunderstood. As a result, the conversation would almost inevitably end poorly.

One day Anne took me on a date to one of my favorite restaurants. After a great meal and lots of good conversation, she began to talk about our marriage. I was all ears as she started listing things she respected about me. She even mentioned some specific things she had recently noticed.

Soul Oneness

Then she said, "Hon, I'm so thankful for you, but there is one little thing I want to talk with you about… It's about our different styles of relating."

Uh oh. I have known Anne almost my entire life, and we've been down this road more times than I can count. Based on past experience I interpreted the phrase "style of relating" as code for, "Tim, you might think you are a low-maintenance-strong-leader-type guy…but you are more of a high-maintenance-controlling-type guy."

But this time, Anne took the conversation in a new direction. Instead of hitting me with a verbal 2-by-4, Anne gently made some observations about my style of relating. I listened to what she had to say. Although part of me wanted to defend myself, I knew in my heart that she was speaking truth to me in love. In her winsome way, Anne used a story to make her point. She reminded me how much I love to drive. That is true, I love driving cars, trucks, motorcycles, anything with wheels. I drove the hook-and-ladder for ten years. I probably love driving because when I'm driving — you guessed it — I'm in control.

Knowing my love for driving, Anne asked me a question. "Have you ever been driving along the highway just enjoying your day when someone suddenly pulls into your lane and cuts you off?"

I replied, "Oh yeah, I can't stand being cut off."

Anne responded, "Hon, at times in our marriage I feel I am in the driver's seat. I have a plan. I know what I'm doing and where I'm going. Then you walk into the house and it feels like you swerve into my lane and cut me off. I know you're not trying to take the steering wheel out of my hands, but it often feels that way to me. I really don't want to keep arguing about this or try to defend my position. I know that you don't see this as a control issue. But in the future when this happens…how about if I gently remind you of this conversation by simply asking you to 'stay in your lane'?"

Anne's illustration hit the bull's-eye. I understood her example of being cut off. I could see how my desire to lead could have a negative effect on her. If she had said, "Tim, you are one of the most controlling people I know," I would have responded defensively. Before long, things would have gone south. However, her words were life-giving. She spoke truth in

Soul Oneness

love. I did not feel disrespected or parented. I apologized and asked her for forgiveness. More important, I made a commitment to work on "staying in my lane."

That simple slogan, *stay in your lane*, has served us well over the years. We use it often to defuse potential misunderstandings. In fact, when the assorted donuts were being ordered at the drive-up window, Anne leaned over and whispered to me, "Hon…stay in your lane!"

A NEW APPRECIATION FOR EACH OTHER

In marriage, God invites a husband and wife to deeper levels of intimacy, grace, and forgiveness as they start to see their spouse's behaviors, mannerisms, and character traits from a different perspective. Learning to celebrate your spouse's uniqueness and strengths gives you an opportunity to look inside yourself to see the areas God wants to redeem, restore, and renew.

As husbands and wives choose to appreciate their spouse's unique design rather than letting it be a divisive issue, they open the door to unity and to Ruling together in soul oneness.

Soul Oneness

+ Chapter 10

Learning a New Dance Together

Recognizing the Influence of Your Family of Origin

We have worked with couples long enough to know that when you marry a person, you marry into their family. When our children began dating seriously we encouraged them to get to know the family of the person they were dating and to pay close attention to how family members relate to one another. How do family members communicate? How do they resolve conflict? How do they handle stress? How do the parents relate to each other? What kind of relationship do the children have with their parents? Are family members able to admit when they are wrong? Do they easily apologize to one another? Are they able to forgive?

I (Anne) remember when our daughter Colleen started getting serious about a young man she'd been dating. His name was Johnny Stickl. Johnny was completing his master's in Christian leadership at Denver Seminary. He was also interning at our church and attending classes at the World Prayer Center where Tim and I worked. In fact, Tim was the one who set up their first date (that's another story!). So Johnny got to know our family pretty well.

But Johnny's family lived in the East, so Colleen hadn't yet had the opportunity to see him in his home environment. As we saw their relationship progressing and started to sense that this young man could be the one for our daughter, Tim and I encouraged Colleen to spend time getting acquainted with Johnny's family.

The two of them flew to New York for a visit with his family. One night Colleen called from Grand Island to let me know how things were going. They had just finished dinner. "Mom, their family is so different from ours," she said. "When we sat down to eat, only one person talked at a time. Can you imagine that? At our house we have to talk over each other if we want to be heard. Johnny's family actually listened to every word I said. It was amazing! They let me complete an entire thought without anyone interrupting. When I was done, there was a long pause. Johnny's mom said something like, 'Oh, Colleen, that's so interesting. Let me ask you a question about that.' Mom, it was unbelievable — "

"Honey," I interrupted, "that's how *normal* people relate to each other!"

As illustrated by Colleen's comparison of her future husband's family with her family of origin, every family is unique. They have their own way of

Soul Oneness

doing things. They have their own traditions, beliefs, and priorities. When we counsel couples and when we teach at REAL LIFE Marriage Advances, we often refer to some of these distinct family traits, patterns, and behaviors as the *family dance*.

You have probably heard that the lessons children learn are "caught rather than taught." Children learn how to navigate their world by observing their families: how they communicate, how they listen, how they forgive, how they honor God and each other, and how they handle real life. Children grow up with a perception of who they are based on what they have observed. All of these observations influence the way they negotiate their world, even as adults. Their belief system, perceptions, and general approach to life are a part of the *dance* they learned from their family of origin.

Stop and think about it. Most people can predict how their family will respond to any given situation. For example, a person knows what their family considers funny and what is not funny. They know what is acceptable and what is absolutely forbidden. How do they know this? Because as a child they watched the same dance, the same steps over and over throughout life. Sometimes the message was clearly verbalized, but more often it was conveyed through nonverbal means.

The dance pattern can vary dramatically from family to family. For example, in some families divorce is absolutely prohibited; even when marital conflict arises, divorce never pops up on their radar screen. In other families, divorce is seen as a perfectly acceptable alternative. In our premarital counseling to engaged couples, some individuals have actually told us, "If this marriage doesn't work out, we can get divorced just like my parents did."

Obviously, when two people bring into marriage their own distinctive family dance, they will find it difficult to Rule together in unity. Imagine two people on the dance floor, one doing the tango, the other doing the hokey-pokey, and both trying to move in unison. Inevitably, they will collide or drift apart rather than enjoying the intimacy and beauty of a shared rhythm.

Soul Oneness

WHO'S LEADING YOUR DANCE?

When we got married, it didn't take long before we discovered that Anne's family dance followed a very different pattern from Tim's family dance. So typically when we tried to dance together, we would step on each other's toes. We couldn't believe the other person didn't dance the same way we did. We even accused each other of coming from a family of dysfunctional dancers. Such accusations turned into offenses, which led to arguments. Arguments became power struggles. Before long, each of us was trying to control the dance and fighting over who was going to lead.

Like many married couples, we wondered, *Since we each come from two different families with their own way of doing things, which dance is the right dance? How can we learn to dance together as a couple?*

About ten years ago I (Anne) had a dream that vividly illustrated the answer to these questions. In my dream a man and a woman both dressed in white stood on separate sides of a large stage, unaware of each other's presence. Directly above each of them shone a bright spotlight. Somehow I knew that the spotlights represented the Lord. He was the light in their dark worlds.

Orchestra music began to play, and the spotlights started moving around the stage in perfect time to the music. The man and woman each danced in unison with their light. I felt like I was watching a ballet as I observed their soft and slow movements. I realized the Lord was teaching each of them dance steps as He led them around the floor. In essence the man and woman were being discipled by Jesus, learning all their moves from Him. In my dream I recognized the dances: the dance of love and forgiveness…the dance of joy…the dance of communication…the dance of discipline…and the dance of intimacy and sexuality.

At some point the music stopped. The man and woman suddenly became aware of each other. They turned and looked into each other's eyes for the first time. With their gazes locked in mutual fascination, they began to walk toward one another from across the room, following their separate spotlights. Soon the man and woman stood face to face, and their two separate spotlights merged into one single bright light above them. The music started up again. A new song began to play. The man clasped the woman's hand in his. With his other arm encircling her waist, they started to dance together. Again their movements were soft and slow. Rather than being awkward in their first dance as a couple, they flowed together in unity. They danced as one. They knew every single step of every dance and moved beautifully together because they had spent a lifetime dancing with the Lord. He had prepared them to dance together as one.

When I woke up, I knew that God was inviting me to dance with Him. He wants to teach every husband and wife the steps of unconditional forgiveness, love, joy, peace, servanthood, and sacrifice. God leads, and He invites couples to follow.

DESIGNING A LEGACY

Dancing in unity to the steps God has designed for you as a couple may require unlearning some of the moves each of you picked up from your family dance. To do that, you first must take a careful look at your respective families of origin. Carefully and prayerfully processing various aspects of each spouse's family dance will help the two of you grow in soul oneness and intimacy.

Every person has received a legacy — "something that is handed down or remains from a previous generation or time."[1] And every person will leave a legacy to those who come after them. Legacies include many components; spiritual, emotional, relational, physical, sexual, and even health-related components with associated behaviors and propensities are passed down from generation to generation. All of these components include both positive and negative aspects.

In counseling couples over the years, we've learned that it is critical to explore and identify repeated family of origin propensities, patterns, and behaviors. Couples are equipped to move toward increased intimacy and unity when they better understand who they are, where they have come from, and what they have received from their ancestors. Knowing and understanding histories and families of origin enables a couple to identify positive godly components and to build on them. It also enables a couple to identify negative, ungodly components that they do not want to continue in their marriage.

Soul Oneness

Some time ago, the two of us counseled a couple from church who were planning to get married. We'll call them Scott and Sandy. As we reviewed their histories, we made notes on their families of origin. They both came from divorced homes. Family members on both sides struggled with alcoholism and other addictive behaviors.

At first Scott and Sandy were unaware of how much their families of origin had influenced them. As we continued to meet, they began to see propensities in their lives that were very similar to their parents' behaviors. Sandy had strained relationships with her father and her stepfather. Scott, like his father, was prone to outbursts of anger. They realized that they had become caught up in a destructive cycle of negative family behaviors, and it was affecting them individually and as a couple.

Sandy and Scott were a teachable couple who genuinely wanted to live as new creatures in Christ. They also were determined to pass on godly traits to their children and future generations. Recognizing the value of counseling, they submitted themselves to a healthy process. They were open to looking at their past to see how it affected their present and their future together as one. They began to develop tools to help them advance in intimacy with God and each other. These tools helped them make different choices than their families had made. Learning how to process their stress and express their emotions in healthy ways was key to their health and healing. Their process included prayer, study, inner healing, and deliverance.

An old adage says, the apple doesn't fall far from the tree. A tree produces both good and bad fruit. A family tree also produces good and bad fruit. The Bible refers to these positive and negative generational behaviors as blessings and curses. In the Old Testament we read how personal decisions affect generational lines. The Bible says, "I, the LORD your God, am a jealous God, punishing the children for the sin of the fathers to the third and fourth generation of those who hate me, but showing love to a thousand generations of those who love me and keep my commandments."[2]

The decisions of one generation affect the next. Every man and woman has a father, a mother, and grandparents that went before them and passed on certain qualities and behaviors to succeeding generations.

A person is considered to be blessed when their ancestors exhibited godly character traits and behaviors, such as honesty, trustworthiness, financial integrity, prosperity, and a good work ethic. On the other hand, a family with ungodly character traits and behaviors produces bad fruit: unrighteous judging, unforgiveness, marital stress, addictive behaviors, lying, violence, pride, rebellion, dishonesty, or financial insufficiency. These negative behaviors are often referred to as family curses.

Although each generation is impacted by those who have gone before, we also have the ability to break negative generational cycles, as Sandy and Scott chose to do. Every person is created with the ability to make choices. They can choose obedience or disobedience, and their choices carry consequences that result in blessings or curses. The key to dancing together in unity, following God's design, is to build on positive behaviors while identifying and eliminating negative behaviors.

As a husband and wife process what they've brought into marriage from their family of origin, they can then begin to choose which propensities, behaviors, and beliefs are worth passing on and which need to be pruned away. The promise of blessing motivates a couple to continue living for God, knowing it will result in blessings to them and to future generations.

TRIPPING OVER OURSELVES

As mentioned earlier, from their family of origin people inherit not only generational patterns of behavior and faith but also physical features, character traits, mannerisms, temperament, speech patterns, and much more. Blending this complex family DNA is not as easy as it sounds, particularly when it comes to valuing each other's cherished family traditions. Complicating the process is the tendency to stay in our own comfort zones rather than creating a "new normal" in unity with our spouse.

Thanksgiving is my (Tim's) favorite holiday. You don't have to decorate the house, put up a tree, or shop for gifts. I love everything about Thanksgiving: the smell of turkey, the family bonding, and the nonstop football. In my family of origin, every Thanksgiving was a laid-back, relaxing day. We ate great food, watched sports on TV, and played our traditional family football game on the dead-end street where I grew up.

When I started working at the fire department, life as I knew it changed drastically. Working shift meant that I was on duty twenty-four hours and off duty the next forty-eight hours. Basically I spent every third holiday at the firehouse instead of with my family, so I really looked forward to those holidays when I was off duty.

One year I ended my shift at 8 a.m. on Thanksgiving morning and couldn't get home fast enough. Since each of our families lived just a few miles apart, we planned to start the holiday at the O'Shaughnessys' and then head over to my parents' house for dessert. This seemed like a great plan. I was totally pumped and ready to enjoy my favorite holiday.

When I arrived home, Anne was ready. She had our son, Timmy, all spiffed up. His diaper bag was packed and some baked goods were stacked near the door. All I had to do was change clothes and load the car. Anne wanted to get to her mom's early to help with the preparations.

I went into our bedroom to change and noticed some clothes laid out on our bed. But since they were clearly too dressy for the relaxing day I had planned, I put on my ripped jeans and favorite flannel shirt. As I headed out the door, I noticed Anne giving me The Look. She was eyeballing me from head to toe. Obviously, she disapproved of something. With a firm voice noticeably lacking in holiday cheer, she said, "You are not going to my mom and dad's house looking like that!"

Confused, I responded, "Looking like *what*?"

"Tim, this is Thanksgiving," she said. "It's a holiday. We are going to a family sit-down dinner. My mom works really hard to make it special. The table will be beautifully set. You cannot show up looking like that."

Feeling defensive, I said, "What does any of that have to do with what I'm wearing?"

She replied, "Tim, there is more to Thanksgiving than just eating food at a table."

To which I replied, "I know. There is food, football, and fun."

"My family doesn't watch a lot of TV on the holidays," Anne said. "My mom would prefer we spend our time together talking and enjoying each other's company."

That was the last straw. "You have *got* to be kidding me," I spouted. "No TV? That's just unAmerican. This is my favorite holiday: food, football, fun…more food, more football, more fun! Babe, it doesn't get any better than that. Besides, I don't care what your family thinks about how I dress. When we get to my family's house, we'll all end up outside playing football, so why would I want to wear dress clothes?" (Note: I was raised with four boys and one girl. Anne was raised with three girls and one boy.)

Anne was getting increasingly frustrated. She could see that she was losing the fight, so she decided to step up her game. She said, "Tim, you look like a homeless person who is having hard luck and is going to a soup kitchen for dinner."

I replied, "At least the people at the soup kitchen would not judge me for what I'm wearing."

Running out of ammunition, Anne decided to close with a final, declarative bang: "Fine. Then I don't want to go."

I responded, "Great, I can stay home and turn on the games." Then realizing how ridiculous we sounded, I said, "Honey, why are we even fighting about this? This is my favorite holiday. Can't you cut me some slack?"

She stood firm. "Tim, you are dressed like a slob!"

With that, we retreated to different rooms. I remember grumbling about how I should have stayed at the firehouse. At least I could have enjoyed food, football, and maybe even a good fire.

Anne was in the living room staring out the window. I noticed Timmy toddling around the room. As I picked him up, I took a closer look at his outfit. It was a white sailor suit with a blue tie and leather saddle shoes.

Soul Oneness

I thought to myself, *She's dressing him like a girl. It's Thanksgiving. Where's his Bears jersey?* Resisting the urge to comment aloud on her choice of clothing for Timmy, I attempted to talk some sense into my young bride.

"Hon, why is getting dressed up such a big deal? Why can't I enjoy my favorite holiday in my most comfortable clothes? Seriously, who are you trying to impress?"

"Tim," she said, "this is our first Thanksgiving together with my family. I want it to be special." It dawned on me that Anne was holding back tears as she spoke. "I want you to look nice. I want us to enjoy the day together. We have so much to be thankful for…look at all God has blessed us with."

I thought to myself, *Great. Now she's pulling the God card.* I could feel myself beginning to cave. I asked, "Okay, what do you want me to wear?"

"A tie would be nice."

"A tie?" I was not happy with that answer. "The only time I'll be comfortable wearing a tie is when I'm in a coffin!"

She was not laughing.

I made a peace offering: "Okay, how about my good jeans and my plaid shirt?"

She countered with, "How about your beige dress slacks and navy long-sleeve, button-down shirt?"

I said, "How about my Dockers and my fire department sweatshirt?"

She said, "Okay on the Dockers, but how about your black sweater?"

I thought for a moment, then said, "Okay, but I'm gonna leave for a few hours to play football with my brothers."

She agreed, so I pushed my thin advantage: "One other thing. Get Timmy out of that girlie outfit and put him in his Bears jersey."

"I bought this outfit especially for Thanksgiving," she replied. "I'll bring his jersey and put it on after dinner."

With our complicated negotiations finalized, I changed clothes and we drove off to the O'Shaughnessys'. But neither of us was happy. I felt like I was going to the prom, and Anne felt like I had already ruined the holiday. Somehow we managed to put on our happy faces as we walked in the door at her parents' house and we both survived the day.

However, I realized that if we were going to make it through future holidays, I needed to get some help. As a new follower of Christ, I called my spiritual dad, Dick Swetman. We met for lunch so I could tell him my side of the Thanksgiving drama. I just knew he would understand. As I recited my long list of reasons why my way was the right way, Dick listened and ate his lunch.

I finished making some excellent points, then Dick said with his quiet, raspy voice, "Timmy, you need to bring this to the Lord."

I said, "Okay, Dick I'll do that. But what do you think I should do about all this holiday stuff?" I knew he loved sports; he had four sons. He knew the real meaning of Thanksgiving. I was hoping for some biblical ammunition to bring home and use against Anne.

Instead, he just repeated, "Timmy, you need to bring this to the Lord. Remember the verse you memorized? James 1:5 says, 'If any of you lacks wisdom, let him ask of God, who gives to all generously and without reproach.' God will give you wisdom on this."

I remember thinking, *Hey, wait a minute. I bought this lunch and I need some answers.* I gave it once last try and pressed him further: "Dick, you know the entire Bible by memory. You have to tell me what to do."

He just smiled like old Doc Graham in the *Field of Dreams* movie. Then he got up to leave the restaurant, looked me directly in the eyes, put his hand firmly on my shoulder, and said, "Timmy, bring this to the Lord, then listen and do whatever He says." He turned around and walked out to his car as I paid the bill! I remember driving home thinking, *What a waste of time and money. I'm sure God does not care what I wear on Thanksgiving. He has global issues like starvation, pestilence, and wars to deal with.*

The next morning I woke up early and went for a jog. There was a park near our house with a bench that I referred to as my prayer bench. After my jog I headed there to spend some time with the Lord and go through my prayer list like I did every day. After finishing my list, I casually prayed, "Lord, Dick said I should ask you what I should do about the holiday clothes thing with Anne."

I waited a short time and then — well, this is difficult to describe, but I thought I heard something in my heart. It wasn't an audible voice, but it was clear to me. It sounded like a question: *Who are the holidays about, Tim?*

At first I thought, *This can't really be God.* Then I thought, *Well, here goes…* and I began to pour out my complaints: *Why should I get dressed up for holidays? I never had to get dressed up for holidays growing up. I work hard. I provide for our family. I am a pretty good husband and dad.*

When I paused for a moment, I thought I again sensed that voice in my heart saying, *Tim, who is this really all about?* I sat on my prayer bench thinking about that for a while. I began to analyze what was happening. If this really was God, the great I AM, the Creator of the universe, and if I said it was all about me that would sound pretty selfish. After a couple of minutes, I reluctantly admitted, *Well, maybe it is a little about me.*

There was silence, then I sensed this response: *Well, Tim, there's your answer.* I walked home thinking about what had just happened. What could all this mean?

Over the next few weeks I began to see things in different ways. I realized I had been living in the **smaller story**, and in doing so I was stepping on Anne's toes. The result was that neither one of us was enjoying our marriage dance. I knew I loved Anne and I wanted to be a good husband. I realized holidays could be an opportunity to show Anne that I loved her and wanted to make her holidays great.

A few months later Easter rolled around — another off-duty holiday for me. We planned to go to Anne's family's house for Easter brunch. When I

Soul Oneness

arrived home from the firehouse, she already had Timmy dressed for church. But when I went in the bedroom, there were no clothes laid out for me. Obviously she did not want to get into an argument about what I was going to wear.

I opened the closet and took a deep breath. I pulled out my dress slacks, white shirt, and…t-t-tie! I put them on and walked out to the living room. "Let's get going," I said.

Anne almost fell over. "Honey, you look great! Why are you all dressed up?"

I said, "Because I want this holiday to be all about you and not about me."

She was in shock. All she could say was, "Really?"

We went to church, then to her family's house. I made it through the day all dressed up. After the meal Anne leaned over, gave me a kiss on the cheek, and whispered, "Hon, you can take off your tie now." The twinkle in her eye conveyed to my male brain that before this day was over I would be taking off more than my tie!

LET THE DANCE BEGIN

Negotiating and evaluating family of origin differences is a lifelong process for a couple committed to advancing in intimacy and soul oneness. As together you put your family dance aside and choose to let God guide your new dance steps, you will find yourselves moving to a rhythm of unity that blends the best of both families with fresh elements. This is a key part of knowing and being fully known.

+ Chapter 11

The Traffic Light Principle

A Practical Way to Live Out Rulership in Unity

In the past few chapters we've looked at a variety of things that can either enhance or destroy a couple's ability to rule in unity. We've looked at a man's need for respect and a woman's need for love, as well as God's differing visions for husbands and wives. We've looked at spiritual gifts, temperaments, relational styles, love languages, and family of origin legacies. Each of these areas provides the basis for living out God's design for marriage as each spouse learns to appreciate the uniqueness of the other. But each of these areas also can be a place the enemy will try to gain a foothold by causing division.

As we've seen, identifying, processing, and learning to value these differences is all part of advancing in soul oneness. But real life is packed with unexpected challenges and decisions that will at times severely test the strength of your marital "**We.**"

To help you transform these potentially divisive moments into opportunities to build trust, we'd like to share with you one very practical tool we've discovered that helps us daily live out our God-given responsibility to rule in unity.

STOP, WAIT, GO

We had not been married long before we realized that we each processed information and came to conclusions in different ways. Tim tended to focus on the big picture and long-term effects of decisions, while I (Anne) was concerned with immediate results. We were limited in our ability to process decisions in ways that brought unity to our marriage. In fact, at times we felt as if we were wrestling with each other rather than working together. Both of us believed we were right and wanted things to go our way.

As we reviewed our decision-making process, one thing that became obvious was that we were not including God. We wanted God to be a part of our decisions, but on a practical level we just did not know what that looked like.

Then one day while running errands I found myself at a stoplight, waiting for the light to turn green. It occurred to me that every car in that intersection was being directed by one small traffic light. The government had set up a system that protected every driver by helping us determine our next move.

According to this uncomplicated system, every licensed driver knows that red means *stop*, yellow means *slow*, and green means *go*. Age, gender, family of origin, and personal desires have nothing to do with the decision. Every driver is responsible to comply with traffic signals or face consequences determined by the government.

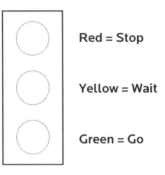

Red = Stop

Yellow = Wait

Green = Go

Can you imagine what would happen if the state left driving decisions up to each individual driver? The driving handbook could read: "If you feel like stopping, then stop. On the other hand, if you're in a hurry and have to get somewhere quickly, then go right on through. Because it's all about you!"

Or what if the manual read, "If you are in the mood to slow down and yield, go ahead. But if not, don't bother."

Or, "If a male and a female are approaching an intersection, the male has the right-of-way."

What if each driver responded to the color of the traffic light according to personal feelings and interpretations? For some drivers, red could mean *go* and green could mean *stop*.

What if you didn't like traffic lights? What if you didn't like to obey laws?

What if you believed that driving with the safety of others in mind is not nearly as important as having it your way?

Soul Oneness

The Traffic Light Principle

Imagine the chaos there would be if each person did things their way.

As I reflected on the traffic light system and its remarkably simple approach to getting drivers to work together, I thought, *Why couldn't Tim and I set up a system that provides unity in our marriage? Why couldn't we set up a system to protect us from our natural desire to do life our way?*

When I got home, Tim and I spent time discussing how a traffic light system could benefit our marriage in terms of decision making. What if we both agreed to let the Lord be our traffic light? Over time we devised the Traffic Light Principle. Here's how it works:

First, whenever we need to make a decision, we begin with prayer — first individually, then together as a couple. Prayer reminds us to invite God into our process. Prayer provides a spiritual discipline that reaffirms our priority of focusing on God and listening to Him. Listening and waiting for God protects us from running ahead with our own agenda.

We pray something like this, "Lord, speak to us in a language we can understand. Give us a red light if You want us to stop. Give us a yellow light if You want us to wait. Or give us a green light if You are saying 'Go.' "

The second part of the Traffic Light Principle involves coming together after we pray and sharing what direction we sense the Lord is leading us. When we first began to test out this principle, we had lots of questions: What happens if we come together and do not have the same color light? What if God gives one of us a green light and one of us a red light?

To address these issues while keeping our process simple, we agreed on the following guidelines:

1. We will proceed only if we are in unity. If we come back together and do not have the same color light, we will agree to wait.

2. While we are waiting, we will continue to pray, listen, and discuss the decision. If appropriate, we will pull in a third party for insight and feedback.

3. We will continue waiting while regularly revisiting the decision until we both sense God giving us the same light signal.

NAVIGATING A DIFFICULT ROAD TEST

As we put the Traffic Light Principle into action, we both agreed that being united did not mean that we had to think exactly the same. We acknowledged our differences and were committed to celebrating them. We decided to focus on unity by being mutually submitted to God and to each other. We would not move ahead until we both agreed. We would resist the temptation to justify our position, power up, or allow the stronger personality make the final decision.

Having talked all these things through up front, we felt pretty good about our new plan. However, not long after we agreed to implement this principle we realized that walking it out was not as easy as we first thought.

I (Tim) have loved motorcycles my entire life. Well, no…I *love* people, I *like* motorcycles. A lot. Growing up, my brothers and I always had motorcycles.

Now, I have never been the kind of person who has to have new things. I am just as happy with a used car as with a brand-new one. In fact, I used to regularly purchase vehicles from firemen who took extra special care of their cars. I purchased three vehicles from my buddy Murph. He's the kind of guy who waxes under the hood of the engine. Rumor has it he puts a blanket over the entire car as he tucks it in to the garage and kisses it good night! When Murph wanted to buy a new car, I got first dibs on his old one and encouraged him to buy a specific color car since I knew it would eventually be mine.

Dave Grant is another fireman friend who takes great care of his vehicles. He also loves motorcycles. When he wanted to purchase a brand-new 1981 Honda CB 750 custom motorcycle with the stock Hondaline fairing, stereo, and all the options, I encouraged him to buy the two-tone blue (my favorite color). So Dave purchased my future motorcycle.

One day when I reported to the firehouse, Dave grabbed me and said, "Hey, Timmy, I'm selling my bike. Do you still want it?"

I said, "Are you kidding me? I've been dreaming about that bike since I

Soul Oneness

helped you pick it out." When he told me the price, I said, "Great."

Dave mentioned that three other firemen wanted him to skip me and sell it to them, but he'd told them, "No way. Timmy has been bugging me for this bike for years."

I couldn't wait to tell Anne I was getting my new bike, the one Dave had been keeping for me. The next morning I got off duty, went home, and told her the great news. Anne was also excited for me to get the bike. But then, as I was heading back out the door to my side job, she casually said, "Hon, should we do the 'red-yellow-green light' thing we agreed to do when making decisions like this one?"

I said, "Sure, pray about it and let me know what your light is," then I headed to work, totally confident that the bike was mine.

Seeing Red at a Yellow Light

That night after we put the kids to bed Anne said, "Can we talk?"

"Sure. What's up?" I noticed Anne was in a somewhat serious mood.

"Tim, you are such a great provider for our family. I know there are very few things you really want. You are not the kind of husband who buys a lot of things or has a long toy list…"

"Anne, what's your point?"

She said, "Tim, I know how long you have wanted Dave's motorcycle — "

Her words hit me like a Dick Butkus–blindside tackle, and I immediately interrupted her. "Anne, I have been riding motorcycles forever. I am a safe driver, I wear a helmet, I don't drink and drive — "

It was her turn to interrupt: "Tim, I know all that, and I agree with you on all those points. It's not any of that…"

"Then what is it?"

She hesitated, then softly said, "Remember our agreement to pray before making any major decisions? Well, I did that. The kids went down for a nap this afternoon. I got on my knees and asked God about the motorcycle, fully expecting to get a green light. But when I prayed, I sensed a yellow light. I thought to myself, *This can't be happening.* I know how much and how long you have wanted Dave's bike. So I asked God again, and again I sensed a yellow light. I could not believe what I was seeing."

My mind kicked into rapid-fire-power-up mode. "Hon, this can't be right! My green light is so green it's like I am on the Emerald Isle! Do you have any idea how many hundreds of times I have bugged Dave to give me this bike? I even helped him pick out the color when he bought it. Plus, I already told him yes. If it's the money, I am selling my old bike and I have some firehouse locker money saved. Hon, do not tell me you don't have a green light."

Anne said, "Tim, I'm sorry, I know how bad you want this bike. Hear me: I want you to have it too. I am sick about this. I wish I could tell you my light was green…but honestly, when I asked God, I kept sensing a yellow light."

I said, "Whoaaa…I have to think about this." I deserted to the garage, where my mind continued to race. *I can't believe this. What is Dave gonna think? Now Dick Munch will buy it.* I mentally grumbled, *Whose idea was this traffic-light thing anyway?* Then I had a new thought: *Wait a minute! What if I give Anne a free coupon that would be like a get-out-of-jail-free card next time she wants something? No, wait. I know…I will agree with her and then secretly buy the motorcycle and keep it at the firehouse. When I want to ride it, I'll drive my old bike to the firehouse, leave it there, and take my new one for a ride. She'll never know. In a few months this will blow over, Anne will have a green light, and I will have my bike.*

This seemed like a great plan. But that night I couldn't sleep. Uncomfortable thoughts flooded my mind. *Do I really want to lie to Anne? We did agree to implement this deal. On the other hand, she has no idea the razzing I will get if I back out after harassing Dave about "my" bike. What should I do?*

Then it hit me: *I'll call Dick Swetman. He is so close to God, he can ask Him to change her yellow light to green.*

The Traffic Light Principle

The next day I phoned Dick, and we met at our usual place. Since I had called the meeting, I had to buy lunch. As we ate, I poured my heart out to my spiritual dad. I told him how I had picked out the color of this bike and stressed the fact that, if I didn't buy it, three other guys would buy it on the spot. I explained that we had the cash. My friend and mentor listened attentively as I explained all the reasons why I should buy the bike, wrapping up with the words, "Dick, this bike is mint, and it has my name on it."

When I finished, Dick paused and looked me directly in the eyes. He said in his raspy voice, "Timmy, did you really ask God to give you a red-yellow-green light?"

"Well, sort of..."

Then Dick said, "Maybe it would be a good idea to really ask God for a traffic light." Sensing my disappointment, he softly said, "Timmy, it's only a motorbike."

I thought, *What does he mean, "only a motorbike"? He didn't even say it right; it's called a motorcycle or a bike, but not a motorbike!* But what I said was, "Dick, this thing is perfect. I have to get it. Can't you support me on this?"

He grabbed my shoulder and looked me directly in the eyes. He firmly said, "Timmy, you need to bring this to the Lord." Yet again he reminded me of the verse he had required me to memorize: "If any of you lacks wisdom, let him ask of God, who gives to all generously and without reproach."[1] He said, "Timmy, ask for God's wisdom and do what He says" — and then he walked out!

I thought, *Why do I bother with this guy? What does he know? He has probably never even ridden a "motorbike."* As I got up to pay the bill, another thought came to me: *I am actually paying for this guy's lunch... again! What did he tell me that was of any real value?*

Shifting into Reverse

On the way home I started to calm down and my thoughts toned down a bit. *Okay, Dick is a good guy. He loves Anne and me and our family.* Remembering his words, "Timmy, bring this to the Lord," I pulled the car into Campanneli Park near our home and sat for awhile. Finally I said, "Okay, God, do you have anything for me on this?" A minute or so passed, but it felt like an hour. Eventually, I moved to put the car in reverse, impatiently thinking, *I have stuff to do.* Just then I sensed this message penetrating my brain: *Tim, this is not about the motorcycle.*

I said, "What? That's crazy! This is *all* about the motorcycle. It's about making a deal with Dave years ago. It's about not having to borrow money. It's about one of the few things a hardworking guy like me enjoys…" I rambled on for a bit. Then I calmed down and asked, "Okay, if this is not about the motorcycle, then what is it about?"

After a short pause, I again sensed a response in my mind: *This is all about you, Tim.*

I said, "All about me? I don't ask for much. I work my tail off, I provide for my family…" All of a sudden I realized I was using the word I a lot. I reluctantly faced the question, *Could this really be all about me?*

I sat in the car for a half hour, trying to overcome my inclination to go back to my plan for buying that motorcycle, with or without a green light from Anne. I reviewed the facts of the situation. Anne and I had agreed to do the traffic-light thing. I knew she wanted me to have the bike, and I definitely respected the way Anne heard from God. Okay, even Dick's counsel was probably right on. But…I *really* wanted this bike.

It was a moment of truth in my young heart and life. As I sat there, I thought about everything I did have and reviewed my list out loud: "I do have a great marriage, great kids, good friends. I love my job and our church. And I already have a motorcycle." As I reviewed the cards on my table, in my heart I realized that my plans were all about me. I knew in my gut what I had to do. I also knew that if I went home right then I would probably try to guilt Anne into a pseudo-green light. So I headed directly to the firehouse, where I knew Dave was on duty.

Soul Oneness

I walked into the firehouse and found Dave cleaning my bike. "I've got it spotless for you, Timmy," he said.

I responded, "Bud, can we talk?" We walked back in the alley. I didn't quite know what to say. "Dave, you know how much I want your bike — "

He cut me off. "Timmy, if this is a cash problem, I can take payments."

"Thanks, no. It's…well, you see…" I stammered. "Anne and I kinda made this deal we would first pray about stuff…and if we both didn't get a green light…well, then…we kinda said we would wait until…we both got green lights."

Dave's response was blunt. "Let me get this straight: you are not going to buy the bike you helped me pick out, the one you have been harassing me about for years, because Annie doesn't have a green light?" Then he launched a missile that landed a direct hit to my heart. "Timmy, is this a *Jesus* thing?"

I nodded my head. "Yeah…I guess it kinda is." Then I told him I had to get home.

Dave slapped me on the back and jokingly said, "Well, it's nice to see who wears the pants in your family."

Worn out, I headed home. As soon as I walked through the door, Anne could tell I was totally bummed. When I explained that I had stopped by the firehouse and told Dave no on the bike, she just looked at me in silence, but I noticed she looked as sad as I felt.

At 7 a.m. the next day I walked into the firehouse to report for duty. I put my gear on the rig and went to open my locker. Pictures of traffic signals were taped all over my locker. The razzing started and never let up. That day the firehouse cook came up to me and said, "Hey, Timmy, I was thinking of having BLTs for lunch — that is, unless you don't have a 'green light.' Then I'll make burgers!"

About the only highlight of the day was when I got a phone call. I immediately recognized Dick's soft raspy voice. "Timmy, Annie called me.

She told me about the motorbike — " his voice cracked. "I'm really proud of you, son. How about we meet for lunch tomorrow? I'll even buy."

I thanked him and hung up. At that point, even a free lunch sounded like a downer. The jokes continued as other firehouses got wind of the *red-yellow-green* light deal. Let's just say it was one very l-o-n-g day.

The Turning Point

I (Anne) would like to add a brief note here from my perspective.

What complicated the situation surrounding the motorcycle was the fact that both of us wanted to purchase Dave's bike. We had the money. I was excited to think of Tim purchasing something he would enjoy. I trusted him as a driver. Yet the Lord was clearly showing me *yellow — slow,* not *green — go.* I couldn't understand it.

Now, after being married over thirty years and implementing this principle countless times, I realize that God is much more interested in unity than He is in either one of us getting our own way. God used the motorcycle as a turning point for us. It was the first time I recognized that Tim's response to my decision came out of his deep love and respect for me and my relationship with the Lord. Seeing Him submit to God by submitting to what I was hearing encouraged me to look for ways to out-serve him. The fruit of our decision to include God cost us the bike, but what we gained in trust and unity was priceless.

What's more, the story of the motorcycle wasn't over. I'll let Tim take it from here.

+ + +

That day at the firehouse was not the last chapter for me (Tim) regarding Dave's bike. After I said no, another fireman named Dick Munch bought the bike and put lots of upgrades on it.

A few years later he called me and said, "Hey, Timmy, do you remember Dave's bike?"

Soul Oneness

After a pause, I sarcastically said, "Yeah, I seem to recall that."

"Well, it's just been sitting in my garage," he continued. "I rode it for a while, then my wife got pregnant. Life happens, you know? Anyway, the bike hasn't been started for a few years. Any chance you'd be interested in buying it? That's of course, if Annie has a 'green light'?"

I said, "Let me get back to you." Then I hung up the phone and said to Anne, "You're not going to believe this. Dave's bike is for sale again. What do you think?"

She said, "Tim, as you were talking, I quickly brought it to the Lord and—I am not kidding—I immediately got a huge green light."

The only problem we could see was that, at the time, our finances were tight. I called Dick back and offered to get the bike out of his garage for five hundred dollars.

At first, he just laughed and said he'd put that much into it after he bought it from Dave. Then he paused and said, "Oh, whatever. I just want to get rid of it. You can have it for five hundred dollars."

I couldn't believe it. I called a friend at the firehouse, Butch Adams, who owned a motorcycle shop. The next morning we loaded the bike on his truck, brought it to his shop, bought a new battery, cleaned the carbs, and tuned it up. A few days later I was riding my bike.

This all happened more than twenty years ago. And as I type this, that same old two-tone blue 1981 Honda CB 750 custom motorcycle with the stock Hondaline fairing, stereo, and all the options is sitting in my garage. That bike represents so much more to me than just an old motorcycle. To this day, every time I throw my leg over it to go for a ride, I just smile and shake my head, thinking, *Only God would use a motorcycle to make such a difference.*

Soul Oneness

CHECK THE SIGNAL BEFORE PROCEEDING

In the years since, we have used the Traffic Light Principle for countless decisions involving parenting issues, career changes, promotions, moving, vacations, purchases, and even getting a dog. We continue to find it a useful tool for exercising Rulership together in unity. Because it is centered in prayer, listening to God, and submitting to one another, this principle also provides opportunities to Reflect and Reveal God to each other.

We challenge you to implement the Traffic Light Principle and see how it transforms the decision-making process in your marriage. Remember that oneness, mutual submission, and reciprocal servanthood are the heart of marital unity.

The key to successfully walking out Rulership in unity is to keep in mind that "marriage is not about me." Marriage is about living in the **Larger Story** with God as the main character.

Soul Oneness

+ Chapter 12

Straight to the Heart

Experience the Healing Power of Forgiveness

On a cold December morning a young man wearing a black trench coat walked onto our church's campus after the 11 a.m. Sunday service. Armed with an automatic rifle, handguns, and enough ammunition to kill hundreds of people, he began randomly shooting at people in the parking lot. In his rage he killed two sisters and wounded their father as they were getting into their van. In an instant this family was changed forever. Then the gunman entered the church building, where a security guard met him in the entrance hallway. Shots were exchanged, and she managed to take him down. Later the police investigation determined that, after being wounded by the security guard, the gunman shot and killed himself.

The entire community was reeling in the wake of this random act of violence, which received worldwide media coverage. Our church went into emergency crisis mode. Pastor Brady Boyd led us with strength and passion through this difficult time. He surrounded himself with friends and experienced leaders. At an emergency prayer gathering after the shooting, one of the first statements from our pastor was, "We will not be ruled by fear." He continued by saying, "As Christ followers we forgive this man."

A month or so after the incident, church leaders encouraged Pastor Brady to take some time away to recharge. He had been running point on the front line since the first shots were fired. He decided to spend a day with God.

While spending time alone with God, Pastor Brady felt the Lord wanted him to invite the parents of the gunman to visit our church and to see where their son spent his last few moments. In faith he contacted the parents, who are both followers of Christ and were utterly devastated by their son's choices. They humbly accepted Pastor Brady's offer.

As prayers and preparations were made in anticipation of the visit, the parents of the two girls who died in the attack learned about the planned meeting. This grieving mom and dad, also passionate followers of Christ, asked if they could come and meet the parents of the young man who killed their daughters.

When Pastor Brady later described the meeting between these two sets of parents, he said his office felt like holy ground. He stood by in awe of the God who orchestrated this intimate encounter. He listened as the parents of the gunman apologized and watched as the two couples embraced one another and wept. He described how the hearts of these total strangers were knit together through forgiveness. He told how they tearfully shared stories about God and their children. This gifted teaching pastor could barely find words to convey his experience of witnessing the power of God's grace and forgiveness at work.

Shortly after this remarkable event, Dr. James Dobson hosted a *Focus on the Family* radio broadcast with both couples. The father of the shooter said, "[We had been] praying for the day we would be able to meet with [this] family and express our deep sorrow over what happened, and the great loss of their daughters at the hands of my son. And they [have been] gracious enough to extend their hand of friendship, love and forgiveness to our family."[1]

The father of the girls, who was seriously wounded himself, said on the same broadcast, "Over the years, you learn through life's experiences to forgive, because your only other choice is to be bitter. And I refuse to be bitter."[2]

INEXHAUSTIBLE FORGIVENESS

Thankfully, few of us will ever face a situation as tragic as the one that confronted these parents. But every person will inevitably experience disappointment, pain, humiliation, or distress at the hands of others. And in each situation we can choose either to cling to our wounds or to offer forgiveness.

Forgiveness has life-transforming power. It holds the potential to set a person loose from the chains of the past, freeing both the offender and the wounded party to pursue a second chance. Forgiveness replaces bitterness and sorrow with hope and joy. Forgiveness is an *absolute necessity* for couples who want to experience spirit, soul, and body oneness.

Why is it so necessary? Because real life marriage involves two fallible people who will inevitably make mistakes. Even two people deeply in love will disappoint and hurt each other. In the past few chapters we've looked at a number of areas where conflict often arises naturally just because of each person's unique design. Additionally, the consequences of sin make life difficult and relationships complex.

In marriage, forgiveness directly impacts a couple's level of intimacy. It is the oil that keeps the friction of offense from doing irreparable damage. Every act of forgiveness within marriage provides an opportunity to Reflect and Reveal the heart of God to your spouse. Forgiveness restores intimacy and enables a couple to Rule together in unity.

Because we recognize the vital importance of this issue and because we've seen so many couples struggling under the burden of past disappointments, we begin every REAL LIFE Marriage Advance by teaching on forgiveness. We open the session with this two-word definition of marriage: *inexhaustible forgiveness.*

The word *inexhaustible* means incapable of being used up, wearied, or worn out.[3] Isn't this a great description of God's heart toward us? No matter how many mistakes we make, He never grows weary or worn out. His capacity to forgive our sin is unlimited and unconditional.

Inexhaustible forgiveness as a definition of marriage means "never growing weary in showing grace toward one's spouse." It's a cornerstone of Reflecting and Revealing the very heart of God to each other. But we can't give away something we have not received. In other words, a couple's ability to forgive is directly related to their personal relationship with God. Only by accepting God's forgiveness for ourselves can we offer that same gift as an expression of love for our spouse. Forgiveness in marriage flows out of the continual flood of God's mercy in our own lives.

REPEATING HISTORY

Most people would acknowledge that forgiveness is an important aspect of any relationship, especially marriage. The problem comes in actually living it out!

In our work with couples, we've seen that a person's view of forgiveness often derives from their family of origin and significantly impacts how they respond to conflict within their marriage. This is one reason why we regularly challenge couples to look at their family of origin and answer these questions:

+ Did you come from a forgiving family?
+ How did your family handle offenses? How did they process conflict?
+ What kinds of communication skills were modeled to you as a child?

The answers to these questions can help pave the way for a couple to work through some painful issues, choose forgiveness, and begin the process of healing.

A few years ago we counseled a couple we'll call Jim and Joan. At our first meeting, Jim explained that Joan had recently — after five years of marriage — revealed new information about her sexual past. We decided to meet alone with Joan and quickly learned that she had difficulty sharing her emotions. She was ashamed of her sexual past. She was also angry and afraid Jim would judge her.

In the past, whenever the topic of their sexual histories came up in conversation, Joan's shame and fear drove her to try to control the situation by lying to Jim. The more lies she told, the more lies she needed to tell. The information she withheld became a major obstacle to advancing their intimacy. This led to conflict as Joan withdrew emotionally from Jim. Her inability to forgive herself had begun to affect every area of her life.

It took some time for her to work through issues that resulted in her decision to withhold the truth from Jim. She needed to start with believing in God's goodness and the fact that He had forgiven her. Once she was able to receive His forgiveness, she could deal with her fear of being unrighteously judged by her husband. Her next step was to apologize to Jim and ask him to forgive her for lying to him.

When the four of us met together, we explored family-of-origin issues. Joan came from a very controlling family while Jim's family heritage included a lot of unrighteous judging. Jim's parents were willing to forgive, but they never forgot an offense. Jim realized that he tended to respond to conflict much like his parents had, and this contributed to Joan's propensity to lie to him. This couple realized their disunity was rooted in large measure to their misunderstanding of forgiveness.

Healing does not take place overnight, and it took time for this couple to work through root issues in their personal lives and marriage. However, as Jim and Joan grew in understanding God's forgiveness and in Reflecting and Revealing that forgiveness to each other, the rift between them grew smaller and eventually healed.

WHAT FORGIVENESS IS NOT

Making a connection between the way your family of origin responded to forgiveness and the way you respond to your spouse is an invitation to advance in intimacy. But before you can effectively reshape your definition of forgiveness, it's helpful to identify any ways in which your current definition is wrong. Let's look first at some things that are *not* true about forgiveness.

Forgiveness is *not* a feeling. A person may never *feel* like obeying God by choosing to forgive. Yet God promises that obedience to His commands will bring blessings.

Forgiveness is *not* pretending you weren't hurt. Your level of personal pain should never be the deciding factor in choosing to forgive your spouse or another person. In fact, forgiveness and pain are separate issues. God created us as emotional beings. Therefore, when you are hurt or offended, an emotional response of sadness, anger, or fear is appropriate. However, these feelings don't give you permission to withhold forgiveness. Instead, God commands you to forgive, just as you have been forgiven by Him.

Forgiveness is *not* ignoring the fact that the other person was wrong. The decision to forgive does not excuse wrong behavior or eliminate the need to engage in a healthy conflict resolution process. However, forgiveness provides an opportunity to Reflect and Reveal the character of God by extending grace to someone who doesn't deserve it. Remember, the Lord is working on your spouse just as He is working on you.

Forgiveness is *not* relieving the other person of responsibility. Every one of us stands before God and is responsible to Him for the choices we make. When it comes to your spouse, God is the final judge and jury, not you. Choosing to forgive your spouse doesn't release him or her from responsibility, but it does protect you from taking on the unhealthy role of the parent.

Forgiveness is *not* an act that always requires confronting the other person about their wrongdoing. The process of working through issues of forgiveness is different for every situation. Sometimes God uses conflict as an invitation to advance in personal growth. The process of forgiving your spouse may expose something in you. This is why we encourage couples to bring their offenses to the Lord *first*. Individuals who are living in the **smaller story** may allow emotions to direct their decisions. But when you choose to step into the **Larger Story**, God is directing your life. His Word reminds us to first remove the speck from our own eye before worrying about the plank in our spouse's eye. We would suggest you involve Him in your process by asking, "Lord, do I need to confront my spouse about the offense, or is this something you want me to resolve alone with You?"

Definitely, there are circumstances where confrontation is appropriate, but learning how to engage in healthy conflict is a process of discipleship. Immature communication skills can cause a couple to overreact emotionally and lose sight of the presenting issue.

How one person confronts another sets spiritual laws in motion. One of these spiritual laws is the principle of sowing and reaping. When one spouse confronts the other with grace and mercy, they reap grace and mercy. If they confront in anger, with unrighteous judgment or accusation they reap the same. Ask the Lord to give you His heart for your spouse and to impart a godly attitude that helps you convey your feelings appropriately.

Forgiveness is *not* dependent on trusting the person who has hurt you. Whether a couple is facing serious issues that threaten the trust level in their marriage or just everyday forgiveness issues, it is important to remember that trust and forgiveness are two separate issues. God knows that husbands and wives will disappoint each other. They sin against each

Soul Oneness

other in ways that violate trust. Often, when that happens the offended spouse will choose to withhold forgiveness until trust is restored. But forgiving someone doesn't mean you have to trust that person. Instead the Scriptures command us to "trust the Lord completely; don't ever trust yourself. In everything you do, put God first, and he will direct you and crown your efforts with success."[4]

In marriage, husbands and wives who choose to forgive do so as an act of obedience and a demonstration of their trust in the One who is trustworthy. Certainly trust is an important part of every marriage relationship, but it should never supersede a person's ultimate trust in God.

Forgiveness is *not* a guarantee of restored relationship. In every situation restoring a marital relationship requires the participation of both parties. There may be times when one spouse is unwilling to take responsibility for their part of the breakdown. In this case, we encourage you to stay focused on God and your choices for healing rather than focusing your expectations on getting your spouse to respond in a particular way.

WHAT FORGIVENESS IS

Now that we've identified some mistaken definitions to determine what forgiveness is not, let's look at forgiveness is — with God's Word as our starting point. Knowing how foundational forgiveness is to maintaining healthy relationships and yet how difficult it is to live out, God provided clear guidance regarding this important topic.

Forgiveness *is* a decision to obey God. God commands His followers to forgive others. Jesus said, "For if you forgive others for their transgressions, your heavenly Father will also forgive you. But if you do not forgive others, then your Father will not forgive your transgressions."[5] In other words a person who does not forgive will not be forgiven by God. This verse should provide enough motivation for us to forgive.

Of course, the choice to obey is not always easy, but the Lord never asks a person to do something that He Himself has not already done. Colossians 3:13 says, "Be gentle and ready to forgive; never hold grudges. Remember

Soul Oneness

the Lord forgave you so you must forgive others."

It is important to recognize that although forgiveness is a decision, healing is a process. Depending on the severity of the hurt, healing may take months, seasons, or years. However, in every situation healing will increase after the decision to forgive is made.

Forgiveness *is* living out the truth that life is "not about me." It is a natural human response to feel hurt when your spouse offends you. Whenever you focus on yourself and your own perception, it's easy to spiral down and begin living as if "it's all about me." Allowing yourself time to receive the Lord's perspective is key to how you respond when you are wounded or offended. Practically, this involves stepping into the **Larger Story** with God as the main character. Ephesians 4:31-32 reads, "Let all bitterness and wrath and anger and clamor and slander be put away from you, along with all malice. Be kind to one another, tender-hearted, forgiving each other, just as God in Christ also has forgiven you." Again, the Lord instructs every person to forgive as He forgives, because life is about Him, not us.

Forgiveness *is* moving forward rather than continually looking back. Jeremiah 31:34 reminds us to put sin behind us and to stop bringing up mistakes or past sins. When God forgave us He didn't keep a little black book. Instead He says, "For I will forgive their wickedness and will remember their sins no more."[6] Even though forgiveness is a decision to obey God, it is often necessary to process the past before you can move into the future in healthy ways. As you do this and commit to forgiveness, it is important to resist the temptation to look back. Instead focus on your decision to forgive even as you take necessary steps in your process of healing. As you do, you will experience a sense of peace and find yourself freed from the past.

Forgiveness *is* getting out of God's way and allowing Him to deal directly with the other person. "The anger of man does not achieve the righteousness of God."[7] The issue of forgiveness does not hinge on whether or not your spouse is wrong; forgiveness is about whether or not you will obey God and trust Him to take it from there.

In every situation that requires forgiveness, our recommendation is to obey God. Forgive your spouse, pray for him or her, extend much grace,

Soul Oneness

and wait on God. Remember God is working on your spouse just as He is working on you.

Forgiveness *is* the cornerstone to being in relationship with God. In order to Reflect and Reveal the goodness of God to your spouse, you must understand God's forgiveness. Those who have received forgiveness from God know what it means to have their debt canceled. Overwhelmed by this undeserved gift, they gladly turn to their spouse and Reveal the heart of God by offering a Reflection of what is means to forgive.

A MODEL FOR FORGIVENESS

Becoming a forgiving person is a process that takes a lifetime. And learning to humbly seek forgiveness can be just as challenging.

We began to learn the importance of forgiveness early in our marriage and so we made it a priority as we were raising our four children. We decided to institute a simple forgiveness model that benefited us as a family. Whenever one person offended another, the person who caused the wound, intentionally or not, was to respond in this way:

I am sorry for _____ (name the specific offense). *Will you forgive me?* (allow the other person the choice to respond with *yes* or *no*).

This simple model helped the two of us and our family process forgiveness issues in a more thorough way. Too often it can be tempting to try to move past offenses by offering a quick "I'm sorry." But such a quick apology fails to address the heart of the issue.

We've learned that it is very important for the offender to name the offense and ask the other person for forgiveness. It initiates healing and growth for all parties involved when the offender acknowledges and takes responsibility for any pain that was caused. This model honors the person who was offended. It also gives the offended person time to process the situation before responding.

Remember: forgiveness is a decision, healing is a process.

SIGNS THAT YOU HAVE NOT FORGIVEN SOMEONE

God's Word is clear on forgiveness: every Christ follower is commanded to forgive. However, the reality of living in a sinful world reminds us that obedience is not easy. While most men and women would describe themselves as forgiving people, upon honest inspection they often discover that signs of unforgiveness are present in their lives.

Attempts to *advance* in intimacy with God and your spouse are blocked when unforgiveness is present. Therefore, we encourage you to be open to examine and explore the patterns and choices that are present in your life. We invite you to carefully consider the following questions: *When you have been offended by your spouse or someone else, do you ever...*

+   replay the offense in your head? When this occurs, only one side of the story is being told. Your version of reality automatically places you in the position of judge and jury. This process controls the outcome by blocking the other person from being a full participant.

+   engage in internal conversations? Carrying on a one-way dialogue to justify your position may give you a sense of power or vindication, but it doesn't help you move toward resolution. The issue may appear to be black and white with little room for discussion, but things are always off balance when you feel 100 percent right and view the other person as 100 percent wrong.

+   have an intense emotional response? Feelings that have been buried often surface at the most unexpected times. Exaggerated, inappropriate, or out-of-control emotional reactions to someone in particular are always a red-flag warning, a sign that you may have not forgiven.

+   experience physical symptoms? You may feel your heart race, your face flush, or your mouth get dry when an offensive or hurtful situation comes to mind. A negative physical response like this invites you to explore possible areas of unforgiveness.

Soul Oneness

+ withhold positive emotions? Intentionally withholding a positive emotion is a passive form of punishment and a subtle form of control. Choosing to focus on the offense and withhold forgiveness makes it difficult to enjoy being with your spouse or another person. This is another example of dealing with conflict in unhealthy ways.

+ stop praying for that person? Prayer is an act of intimacy. When you have not forgiven someone, it is difficult to pray for them. When you find yourself consciously or unconsciously leaving a person off your prayer list, this is an invitation to look at what is going on in your heart.

People may choose not to forgive for a number of reasons. Some individuals admit to intentionally withholding forgiveness as a means of control. Or a person may withhold forgiveness because he or she has prejudged the motives or actions of the other spouse. Being ready to forgive means being willing to presuppose the best.

Other couples have trouble choosing forgiveness because conflict avoidance was modeled in their family of origin. In such cases, the lack of forgiveness may be a by-product of unhealthy communication skills. A conflict avoider may mistakenly conclude that burying their feelings is a more godly choice. They assume that withholding their feelings is better than failing at an attempt to engage in healthy conflict resolution. This decision only complicates an issue, inhibits a person's maturity, and delays resolve. There is truth in the familiar saying, *when you bury your feelings, you bury them alive*. Intentionally ignoring or overlooking a problem can be the first step in a destructive cycle.

We counseled a couple we'll call Robert and Julie, whose twelve years of marriage had been impacted by this problem almost from the very start. At our first meeting they told us about an explosive argument with Robert's parents that took place during their first year of marriage. Julie explained, "I didn't grow up in a home with that level of rage, so when his parents exploded, I just shut down."

Without the tools and biblical principles needed to engage in a healthy conflict-resolution process, they simply severed their relationship with Robert's parents. It had been almost ten years since either of them had spoken to Robert's parents. The couple's three children had never met their grandparents.

When we asked Robert to give his perspective, he said, "I grew up in a home where my parents were always fighting and saying hurtful things. No one in our family ever apologized; we just moved on. I keep telling my wife she needs to put the past behind her so we can move on, but she can't seem to forgive my parents — or me."

It became apparent that their decision to sever their relationship with his parents may have temporarily solved one problem, but it exposed the root of another.

Julie said, "What started out as a horrible argument has only gotten more complicated. At the time, I guess I was waiting for my husband to say something to them...to stand up for us...to protect us from their painful accusations." She started crying. "But he didn't say a word."

Robert seemed uncomfortable with Julie's show of emotion and just looked down at the ground.

Julie continued, "It's not that I can't forgive Robert or his parents. The problem is, we don't know how to process conflict as a couple. For Robert, the answer to everything is to just forget about it and move on. Everything seems to get shoved under the carpet. I just can't do it anymore. I won't do it anymore. We have so many unresolved issues that I feel like I'm dying inside."

When we first met with this couple, they were just beginning to grow in relationship with God. Their faith in His principles caused them to rethink their estranged relationship with Robert's parents. They began to understand that obedience to God is accompanied by blessing. We reminded them that the fifth commandment to "honor your father and your mother" ends by saying, "so it may go well with you."[8] Up to this point, things weren't going too well for this couple. A lack of forgiveness had infiltrated other relationships in their life, including their own marriage. We challenged them to trust God by obeying the fifth commandment and see what might happen.

After much prayer, the husband initiated contact with his parents. His phone call opened the door to communication. It became obvious to Robert and Julie that God had been working in his parents' hearts as well. Slowly things began to turn around.

By focusing on God instead of their own needs, they realized they no longer needed an apology from Robert's parents. At some point this couple took responsibility for their part in the breakdown of the relationship. They apologized to Robert's parents and asked for their forgiveness.

The rigid barriers created by withholding forgiveness began to melt away. Once their hearts were reconnected, Robert and Julie introduced their children to their grandparents for the first time. We sat together while they told us about the changes taking place, and tears rolled down their cheeks as they grieved over all those wasted years.

The gift of unconditional forgiveness that God offers every person has the power to transform lives, marriages, and families. With the decision to forgive, this couple stepped into the **Larger Story** and allowed God to be the main character. Not only was their family reunited, but this couple also received the blessing of advancing in soul oneness and marital intimacy.

The truth is, no matter how great a rift has taken place in a relationship, the decision to forgive is always the healthiest choice.

God's Word says, "There is a way that seems right to a man, but in the end it leads to death."[9] In marriage as well as other relationships, the decision to withhold forgiveness often seems right to a person. We may justify the decision to withhold forgiveness by convincing ourselves the timing isn't right or that we need to further process the situation. We may find ourselves unrighteously judging the other person and come to the conclusion they don't deserve to be forgiven. Withholding our heart by not obeying God's command to forgive can give a person a false sense of power or control. One familiar saying captures the consequences of refusing to obey God in this area: "Unforgiveness is the poison you drink every day hoping the other person will die!"

We believe the decision to freely offer forgiveness defines a person. As a Christ follower, withholding forgiveness is not an option. Jesus Christ is the quintessential example of forgiveness. No person in all of history had more right to be offended or to withhold forgiveness. Instead He responded with these words, "Father, forgive them, for they do not know what they are doing."[10]

In some situations — including those that involve adultery, addiction, or abuse — the help of a counselor may be needed to help you process your wounds and choose to forgive. Rather than remaining stuck in or feeling guilty about your inability to forgive, we suggest you view it as a sign that you still need work in this area, whether that means asking another person to come alongside you or asking God for His help.

God's command to forgive leads to life. When a person chooses to forgive they reap the blessings and benefits of obedience. These blessings will be passed on for generations.

Soul Oneness

Review Part 2

In Part 1 we examined the basics of **Spirit Oneness** as we looked at God's original Plan A design for marriage. We saw that marriage was designed to Reflect and Reveal the plurality of God. To accomplish this purpose, a husband and wife must be in covenant with God and each other.

In Part 2 we considered what it means for a couple to enjoy **Soul Oneness**. We saw how Rulership was lost in the Garden, but it was later reclaimed by Jesus, freeing couples to live out God's Plan A design for marriage in which Rulership, dominion, and authority are given to *both* the husband and wife. The key to successfully walking this out is by choosing to live together in unity. This involves **Larger Story** living where "marriage is not about me."

The heart of **Soul Oneness** is genuine intimacy — to know and be fully known. Advancing in intimacy means focusing on the "**We**" of marriage. This includes learning how to delight in each other's differences — in spiritual gifts, styles of relating, temperaments, families of origin, and more — as you dance as one in a rhythm of unity. We looked at implementing the Traffic Light Principles as a practical way of making decisions in unity. We concluded Part 2 by challenging couples to demonstrate *inexhaustible forgiveness* to one another, which opens the door for you to advance in **Soul Oneness**.

Before moving on to Part 3, in which we explore **Body Oneness**, we encourage you to take a closer look at your marriage and review your story, using the following exercises:

+ What marriage model are you living? (for example: rulership, hierarchical, or God's Plan A)
+ What does it mean to walk out Rulership, authority, and headship in your marriage?
+ How do you view your relationship in the context of a marital "**We**"?
+ Describe your marital dance.
+ Discuss examples of how you could implement the Traffic Light Principle in your decision-making process.
+ Describe how *inexhaustible forgiveness* could advance intimacy between you, God, and your spouse.

Soul Oneness

REAL LIFE *Companion Journal* is available for study questions and
personal applications for each chapter.

3

REAL LIFE MARRIAGE
it's not about me

Body Oneness

+ Chapter 13

Body Oneness

Naked and Not Ashamed

Rediscovering God's Intentions for Sex

In the summer after my (Anne's) fifth-grade year, my mom decided it was time to talk to me about sex. At eleven years of age, surely I must have heard something about the subject in playground conversations or whispering between friends, but this particular evening with my mom is my first real memory of learning about sex.

I remember sitting in the back of the living room, where our family had gathered one evening to watch TV. I felt a tap on my shoulder. Turning around, I saw my mom motioning me to follow her down the hallway that led into her bedroom.

Since I grew up in a large family, I didn't often get to spend time alone with my mom, so this felt like a special moment. I still remember climbing up on her bed as she closed and locked the door. Then she reached inside the drawer of her bedside table and pulled out a little pamphlet she had received in the mail from Kotex. It was titled something like *What Every Daughter Needs to Know about Sex.*

A sensitive child, I couldn't help but notice how uncomfortable my mom seemed as she began to read to me from the booklet. It felt more like story time than a conversation. I don't remember having any interest in learning about sex at age eleven. In fact, I wasn't quite sure why I had to leave my TV program for this. There seemed to be absolutely no connection between the pamphlet my mom was reading and my own personal life.

As my mom flipped through the pages, I noticed pictures of some birds in a flower garden, some bees pollinating the flowers…and then suddenly there was a diagram of a female body with the uterus highlighted. It looked to me like a big baked potato with wings sprouting off each side. My mom nervously talked about the production of eggs and sperm. Then we advanced to the monthly "shedding" of the uterine wall. To be honest, the whole thing was a little hard to follow. I was much more aware of my mom being uncomfortable than about what was happening in the story she was trying to tell me.

As we approached the part explaining how the sperm actually got to the egg, my curiosity was piqued. That was probably the only part of the entire booklet that was of any interest to me. At that point I sat up straight and tuned in to every word. As I waited for my mom to turn the page, I noticed something strange. My mom had taped the next few pages together, and she skipped to the end of the pamphlet. I thought to myself, *Wait a minute. How am I ever going to find out how the sperm gets to the egg?* The story came to an abrupt end with a happy couple holding their new baby.

My mom always referred to the story of reproduction as a "beautiful story," but I often thought to myself, *If it's such a beautiful story then why did you tape the pages together and completely skip the part about how the sperm meets the egg?* I grew up feeling like I only had part of the story. I had an uneasy sense that I was still missing some vital information. Surely it was hidden inside those taped pages!

+ + +

I (Tim) vividly remember one day when my dad said, "Timmy, I need to see you in the bedroom." At the time I was in the sixth grade, and I knew those words usually signaled that discipline was coming my way. In most cases, the discipline involved two things: my dad's belt and my butt.

I walked into the bedroom and sat on my parents' bed. My dad closed the door and lit a cigarette. I noticed he didn't have the usual look on his face that preceded my getting whacked. Something was about to happen, but I had no idea what it might be.

My dad paced back and forth for a few minutes. Then he stood still for a moment and said, "Timmy, I have to talk to you about a stepping stone."

As soon as I heard those two words, I felt an immediate sense of relief. "Stepping stone" was a familiar term in my family, a way of referring to little life lessons that my dad thought were important. For example, when my grandma died, my brothers and I were pretty young and none of us wanted to be pallbearers. We were afraid we might drop the coffin. Dad called us together and said, "Boys, this is a stepping stone. It is an honor for you to carry Grandma to her grave." Stepping stones were such a big part of our family life that when Dad died we engraved his headstone with these words: My Final Stepping Stone.

My dad was a man who never had trouble saying what he thought. He was a good athlete, a Golden Gloves boxer, a decorated World War II veteran, and a hardworking, union-card-carrying milkman. Yet here he was pacing across the bedroom, seemingly flustered about talking to me about a *stepping stone.*

Once again he stopped pacing, took a long drag on his cigarette, and said, "Timmy, one of my jobs as your dad is to talk to you about sex." When I heard my dad say the word *sex,* I almost fell off the bed laughing. Realizing that would not have been a wise choice, I decided to just listen.

Dad returned to his nervous pacing until he stopped and looked me straight in the eyes. Finally, he said, "Timmy, if you ever have any questions about sex...ask your mother!" Then he opened the door and walked out.

I sat on the bed for a few seconds and thought, *What just happened?* My older brother Billy was in the room across the hall. When he saw me walk out, he asked if I got whacked. Confused over what had happened, I told him, "I think Dad just had a sex talk with me."

Billy burst out laughing and said, "Let me guess. Dad told you if you have any questions, ask Mom." When I nodded, he said, "That's the same talk he gave to me last year!" We both laughed about Dad's sex stepping stone!

Beyond that talk, the subject of sex was never addressed in our home. Since I didn't hear about sex from my parents, I heard about it from my older brother, in the locker room, on the ball field, and at the firehouse. Let's just say that what I learned had absolutely nothing to do with God's design for sex.

IN THE BEGINNING...

Think back to your growing-up years. Were you ever taught God's purposes for sex? If you didn't learn about God's purposes, then what did you learn about sex? In our conversations with people across the nation, we've discovered that most received little if any sexual training in their family of origin. For the most part, the church has dropped the ball as well. The media has stepped in to supply much misinformation, while Hollywood mocks God's purposes.

With all this confusion swirling around, it can be easy to lose sight of what sex is meant to be. However, from the beginning God had a plan and a purpose in mind.

Imagine what it was like in Paradise for Adam and Eve before sin entered the world. The text reads, "The man and his wife were both naked and were not ashamed."[1]

To be naked means "to be without cover or protection," and to be unashamed means "to have nothing to hide." Recently our grandson slipped away during a diaper change. Naked and without shame, he ran around the house in his birthday suit — a picture of innocence, freedom, and joy.

God paints a similar picture of the first couple to illustrate His original design for marital intimacy. Before sin entered the world, the first man and woman lived without fear or shame and had no reason to hide. They had no secrets from God or from each other. Fear and shame were not in their vocabularies. They *knew* God intimately and were *fully known* by God. As the Bible declares, things were *very good!*

And because Jesus restored our innocence by taking the penalty for our sin and reclaiming Rulership from the enemy, married couples can once again live in God's original design for marriage. This means living out the following principles:

+ **Spirit Oneness**, with both the husband and wife living in relationship with God, Reflecting and Revealing His character to each other and to the world around them.
+ **Soul Oneness**, with the couple Ruling together in unity, intimacy, and friendship.
+ **Body Oneness**, with husband and wife joining together and becoming one sexually in a celebration of being *naked and not ashamed*.

Body Oneness

All three of these are intertwined. For example, physical nakedness is symbolic of a couple's willingness to be emotionally naked. A husband and wife who understand what it means to become one are willing to take off much more than their clothes. God designed emotional nakedness to come before physical nakedness. This enables married couples to grow in intimacy with God and each other.

TWO LOVERS, ONE FLESH

Let's return to the creation account. In the beginning, when God first brought the newly created woman to the man, He declared, "For this reason a man shall leave his father and his mother, and be joined [cleave] to his wife; and they shall become one flesh."[2] In short, here were God's instructions to all future married couples:

1. The man is to leave his father and mother.
2. The man is to cleave to his wife.
3. The man and woman are to *become one flesh*.

Let's look at God's pattern for marriage a bit more carefully.

God's design calls for the man to *leave* his most significant relationships and *cleave* to his wife. *Cleaving* involves a husband giving himself totally to his bride. In other words, they are to be bonded together so tightly that no other relationship can get between them as husband and wife. *Leaving and cleaving* is a cornerstone of the intimacy needed to advance in soul oneness, which sets the stage for celebrating body oneness — two becoming one flesh through sex in marriage.

Every married couple is commanded by God to *become one flesh*. This refers directly to sexual intercourse. Becoming one flesh as husband and wife involves a God-ordained process. The man initiates the process when he *leaves* his most significant relationships and cleaves to his wife. Together they enter into covenant with God and each other. After the wedding the wife allows her husband to enter into her life and body. This mutual obedience and celebration of God's design for marriage culminates in the husband and wife becoming one flesh as they experience the orgasmic joy of sex.

God created body oneness, which means sex is His idea. Sexual intercourse in marriage is symbolic of the miracle and mystery of two becoming one. This includes an intangible mutual exchange that is sacred to God, the husband, the wife, and a marriage.

There is so much symbolism in the sexual act in marriage. God created the husband in a unique way so that his reproductive organ is outside his body. His maleness leads out toward his wife, who is also created in a unique way. The wife's reproductive organs are inside her body. A woman's womb is a symbol of the innermost part of her soul. Her heart provides the invitation as her body provides the stimulation. Increased levels of excitement allow her husband to enter, depositing life-giving seed into her womb. Sexual intercourse is the celebration of marriage. It joins two spirits, two souls, and two bodies.

GOD'S PURPOSES FOR MARITAL SEX

As we look at the creation story and God's instructions throughout the Bible to married couples, we believe He designed marital sex for five primary purposes.

1.   Marital sex is for celebration.
The first thing we learn about marriage from the creation story is that every man and woman is made in the image of God.[3] Maleness is an intrinsic part of every man. Femaleness is an intrinsic part of every woman. One man and one woman are intrinsic parts of every marriage. Therefore, God invites a married couple to celebrate their creational design. Sex can become an act of worship toward God, the creator of sex. Colossians 3:17 says, "Whatever you do in word or deed, do all in the name of the Lord Jesus." Body oneness provides a place for a couple to love, serve, and enjoy each other.

2.   Marital sex is for procreation.
Every married couple is commanded to "be fruitful and multiply."[4] A husband and wife are given the ability and instructed to have children. At the start of this book, we alluded to God's four key purposes for marriage: to Reflect and Reveal the plurality and character of God, to Rule together in unity, and to Reproduce, bringing forth new life to

Body Oneness

advance the kingdom. Of course, reproducing isn't limited to bringing biological children into the world. Reproduction can take many forms, including adoption, foster parenting, and spiritual parenting. We'll look at this subject in greater detail in the next chapter.

3. Marital sex is for protection.

Sex creates a strong bond between a husband and wife, a bond that helps protect the marriage relationship. The enemy clearly understands the power of sexuality and uses sexual temptation as one of his key strategies. A healthy sex life helps a couple avoid temptation.[5] Couples who enjoy a healthy sexual relationship feel more connected and emotionally focused on each other as well as more hopeful about their marriage. Studies also indicate a healthy sex life protects a couple from health problems. Positive endorphins released during orgasm help suppress stress and aid the body in self-healing and overall better health.

4. Marital sex is for pleasure.

Despite anything you may have heard to the contrary, God is pro-sex and pro-pleasure. His desire is for married couples to enjoy a mutually satisfying sex life. God created orgasms so a couple could experience deep pleasure and physical satisfaction through body oneness within their marriage. A husband and wife are invited by God to eat, drink, and "imbibe deeply."[6]

5. Marital sex is for comfort.

After the death of David and Bathsheba's son, the Bible says, "Then David comforted his wife Bathsheba, and went in to her and lay with her…"[7] During difficult seasons in marriage, comfort through sexual expression can be a gift from God. These seasons become opportunities to advance in intimacy and strengthen marital bonds by serving a spouse sexually to bring comfort and healing.

HOW DO MARRIED COUPLES RATE THEIR SEX LIVES?

Husbands and wives may have many great friendships that include love and intimacy. But the only person they can enjoy sex with is their spouse. This sacred gift is to be enjoyed exclusively by a husband and wife within

Body Oneness

the context of marriage. A great sex life involves much more than frequency, locations, timing, and positions.

+ "Sex is not the search for something that's missing. It's the expression of something that's been found. It's designed to be the overflow, the culmination of something that a man and a woman have found in each other. It's a celebration of this living, breathing thing that's happening between the two of them."[8] +

Sadly, many couples seem to have misplaced their invitations to this celebration.

At our REAL LIFE Marriage Advances we ask married couples the following question: *Have you embraced God's purposes for sex in your marriage?* Then we ask them to individually write down three words that describe their sex life. The responses vary widely. Some husbands and wives use positive words like *pleasurable, exciting, stress-busting, adventuresome, mutually pleasing, playful, joyful, risky, comforting, the highlight of my day.* Others describe their sex lives in negative ways, such as *boring, routine, a power struggle, frustrating, one-way, non-existent, duty, over in two minutes, controlling, shameful, and fearful.*

At one of our conferences that was centered primarily on body oneness, we took a short, anonymous survey. This was a group of couples, primarily Christian leaders from a local church, who had been married between fifteen and twenty-five years.

We gave each person a piece of paper with two questions:

1. How do you rate your current sex life? _____
2. How do you think your spouse would rate your current sex life? _____

They were to write in each blank a number between 1 and 10, with 1 indicating "nonexistent' and 10 being "off the charts.'

When we tabulated the numbers, we were surprised by the results. As a group, these men and women rated their current sexual satisfaction at 2.7 out of a possible 10. They thought their spouses would rate their current sexual satisfaction at 2.3.

Body Oneness

We have since repeated this survey and gathered similar data.

Our experience tells us that the sexual dimension in many marriages is far from what God intended. For many couples, what God has designed for celebration, procreation, protection, pleasure, and comfort has evolved into control, power struggles, and frustration. On the positive side, married couples who give a high rating to their sex life often rate their marriages high as well.

In the next several chapters we'll be exploring a number of topics that can negatively impact a couple's ability to enjoy body oneness as God intended, and we'll look at ways to turn those negatives around.

We understand that reading about sensitive sexual issues may be uncomfortable for you. Perhaps your family of origin had a negative view of sex or your sexual history is not what God intended. Maybe you've endured abuse in the past. Whatever your initial reaction to this subject, we encourage you to invite the Holy Spirit to walk you through these next chapters. Genesis 50:20 reminds us that what the enemy intends for evil God can use for good.

We're convinced that, as you prayerfully work through these issues with your spouse, the two of you will advance in spirit, soul, and body oneness to an extent you can't now imagine.

+ Chapter 14

Be Fruitful and Multiply

Carrying Out God's Mandate to Reproduce

Nothing changes life like the arrival of a baby. I (Anne) so clearly remember the moments leading up to the arrival of our first grandchild. We had been in Michigan for over a week, anticipating Amy's delivery date. After a few false alarms and an attempt to induce labor, today was the day, so Tim and I drove to the hospital for the grand event.

As we headed toward our daughter's room, we saw the doctor walking out. Amy had just been scheduled for a Cesarean section. Having surgery definitely wasn't their first choice, but it was the best option available in light of the circumstances.

A short time later, they wheeled Amy out of her room, with Curt walking right alongside. He held her hand and spoke words of reassurance as they headed for the delivery room, both of them looking equally scared and excited. Watching them move down that long hospital corridor, I couldn't help but think of their wedding day when, with family and friends gathered around, they had walked hand in hand down another long aisle and stepped into a new life together as one. Now here we were a few years later, looking on as they walked together through the final stages of their nine-month journey leading to parenthood.

Tim and I continued watching until they disappeared behind the double doors to the surgical suite. After all these months of praying, preparing, and dreaming the time was actually here. Within the next few hours we would be holding our first grandchild.

The family gathered in the waiting room. We tried to enjoy casual conversation, but it was hard to focus on anything other than the baby's arrival. Every minute that passed felt like an hour. We kept glancing toward the doors that separated the waiting room from the surgical area.

Finally the doors swung open, and Curt walked out in his blue surgical scrubs. As he approached, his step was light and his smile bright. The look on his face was indescribable. It was as if he were ready to burst.

As a mom I just wanted to stop the clocks and hold on to that moment forever. Before us stood a man who had just witnessed the miraculous birth of his first child. I knew he would never be the same again. No longer was he just Curt…or our son…or our daughter's husband. He was now a *dad*. He was about to experience a depth of love that he had never known before.

We all formed a circle around him. There was a long pause. Then, with a huge smile, Curt proudly announced, "It's a boy! His name is Joel Christopher DeBoer."

The cheers of our family broke the silence. Although there were only a handful of us in the waiting room, my heart heard the sound of cheers from a stadium filled with people. In that brief moment it felt like the whole world was sharing our joy. Some of us laughed, others cried. But we all thanked God for the gift of new life.

After a few minutes Curt motioned us to follow him to the recovery room to see Amy. We walked through the doors that led us into the next season of our lives. Pulling back the hospital curtains we saw our baby holding her baby. His perfect little body was bundled tightly in a light blue hospital blanket, like a gift waiting to be unwrapped. Drawing Joel out of Amy's arms and into mine, I realized I was looking into the eyes of the next generation.

It has now been over three years since Joel's miraculous birth. Since that wonderful day, we've been blessed with three more grandbabies. Two years ago, Tim and I flew to Texas to be with Colleen and Johnny when John William III was born. Then we returned to Michigan to welcome the arrival of Joel's little sister and our first granddaughter, Grace Elizabeth.

Both Tim and I would have to describe becoming grandparents as a mountaintop experience. Tim often says, "There are a lot of things in life that aren't what they're cracked up to be…but being a grandparent is *not* one of them!"

We have found such delight in watching our children embark on the adventure of parenting. In addition to the joy of seeing the world once more through a child's eyes, being a parent leads to a deeper understanding of how God feels toward His children and to a greater vision of His purposes for marriage.

Body Oneness

THE PROCREATION MANDATE

God designed men and women as sexual beings, and He designed marriage as a place for a husband and wife to experience the satisfaction and pleasure of body oneness. Out of this oneness, a husband and wife are to fulfill God's purpose of Reproducing. To reproduce means "to bring forth new life."

In Genesis 1:28 we read, "God blessed them; and God said to them, 'Be fruitful and multiply, and fill the earth, and subdue it.' " This is referred to as the procreation mandate. It is important to understand that the procreation mandate is directly connected to God's blessing. Out of God's blessing, husbands and wives are to have children. This enables humankind to fill the earth and subdue it.

Having children is the continuation of a couple's story and marks the beginning of a new story. Having children is God's way of celebrating marital oneness and connecting one generation to the next. Bringing forth life reminds a man and a woman they were created for more than themselves. Reproducing provides unlimited opportunities to live out the truth "It's not about me." Parenting provides a couple with countless opportunities to Reflect and Reveal the plurality and character of God within their family and to Rule over their home in unity. God's command for couples to Reproduce is intimately connected with fulfilling all of His purposes for marriage.

Of course, sex is not just about making babies. As we saw in the previous chapter, God designed sex not only for procreation but also for celebration, protection, pleasure, and comfort. We'll look more at those other purposes in the chapters to come. For now, our focus is on some of the common questions related to the procreation mandate.

WHAT ABOUT BIRTH CONTROL?

Whenever the topic of reproducing comes up, it inevitably leads to the subject of birth control. Couples ask questions such as, *What if we're not ready for children right now? What kind of birth control, if any, should we use? When should we begin our family? How many children should we have?*

What does God say about this sensitive topic?

The Bible does not specifically address birth control. Some people contend that the story of Onan prohibits any action deliberately intended to prevent sex from culminating in a pregnancy. Onan was an Old Testament character who refused to follow the cultural code of his day, which said that if a man died without heirs, his brother was to take the widow as his wife and raise their firstborn child in the name of the dead brother. The text reads, "Then Judah said to Onan, 'Lie with your brother's wife and fulfill your duty to her as a brother-in-law to produce offspring for your brother.' But Onan knew that the offspring would not be his; so whenever he lay with his brother's wife, he spilled his semen on the ground to keep from producing offspring for his brother. What he did was wicked in the LORD's sight; so he put him to death also."[1]

We don't believe this is a conclusive text about birth control; we see it as directly connected to the responsibility of a brother-in-law to his widowed sister-in-law under ancient cultural laws. However, we'll leave the debating to the biblical scholars.

We will say that, while we are hard-pressed to find any other specific scriptures that deal with birth control, stewardship is addressed throughout the Bible. *Stewardship* refers to "careful and responsible management of something entrusted to one's care."[2] We are commanded to be faithful and wise stewards of our time, talents, and treasures. We are accountable to God for what we do with everything He has given us. In keeping with this principle, we believe a couple is responsible to steward the husband's sperm and the wife's eggs as precious gifts entrusted to them by God.

Coming to a Decision Together

We do not believe there is only one right answer to the questions of birth control, and the issues for each couple may be complex in different ways. Working through the decision together enables a couple to Rule together in unity with regard to their sexuality and reproductive potential. We urge every couple to include God in the decision-making process, using this opportunity to strengthen the marriage, increase unity, and advance in intimacy with God and each other.

Body Oneness

One wife we were counseling honestly admitted, "It never occurred to us to ask God what He thought about birth control. Including Him on these kinds of decisions is new to us. We pray, but in all honesty we never stop to listen. I guess we had our own ideas and our own timetable for beginning a family. We never even thought to ask God to give us His timetable."

It is important for the husband and wife to be on the same page, to support one another, and to stay current with each other in the process. When one spouse decides to fly solo or take a shortcut, other issues often surface.

We met with "Jack and Emily" after they had been married about eight years. Back when they got engaged to be married, the decision to use birth control was simply assumed. Without much conversation or any prayer, Emily chose a method she felt comfortable with.

In the years following, the only time they did not use birth control was when they wanted to get pregnant. They now had two boys, ages five and three, but they weren't sure if they wanted a third child. For the first time, birth control had become an issue in their marriage.

As life continued to demand more from the couple, conflicts surfaced in their sexual relationship. Since their communication was one of their weak areas, Emily discovered that she was able to get Jack's attention when she withheld sexually. In a solo session with us, she acknowledged that she was experiencing some low-level anger toward Jack, partly because she felt as if she was bearing the full responsibility for birth control. Emily realized that another part of her problem was the limited amount of time she had with Jack. They never seemed to have enough time to just talk and catch up on life. Their growing family responsibilities had resulted in their placing each other at the bottom of their priority list.

We talked about the importance of communication and how it impacted their intimacy and oneness. We encouraged Emily to schedule specific times with Jack to express her needs.

When they came in for couples counseling, Emily said to her husband, "I guess I don't feel like you appreciate everything that I do. It seems to me like our decision to use birth control feels more like my job. I'm the one who has to take all the responsibility. I'm the one who makes the appointment and goes to the doctor. I'm the one who fills the prescription and takes responsibility for using it correctly."

Jack seemed confused. "Do you want me to go to the doctor, track your cycle, take a pill, or buy condoms?"

Clearly hurt by his sarcastic response, Emily replied, "It's not that I'm unwilling to take responsibility for birth control. It would just be nice if every once in awhile you acknowledged my efforts. This may sound crazy to you, but it would be nice to hear you say, 'Honey, I do appreciate you. Thanks for carrying the weight of birth control for us. I know it takes time and effort. Just knowing that you are handling it takes off the pressure of always worrying about getting pregnant.' "

As they continued to talk, Jack and Emily were able to recognize the importance of processing their decisions together, especially in the area of birth control. This allowed them to walk in unity, which increased their intimacy.

Seeking a Clear Perspective

In addition to talking openly with each other and listening together to what God is saying, we also encourage couples to consider seeking the insight of others as they process their decisions about birth control. In the context of community a husband and wife may be challenged to consider new perspectives and gain the wisdom they need to reach unity.

While counseling another couple who was preparing for marriage, we asked how they arrived at their decision regarding birth control. The man responded, "Whenever we make a decision on anything, we talk about it together, gather the facts, and make a decision based on that. As far as birth control, we both decided that we do not want to start a family right away. We're still young and want to take some time to travel and have fun before we settle down."

His fiancée added, "Besides, we just bought a house with a pretty steep mortgage payment. Plus, we have two car payments and are paying off a credit card and some college loans."

Body Oneness

This couple seemed to have good communication skills, which allowed them to process their decisions in a healthy manner. However, they hadn't included God. We challenged them to invite God into every area of their life, including their birth control decisions. They both agreed and committed to pray.

In the months leading up to their wedding, they began to see that their motive for birth control was rooted more in concern about their debt than in God's direction for their lives. In reality, financial instability was responsible for the fear they both felt when they considered starting a family. We encouraged this couple to get some financial training and develop a budget. A financial plan would help them get out of debt and make disciplined decisions with future spending, and financial freedom would enable them to make clearer decisions.

Including God and others helped them take Rulership over their finances and directly impacted this couple's decision to start a family.

THREE KEY QUESTIONS ABOUT BIRTH CONTROL

Married couples who already have children and couples who are heading into a second marriage often say to us, "What's to discuss? What do we need to pray about? We already have kids! For us, using birth control is a no-brainer."

Whatever your circumstance, the decision to have children or to delay having children should not be taken lightly. Reproducing is a purpose for marriage that carries eternal ramifications. Including God, your spouse, and others in your process provides protection from disunity and enemy attack. We encourage every couple — regardless of their age, years married, or number of children — to continue processing the topic of birth control. This is not just a one-time decision but an ongoing issue that continually impacts marriage.

We challenge every couple to include God in their birth control decisions by prayerfully answering three questions:

1. What is our motive for using or not using birth control?

When a couple takes an honest look at their motives, it often changes the way they see things. Some examples of motives that affect a couple's birth control decision include religious convictions, family of origin issues, finances, emotional immaturity, health concerns, and fears surrounding parenthood. Since we believe in the importance of processing motives, we challenge couples to ask themselves the following questions:

+   What factors (spiritual, financial, emotional, relational) are motivating our choice for birth control?
+   Do we have a plan for dealing with these factors?
+   What is our timeline for beginning our family?
+   Have we included God as we attempt to understand our motives?
+   Are we in agreement and unity on all these questions?

2. If we use birth control, what method will we choose?

Again, we encourage every couple to seek God's wisdom in their decisions about birth control. The Bible says, "But if any of you lacks wisdom, let him ask of God, who gives to all generously and without reproach, and it will be given to him."[3] Seeking God, processing with a spouse, including others, and consulting medical professionals allows a couple to gather the information they need to make wise choices. Certain methods of birth control are dangerous, immoral, and have potentially harmful side effects. It's important that every couple does their research and talks with their doctor. This will help them thoroughly understand what they are using and how it affects their body, baby, and their marriage. The process of answering this question also should include clear and direct discussions about how each spouse will share in the responsibility for birth control.

3. Is our birth control choice a moral one?

If you've decided together to use birth control, is your method of choice a moral one? We believe life begins at conception. Therefore, any form of birth control that affects a fertilized egg is immoral. On the other hand, we believe forms of birth control that stop the sperm before it fertilizes the egg are morally acceptable. We challenge every couple to prayerfully process the morality of their birth control methods.

Body Oneness

WHEN A COUPLE CAN'T HAVE CHILDREN

We realize that all this talk about reproducing can be painfully difficult for couples who for whatever reasons may be unable to have children.

Many couples deal with sterility and infertility. *Sterility* is an inability to reproduce. This can be rooted in some type of physical abnormality, or it can be a decision for a permanent form of birth control, such as vasectomy or tubal ligation. *Infertility* refers to when a couple is unable to get pregnant after at least one year of regular intercourse without the use of contraception. One survey indicates that just over 7 percent of married couples in the United States deal with infertility, and millions more endure the agony of losing a baby through miscarriage.[4]

Suffering through infertility or living with the knowledge of sterility beyond your control often becomes an obstacle to marital oneness. Couples processing the reality of barrenness in the midst of longing can easily feel isolated from God and each other unless they actively seek to advance in intimacy by walking through this together, looking for ways to serve and comfort one another.

If this is your situation, we encourage you to consider other ways that you as a couple can fulfill the purpose of Reproducing. In addition to alternatives such as adoption and foster parenting, we encourage you to prayerfully consider how God might use the two of you to impact the younger generation for His purposes. We live in a fatherless and motherless generation unlike any in all of history. We sincerely believe the number one need in the church is for God to raise up spiritual moms and dads. Spiritual children provide a couple with unlimited opportunities to Reflect and Reveal the goodness of God to a fatherless generation.

One of the greatest spiritual fathers in the Bible is the apostle Paul. Scripture provides no evidence that he had any biological children, yet in his decision to be a spiritual parent, he fathered countless new believers. Paul's passion and love for his children was evident. He wrote one of our favorite passages, "I have no greater joy than this, to hear of my children walking in the truth."[5] Jesus Christ did not have biological children, yet His fatherly compassion and love for others is the ultimate model for parenting.

If you and your spouse are facing infertility or sterility, please know that God still has a plan for you as a parent. Whether this is through adoption or spiritual parenting, every couple can positively impact the next generation.

A BLESSING LIKE NO OTHER

As we've seen, one of God's main purposes for marriage is for a husband and wife to Reproduce. God invites a man and woman to enter covenant, become one, and *be fruitful and multiply*. In marriage, having children — including spiritual children and adopted children — provides opportunities to Reproduce and pass on godly values to future generations. Being a parent provides a lifetime of invitations to live out "It's not about me."

Raising a family advances God's kingdom. Why do you think the enemy is so committed to distorting and destroying marriage and family as God designed? Raising biological children and spiritual children who know and love God can be compared to a strategic act of war. Godly marriages and children have the potential to destroy the enemy's plans to defeat families. God declares,

"Behold, children are a gift of the LORD,
The fruit of the womb is a reward.
Like arrows in the hand of a warrior,
So are the children of one's youth.
How blessed is the man whose quiver is full of them."[6]

It has certainly been our experience that children are a blessing like no other. I (Tim) remember pulling into the driveway of our small ranch home early one morning. I had just gotten off duty from a busy twenty-four-hour firehouse shift, and now I was coming home to change clothes and then go to my side job. Between the two jobs, I was working over seventy-five hours a week.

Before heading into the house, I sat in the car and took a deep breath. My energy level was at an all-time low as I thought about the two busy days

Body Oneness

ahead working my side job before returning to the firehouse for another twenty-four-hour shift.

Just as I was wallowing in self-pity, the front door of our home burst open and our four children raced out. They tackled me as I stepped out of the car. Timmy jumped on my back as I threw Amy over my shoulder. Colleen and Cate wrapped themselves around my legs and sat on my feet, forcing me to limp into the house.

All four of the kids were competing for my attention, smothering me with hugs and kisses and telling me fragmented stories of their day. The more they giggled, the more energized I felt. All of a sudden I forgot how exhausted I was and how many hours of work I had ahead of me.

As I entered the house with them still clinging to me, our children screamed in unison, "*Daddy's home!*"

In my entire life, those are two of the greatest words I have ever heard!

+ Chapter 15

Processing the Past

Understanding the Importance of Sexual Histories

Every person has a sexual history. Whether you entered marriage as a virgin or with a number of sexual experiences, you brought with you a sexual history, and you continue to add to that history day by day.

A person's sexual history often begins with their earliest sexual memory. For some people, their first sexual memory is hearing someone else talk about sex. Of course, hearing about sex from a parent you love and trust is much different than hearing about sex from friends at school. For others, their earliest sexual memory is rooted in some form of abuse, a violation that skewed their understanding of God's design and purposes.

Each time a man or woman is impacted sexually by a person or experience — whether positively or negatively — it can have a lasting effect on what they believe about sexuality. This process is called sexual imprinting. A person experiences sexual imprinting when they initially hear about sex, receive their first kiss, or have a sexual experience. Further imprinting can occur through visual stimulation, pornography, masturbation, and experiencing orgasm. Sexual imprinting develops a pattern for what a person will expect in sexual experiences.

In every case, a person's positive or negative sexual history and imprinting has a tremendous impact on their life and directly influences their attitudes about sex. It is a part of who they are and how they view God, themselves, and their spouse.

Unprocessed, negative sexual imprinting from the past dramatically affects a person's sexual perceptions and behaviors. For some, the memories are so painful they have never shared their sexual history with anyone, not even their spouse.

I (Anne) met with a woman who was filing for divorce after less than two years of marriage. She felt like her world was collapsing.

At our first meeting she confessed to being unwilling to engage in sex with her husband. Her feelings about sex were so negative that she knew she needed help. Since sexual imprinting has a tremendous impact on how a person views sex, we reviewed her sexual history. She said she was a virgin when she got married. As she relayed stories about her past, I noticed she placed a great deal of emphasis on her virginity. She seemed almost proud of her obedience to God in this area.

As she processed her sexual history, I noticed that she was trying very hard to avoid talking about certain seasons in her life. Eventually, she revealed that as a young girl she had been sexually abused by a family member. Growing up in a Christian home, this negative sexual imprinting had devastated her. She tried to protect herself by denying what had happened. In an attempt to overcome the shame she felt, she became a peak performer and a perfectionist. She also tried to conceal her shame by maintaining rigid physical boundaries with men. This allowed her to stay emotionally distant and gave her a sense of control.

Then in her late thirties, the desire to marry and begin a family became greater than her fear of intimacy. Soon after she was married, her unresolved pain began to surface. Sexual intimacy paralyzed her. Her inability to fully participate in sex with the freedom and joy God intended became an obstacle that ended up destroying her marriage.

Over time she began to see how the enemy's strategy of negative sexual imprinting had influenced every relationship in her life. She realized that her rigid physical boundaries were a form of self-protection rather than a choice to obey God. This woman opened her heart to healing and asked God to give her a renewed perspective on His design for sex.

PROCESSING YOUR SEXUAL HISTORY

Obviously, sexual imprinting and histories are rarely entirely negative. While we all live with the consequences of sin, many people have experienced positive sexual imprinting. They were taught about purity and God's design for marriage, and they were encouraged to protect not only their bodies but also their minds from unhealthy sexual encounters.

However, in our counseling we've worked with countless people who are dealing with the consequences of a sinful past. As they review their sexual history, shame and regret are usually a part of their story. If a person's sexual history is full of guilt or pain, they often deny the impact it has on

Body Oneness

their life. Avoiding the reality of the past becomes a coping mechanism for something they believe they can't change.

People who have not processed their sexual history often struggle with self-condemning thoughts that play over in their minds. Others wrestle with the cycle of shame, fear, and control. They secretly wonder, *What if someone finds out who I am or what I've done?*

One woman we counseled said, "Sometimes I feel like I am punishing myself for the past. I really believe God has forgiven me. The problem is I can't seem to forgive myself. At times I hold back sexually and don't give myself permission to really enjoy sex. My condemning thoughts are like a self-imposed form of penance. Nothing seems to take away the shame."

Sex is more than a physical act. It involves a person's spirit, soul, and body. Therefore, sexual imprinting and sexual histories will influence a person's perceptions, behaviors, and belief system. Taking time to process how your expectations and perspectives on sex, as well as your spouse's, have been shaped by the past is essential to growing in intimacy and enjoying God's design for body oneness.

There is no specific formula or steps for processing one's sexual history. However, we do encourage couples to follow certain principles that line up with the Bible:

Principle 1: Every person is unique. Therefore, each person's sexual history and imprinting will be different, and how each individual processes those realities will vary. As much as people want specific steps, we believe it is wiser to offer biblical principles. The best counsel we can give is to point people to God. The Bible says, "True wisdom and power are found in God; counsel and understanding are his."[1]

Principle 2: Trust is always built on truth. Our experience is that the enemy uses a few familiar strategies to attempt to destroy God's design for sexuality. For example, he tries to convince people to engage in sex before marriage by introducing deceiving thoughts, such as, *Everyone is doing it. Just go for it. What's the big deal? You're in a committed relationship. This is the twenty-first century!* Once a person sins sexually, the enemy introduces even more lies and condemning thoughts. The good news is that once a lie is uncovered it can be exchanged for the truth of God's Word. Processing your sexual history is an opportunity to embrace the truth and to build trust with God and your spouse.

Principle 3: Commitment is foundational to total honesty. In other words, be careful about who you choose to open your heart to. We live in a world where people are emotionally distant and their relationships are layered. After the first sin, the man and woman sewed fig leaves to cover themselves. This was their attempt to create a layer between themselves and God as well as between the two of them.

In the desire to tear away the layers we all have created, people mistakenly conclude that complete disclosure will provide deep levels of acceptance and love. As a general principle we agree with Larry Crabb's comment, "Total openness without total commitment is not the answer to the problem of layered relationships."[2] However, in search of intimacy, people often place a high value on total honesty rather than focusing on commitment.

When the two of us were in our early twenties, we decided to join a small group. We had never been in a Bible study before. In fact, we had never read the Bible. So we were feeling a bit uncertain as we walked into a couple's home for the first time one Sunday and joined a group of *born-again* Christians.

As the evening began we noticed a folder in front of us. It contained a list of icebreaker questions: *Are you married? Do you have children? If so, how many? What are their names and ages? Where do you live? Why did you decide to be a part of this group? Who is your best friend, and why?* After the leader gave a brief introduction, we were asked to take turns introducing ourselves to the group by choosing a few of the questions from the sheet and sharing our answers.

As the exercise began, we noticed that people were offering much more information than they were originally asked to share. It wasn't long before we began hearing stories of divorce and struggles with addictions. We weren't used to hearing such personal information shared so openly in a room of total strangers. Being new to the group, we both were confused by the direction the ice breakers were taking. People shared stories that night that we thought they should have taken to their grave. It felt like we were trapped in a bad episode of The *Jerry Springer Show*. Instead of "breaking the ice," the exercise actually had the opposite effect. We could feel ourselves emotionally withdrawing. As young newlyweds we wondered, *What have we gotten ourselves into?* When it was our turn, we decided to just stick with the questions on the sheet. As a result, our answers seemed to pale in comparison.

We tell this part of the story to illustrate a point. Growing in intimacy with God and others takes time. There are no shortcuts. In fact, the decision to prematurely disclose personal information can often block intimacy with others.

In processing your personal history for the purpose of growth and maturity, it's important to be discerning in who you talk with. Choose someone who is committed to walking with you. For some, that may be a professional counselor. For others, it may be a trusted friend who is wise and perceptive.

Follow the example of Jesus who begins every relationship with commitment. His death on the cross is His commitment to every person. This unselfish act of love invites people to trust Him with the truth of who they are. Jesus never barges into a person's life demanding a public confession. Instead He creates an environment of safety and security where people can enter into relationship with Him and others. It is through relationship that we find forgiveness and intimacy.

The Bible reminds believers, "Watch over your heart with all diligence, for from it flow the springs of life."[3] One way to guard your heart is by choosing godly, trustworthy people who are committed to walking with you as you process your sexual history. Sharing the secrets and intimacies of the heart prematurely with the wrong people can lead to greater levels of pain and confusion. We have witnessed God's healing during powerful public testimonies. However, we encourage people to begin their process of disclosing intimate details of their life first with the Lord, next with their spouse, and then with trusted friends before they decide to go public.

MOVING TOWARD LOVE, FORGIVENESS, AND ACCEPTANCE

The enemy knows the power of sex. He knows that men and women are created as sexual beings made in the image of God. With this knowledge he strategically looks for ways to distort a person's understanding of God's design for body oneness. Some of his strategies include pornography, abuse, promiscuity, and abortion. These distortions dramatically impact a person's sexual identity. They block men and women from experiencing the sexual freedom and celebration God intended for marriage. This is why it is so important for couples to process their sexual history and understand the impact that sexual imprinting has on their marriage.

There is no specific formula for processing sexual histories. Following godly principles and listening to the Holy Spirit is better than relying on programs or detailed steps. Even the best counselors often see as man sees, but the Lord always sees the heart.[4] However, we believe you'll find that incorporating the following practices will help you move toward finding love, forgiveness, and acceptance, first from God and then from yourself, your spouse, and others:

+ Always begin with prayer.
+ Invite and listen to the counsel of the Holy Spirit. He is the Comforter and Counselor.
+ Study Scripture. Ask the Lord to teach you about His design for sexuality.
+ Grow in understanding forgiveness. Those who have not received forgiveness from the Lord will find it difficult to forgive themselves or others.
+ Guard your heart by taking time to process. Don't rush; healing takes time.
+ Involve other mature Christians and seek professional counsel if needed.

Please note: While it's important for couples to share their sexual history, we do not recommend discussing specific details. Our experience is that a spouse will not benefit from having this information. Instead these details only fill their mind with images they inevitably regret having. Detailed

Body Oneness

disclosure of specific events can become an obstacle to advancing in soul and body oneness.

Remember, the goal is not to wallow in the darkness of the past but to expose it to the healing light of God's truth so you can advance in intimacy with Him and your spouse.

I (Anne) remember an event early in our ministry when the two of us were teaching at a premarital seminar. After we completed the session on sexuality, a couple in their midtwenties approached us. The young man walked with a certain swagger. His body language and demeanor gave a definite impression of arrogance. On the other hand, the woman with him looked down at the floor with her shoulders slumped. It was as if she was covered with a blanket of shame.

"Hello!" the young man spoke with confident assurance. "My name is Bob and this is my fiancée, Renee." He gave each of us a firm handshake while Renee stood in the background. "We recently got engaged," he continued, "and we plan to get married next year. When you were talking about processing our sexual history, I was struggling. You see, my fiancée has had a very active sexual past. She had sexual relations with many men before meeting me."

As Bob rambled on sharing intimate details of Renee's sexual history, my heart began to pound. I wondered if he had her permission to share that information with us. I looked at Renee and noticed tears streaming down her cheeks. She looked embarrassed and ashamed but never said a word.

Bob pressed on, seemingly unaware of his fiancée's emotions as he focused on sharing *his* dilemma. It felt as if he was emotionally stripping her in front of us as he revealed her sexual history. I don't think she had a clue about what Bob was going to say next.

He finally concluded his monologue: "To tell you the truth, I am really struggling with forgiving her. I think it's because I am a virgin and have always been able to maintain purity. I don't have a sexual past. But every time we are together, my mind is filled with pictures of Renee with other men. I am really struggling with this. Can you help her?"

I found it interesting he didn't ask if we could help him.

Tim glanced over to me as if to say, "Would you like to handle this or should I?"

I paused for a moment and took a deep breath. Then I looked this young man in the eyes and said, "I really don't know what you should do, Bob."

Turning toward Renee, I said, "I have no idea what to tell Bob, but I have a suggestion for you." I gently lifted her chin with my hand and looked her directly in the eyes. "Renee, we have three daughters. If you were my daughter, I would encourage you to take off that ring and give it back to this man. You deserve to be loved by someone who knows the unconditional love and forgiveness available through Jesus Christ."

Tim switched into damage-control mode. He was squeezing my arm, trying to get my attention and persuade me to change my strategy. But as I continued talking to Renee, her tears stopped. Her demeanor changed as she began to lift her head and shoulders.

Scrambling to keep things from deteriorating, Tim suggested they make an appointment to meet with us so we could discuss the issue further. But Renee interrupted him. She confidently said, "I don't think we need another meeting, Bob. I think I finally get it." She looked directly into his eyes as she took off her engagement ring. Handing it back to him, she said, "I'm sorry, but I won't be marrying you!"

I confess that my response to Bob may not have been my finest hour. If I could go back and replay that scene, I'm sure I would handle it differently. On most days, my personality and style of relating is much less direct and less confrontational than Tim's. However, I believe God saw the intentions of my heart and used them to help this woman begin to heal in spite of my less-than-subtle approach.

That day marked the end of their relationship and the beginning of a new life for Renee as she got professional Christian counseling to help her process her sexual history. She knew she could never fully love and forgive someone else until she loved and forgave herself.

A few years later she attended another premarital seminar we were leading. At the end, she walked up to us and said, "I want you both to meet the man I am going to marry."

Her new fiancé shook our hands and thanked us. He continued by saying, "I want you to know that I love Renee with all my heart. I love her past, her present, and our future together." Tears filled our eyes as he declared his love for his bride-to-be. Looking into this young man's eyes, we saw him as a reflection of Jesus. We congratulated them both and prayed that God would give them a marriage made in heaven.

Renee's story underscores the fact that love, forgiveness, and acceptance must first be found in God. When a person experiences these from God, it is amazing how these same traits can be seen and experienced with others.

We encourage you to move forward in processing your sexual history so that, rather than creating an obstacle in your marriage, it can be an *opportunity* to Reflect and Reveal the love, compassion, and goodness of God.

In the next chapter we'll look at some specific ways to break free of any negative aspects of your sexual history and imprinting that may be revealed as you process your past.

+ Chapter 16

Soul Ties

Breaking the Ungodly Bonds Created by Past Sexual Sin

God designed people to live in community with others. He created men and women to long for and enjoy a full spectrum of relationships, including...

+ a husband and wife relationship
+ a parent and child relationship
+ a relationship between friends such as Jonathan and David. Jonathan's soul was knit with the soul of David. Jonathan loved David as he loved himself.[1]
+ a God-centered relationship between the members of the church[2]

When guided by godly principles and love, these relationships are a good thing. However, since the first sin, the enemy has distorted God's original design by offering a counterfeit.

Whereas healthy relationships create godly bonds and attachments based on Christ-like love, the enemy uses sinful and unhealthy relationships to create ungodly attachments — also called *soul ties* — with other people. The enemy uses these soul ties to block intimacy between individuals and God, their spouse, and others. These ungodly bonds can be sexual or nonsexual. They can occur between people of the same sex as well as between people of the opposite sex.

The terms *ungodly bond* and *soul tie* are not found in the Bible. However, people are warned against ungodly relationships throughout the Scriptures. Here are a few examples of ways the enemy distorts God's original design for relationships:

+ adultery — a sexual relationship between two people, at least one of whom is married to someone else
+ fornication — any sexual relationship between two people who are not married to each other
+ sexual abuse (more on this below)
+ physically, emotionally, and/or verbally abusive relationships
+ unhealthy emotional attachments outside of marriage
+ unhealthy parent-child relationships — parents who do not release their children into adulthood in a healthy manner; parents who are overly involved in their adult child's life; a parent who blocks a child from cleaving to their spouse; a child who is unable to live

independently from their parents; or any unhealthy physical or emotional parent-child attachments

+ unhealthy counseling relationships — an inappropriate bond, whether sexual or nonsexual, between a counselor and client; any behavior by a person in a position of trust that results in an unhealthy dependence or attachment

+ unhealthy friendships — relationships where one or more participants exhibit control, manipulation, exploitive behavior, unnatural affection, guilt, envy, enmeshment, or codependency

A NOTE TO VICTIMS OF SEXUAL ABUSE

The number of men and woman who are victims of sexual abuse is growing each day. Recent statistics report that approximately every two minutes someone in the United States is sexually assaulted. It is estimated that 1 in 6 women and 1 in 33 men will be the victim of a sexual assault in their lifetime. College age women are four times more likely to be sexually assaulted.

What kind of impact do these events leave? Victims of sexual assault are three times more likely to suffer from depression; six times more likely to suffer from post-traumatic stress disorder; thirteen times more likely to abuse alcohol; twenty-six times more likely to abuse drugs; and four times more likely to contemplate suicide.[3]

Sexual abuse is both a sin and a crime that carries an almost immeasurable impact for the victim. As we've noted before, any sexual activity not only touches a person's body but leaves an imprint on the spirit and soul. Thus, any form of sexual abuse has the potential to significantly affect the way a person relates to God and others.

Dr. Dan B. Allender has devoted years of practice to the study and healing of those recovering from the "soul deadening" impact of abuse. His work with victims of abuse has given hope and help to countless people. One of his central messages to victims is that they can experience freedom from the guilt of past abuse. He underscores this message by proclaiming, "What occurred is not your fault!"[4] He goes on to observe, "The damage of past abuse sets in motion a complex scheme of self-protective defenses

Body Oneness

that operate largely outside of our awareness, guiding our interactions with others, determining the spouse we select, the jobs we pursue, the theologies we embrace, and the fabric of our entire lives."[5] In other words, abuse is no small thing. Its effects are far reaching.

Therefore, as we continue exploring the subject of soul ties, it is important to make a clear distinction: unlike other soul ties, sexual abuse is a crime committed by a perpetrator against an innocent person who is no more responsible for the crime than any other crime. This is why we do not place sexual abuse soul ties in the same category as soul ties formed through adultery or fornication. We absolutely do not want to project a sense of judgment on a victim who is already struggling with shame or to imply that the abuse was in any way his or her fault.

In Christian circles, victims are sometimes encouraged to overcome the effects of abuse by simply determining to put the past behind them and move on. While this may seem noble, it diminishes the tragic reality of such crimes. In the next few pages we'll discuss the process of breaking soul ties, an important step for anyone whose sexual history includes negative elements. However, for victims of sexual abuse, it is only a part of the healing process on the road toward freedom and wholeness. If you have endured sexual abuse, we urge you to seek professional help from a counselor trained in this area.

THE POWER OF SEXUAL BONDS

One thing we'd like to make clear from the outset is that sexual sin is not worse than other sins. Jesus had much stronger words for those who committed sins of pride, idolatry, unforgiveness, religiosity, and unrighteous judgment than for those who committed sexual sin. In fact, as we see in the stories of the woman caught in adultery, the Samaritan woman at the well, and the prostitute, He confronted people who unrighteously judged those who committed sexual sins.[6] He said, "He who is without sin among you, let him be the first to throw a stone."[7]

However, Jesus never ignored, accepted, or condoned sexual sins. With love and grace, He addressed the people involved in sexual sins: "I do not condemn you either. Go. From now on sin no more."[8]

So while sexual sins are not worse than other sins, the *consequences* they carry are often much worse. This is why the Bible makes a clear distinction between sexual sins and every other sin.

"Do you not know that the one who joins himself to a prostitute is one body with her? For He says, 'The two shall become one flesh.' But the one who joins himself to the Lord is one spirit with Him. Flee immorality. Every other sin that a man commits is outside the body, but the immoral man sins against his own body."[9]

Sexual sins committed against a person's own body can result in shame, sexually transmitted diseases, divorce, betrayal, children born out of wedlock, abortion, broken relationships, and broken hearts. These consequences often leave lifelong wounds that lead to mistrust, shame, fear, and control.

A woman who made an appointment to see me (Anne) explained that she didn't have anyone she could talk to about the problems she was experiencing in her marriage. She was in her thirties and had been married about a year. What she loved about her relationship with her husband was their ability to be honest with each other. She said, "There isn't anything we can't talk about — except this."

Prior to getting married, they were both honest with each other about their sexual histories. The woman told me that she and her husband each had several sexual partners before they met and married. She continued, "…almost every time my husband and I make love, I have images in my mind of people other than him. Some are past sexual partners, others are just fantasy. My thought life feels like it's out of my control. I love my husband very much," she said, "and I guess I am feeling like I'm being unfaithful to him with my thought life. But I can't seem to control it."

People often admit to struggling with sexual visual images of another person or fantasy while they are having sex with their spouse. They describe their mind as a movie theater that plays the same films over and over again. This distraction during lovemaking blocks a person from bonding to their spouse. When we review their sexual history, they often reveal ungodly bonds with previous sexual partners or from exposure to pornography.

Body Oneness

We can't emphasize enough the fact that sex is much more than a physical act. It involves a person's spirit, soul, and body. God designed sexual intercourse to be so powerful that it makes a lasting impact that becomes a bond between two people. This strong bond, or attachment, is part of the glue that holds a marriage together.

When a person joins sexually to another person, the two become part of each other. The Bible describes this bond as becoming "one flesh." When a person becomes one flesh with another, they are connected spiritually, mentally, emotionally, and physically. This powerful and lasting connection takes place regardless of circumstances. This is why abuse, incest, rape, and premarital or extramarital sexual relationships are such a distortion of God's design. God never intended for people to be bonded or attached to someone they are not in a lifelong covenant with. This is why God reserves sex for marriage.

There are consequences when a person becomes one flesh with another person outside of a marriage covenant. Let's look briefly at these effects, using the simple figures "Roger and Sally" to illustrate the complicated connections that can result from sexual sin.

Roger and Sally had premarital sex. Their decision to engage in sex outside of a marriage covenant resulted in them becoming one flesh.

Roger   **Sally**

Let's assume that, before meeting Roger, Sally had three sexual partners. When she joined her body with each of these partners she became one flesh with each of them. Now Sally has become one flesh with a total of four men, including Roger.

Before Roger met Sally, he also had three sexual partners, which means he has become one flesh with a total of four women, including Sally.

Of course, each of Roger and Sally's sexual partners has a sexual history as well, although people's sexual histories are difficult to track. Most are unaware of the sexual history of the person they engage in sex with. For the sake of illustration, let's say the three men Sally had sex with before Roger each had three other sexual partners.

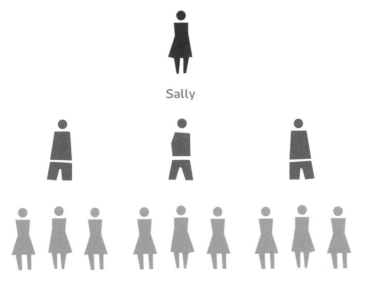

Soul Ties

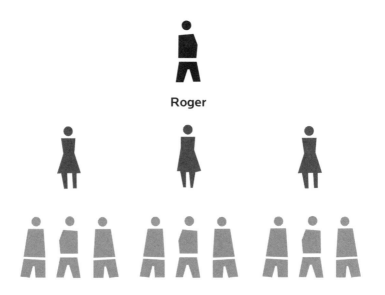

This example illustrates that Sally could potentially have unhealthy connections with twelve other people before meeting Roger. When she begins having sex with Roger, the number increases.

Let's assume Roger's sexual history follows a similar pattern. The three women Roger had sex with each had three other sexual partners.

Roger

This example illustrates that Roger could potentially have unhealthy bonds with twelve other people before meeting Sally. When he began having sex with Sally, the number increased. Together, Roger and Sally could have unhealthy bonds with at least twenty-five people.

BREAKING FREE

Sadly, the preceding illustration is not at all out of the ordinary in describing the ungodly bonds, or soul ties, many people bring with them into marriage these days. The result is that they are inhibited from advancing in marital oneness.

Most couples experience some kind of sexual struggle within marriage, often because their individual sexual imprintings and histories lead to different expectations. When ungodly sexual bonds, or soul ties, are present, they inevitably lead to additional complications that make it difficult for a couple to enjoy spirit, soul, and body oneness.

Some time ago we were leading a REAL LIFE Marriage Advance in the Midwest. The participants were primarily young professionals who had been married between five and ten years, and the majority of the couples in the seminar were new Christians. Knowing this, we had decided not to teach on soul ties, feeling that concept might be too advanced for this audience. The two of us agreed to place a stronger focus on communication and conflict management.

However, at every seminar we invite the Holy Spirit to direct the focus of our teaching, so there are times when we get off our notes. At this particular gathering, the weekend was going great. The group was attentive and eager to learn. At some point during the sexuality session, I (Anne) sensed the Holy Spirit wanted us to change direction and include the teaching on ungodly sexual bonds and soul ties.

Since we were already in the middle of the afternoon session, I was unable to discuss this change in direction with Tim. Fortunately, after years of team teaching, we have learned how to communicate to one another in nonverbal ways. I made eye contact with Tim, then drew a stick figure on my notes to signal him about the possible change in plans. He looked over and nodded in agreement, also sensing that we should teach on soul ties.

Then Tim introduced the topic to our audience by drawing stick figures on the marker board. While he illustrated, I jumped in and explained what the Bible said about two people becoming one when they engage in sex. We went on to show the consequences of multiple sexual relationships and how they affect marriage. As the teaching ended, we encouraged the audience to go back to their rooms and spend some time with the Lord. We suggested they ask the Lord's forgiveness for any past sexual sins and break any ungodly bonds. The couples left quietly.

The following day, everyone returned for our closing session, which is always one of our favorite parts of a Marriage Advance. Each couple has an opportunity to restate their vows to one another. As they place their wedding rings on their spouse's finger, they ask each other, "Will you

Body Oneness

choose me again today to be your spouse?" Couples kiss as a symbol of their desire to breathe new life into one another. After the renewal of vows, we serve wedding cake and have a celebration.

During this time we always open the microphones for personal testimonies. Couples are invited to come up and thank God for what He has been doing in their heart and marriage throughout the weekend. We call this session time a *Say-So*, drawing on the words of Psalm 107, which reminds us to "let the redeemed of the LORD say so."[10] Hearing men and women give God thanks and praise is a great way to end the weekend.

At this marriage gathering, Tim and I looked at each other in surprise as the first attendee approached the microphone. We recognized her as a woman who had been sitting in the front row throughout the weekend and always appeared to be very disconnected from our teaching. Since she sat directly in front of us, we couldn't help but notice as we were teaching that her arms were crossed and she gave us very little eye contact. Her nonverbal, disinterested demeanor communicated, *What are you two going to teach me that I haven't already heard?*

Now, as this woman stood at the microphone, with her husband by her side, she was shaking and seemed to be holding back tears. Her long, pregnant pause quieted the room. Then she spoke, "I really didn't want to be here this weekend. I have been to so many marriage seminars. I didn't really think I was going to hear anything new. Many of you have known me, my husband, and our children for a long time. What you do not know is this is my second husband."

A ripple of surprise moved through the group. She continued, "There is something else that you do not know about me." Here she paused and took a deep breath. "I was sexually abused by my father and grandfather from the age of three to fourteen. After graduating from high school, I left home. In fact, I ran away from home and into a marriage. I thought my husband would give me the love I was so desperately missing. But my sexual abuse had a toxic effect on my life. After I got married, sex was repulsive to me. After years of struggling, my husband finally just left. He said he couldn't stay in a marriage where there was no sexual intimacy."

She began to weep, and her husband put his arm around her. Composing herself, she continued, "Years after my divorce, God brought this man into my life. He is my soul mate. He has stood by me. He has taken me to counselors and to medical doctors. I've attended prayer meetings where they prayed over me. I've memorized Bible verses and have done whatever else I thought would help. But whatever I did, the visual images of my dad and grandfather continued to haunt me.

"To be honest, I didn't want to attend this Marriage Advance. I didn't think I could hear one more thing about God's wonderful design for sex. My sexuality was destroyed as a child and I have never been able to recover it.

"Until this weekend, I've never heard teaching on soul ties. When I saw the stick figures illustration, I applied the principle to my own life. After the session ended, my husband and I went to our room and reviewed our notes. In faith, we knelt down together as I prayed a simple prayer. I asked God to forgive my dad and my grandfather, to forgive me for blaming myself and taking responsibility for what I had no control over. I asked God to break any ungodly sexual ties or bonds that formed between my dad, my grandfather, and me.

"When my prayer ended there were no lights or sirens, but something was different. I felt a sense of freedom that I have never felt before.

"I'm not saying it's all over and I'm completely healed. I don't pretend to even understand it all...but I want to tell you that last night was the first time that I ever made love with my husband without my father and grandfather being in the bed with me. I thank God for leading me into greater freedom by teaching me how to break these soul ties. I stand here tonight with hope and a renewed faith in God."

As she finished speaking, the room was completely silent. The presence of God was so evident. The couple quietly walked back to their seats and sat down. No one stirred, some were weeping quietly. Just then another woman came to the microphone with a story of sexual abuse. Another couple came forward and then another. People began confessing their inability to forgive themselves and others. They confessed anger, bitterness, adultery, abortions, and other examples of **smaller story** living.

Body Oneness

No one wanted to leave the auditorium that night. We all lingered in the room together. Some were praying, some were huddled in small groups, others were just sitting together holding each other.

We witnessed more sexual healing and breakthroughs in two or three hours than we could write in a book. It was a night that only God could have orchestrated. He began by breaking through the heart of one wounded woman and inviting her to trust Him. Somehow He gave her the strength to forgive her abusers. In faith, she asked the Lord to break any spiritual bond with her abusers and to replace it with a bond between herself and her husband.

As Tim and I headed home the next day this verse came to mind: "God sees not as man sees, for man looks at the outward appearance, but the LORD looks at the heart."[11] In looking at the outward appearance of this church, we thought everyone looked so together. We thought the woman in the front row was bored with the teaching. We thought this group was too young to hear the teaching on ungodly bonds and soul ties. Fortunately, we weren't leading this seminar; God was. He looked past their protective walls and heard the cry of their heart. He redirected our teaching and invited many to trust Him. We drove home thanking God for the gift of the Holy Spirit.

THE PROBLEM OF PORNOGRAPHY

Ungodly bonding can take place even without physical contact. The enemy frequently offers counterfeit forms of intimacy to replace God's original design, and one of his favorite tools is pornography.

Pornography can be defined as an explicit display or description of sexual activity or nudity meant to excite viewers or readers. Obviously not all nudity is pornography. Museums exhibit great works of art with nudity. But when sexuality is displayed in unhealthy and immoral ways, it becomes destructive.

Pornography is a rapidly growing, potentially terminal cancer that attacks the heart, mind, and soul of a person. In a society that places a great deal of emphasis on instant gratification, pornography is an issue of growing concern. In a few short decades pornography has grown from a few seedy bookstores to an industry that generates billions of dollars. No longer are people forced to endure the embarrassment of patronizing adult bookstores; instead users both young and old can access pornography with the click of a mouse in the privacy of their homes or offices. The ease in access and the anonymity this provides has enabled pornography to flourish, with devastating results.

Viewing of pornography often is associated with masturbation, and together the images and physical experience provide sexual stimulation that impacts a person spiritually, emotionally, and chemically. A bond is created with the experience or image that results in sexual imprinting.

A Relationship Invaded by Strangers

A woman walked up to us after a Marriage Advance. After introducing herself, she explained that our teaching had prompted her to share the story of how pornography impacted her marriage.

"When my husband and I got married we had never been involved with any kind of pornography. About five years ago we were struggling in our sex life. It's not like we had major problems. I think we were just in a sexual slump. We were facing the normal pressures that accompany marriage and raising a family." She paused for a moment and asked, "Do you ever feel like life is running you instead of you running your life? Looking back, I think our sex life took a hit from all the stress we were facing. We had no time for each other. We always put our relationship last on the list. After a while, our desire for each other was at an all-time low.

"My husband is a solution-based thinker. He's the type of person who likes to fix things. I guess he was trying to fix our sex life. One day he brought home a pornographic video. He said some guys at the office were talking about how porn spiced up their sex life. He asked me if I wanted to give it a try. I don't remember having a strong opinion. You might say I was neutral. I think the truth is, I was too tired to even care. We agreed that our sex life was boring, and since I wasn't bringing any other great ideas to the table, we decided to give it a try.

"The reason I'm telling you all this is so you will continue to teach on this

Body Oneness

subject. I wish we had heard years ago some of what you taught today. It would have saved us from a lot of heartache. What started out rather innocently ended up having a tremendously negative impact on both of us. Pornography introduced other people into our sex life. This influenced the way we thought about sex and each other. The sexual charge that it offered was so powerful that it didn't take long before we were watching it more frequently than I ever imagined. We had no idea about the addictive nature of pornography.

"One day I was reviewing our sexual relationship and realized that our solution had become our new problem. What we thought would be the answer to our sexual slump had now become an obsession. As you said, pornography opened the door to lust.

"Our need for pornography was progressive. Over time it became the focus of our sexual relationship. It all happened so fast. It almost felt like a force that pulled us in. In ways it initially increased our sexual desire. But the desire was a fantasy for someone or something other than our spouse. Sex isn't even about us anymore. It's about two disconnected individuals who use each other's bodies to get their own needs met."

She stopped for a moment to hold back her tears. "I can't even believe I'm telling you this. I am so ashamed of what we've done to ourselves and our marriage. After hearing your teaching, I know we have a problem that needs to be addressed."

One characteristic of a pornography addiction is it is always progressive. What satisfies one day will not be enough to satisfy the next. This cycle of addiction slowly consumes a person as they fall deeper into depravity. Once pornography is introduced to a person, it is difficult to stop.

Pornography had become the mistress in this marriage, and its effects were devastating. The enemy is subtle. He looks for a person's weakness and then offers them a counterfeit solution. In marriages where only one spouse is involved with pornography, the results can be just as destructive. Another woman who told us her husband was addicted to pornography said, "I feel angry most of the time. I feel more like a prostitute than a wife. My husband uses my body to have sex with his most recent fantasy. It makes me want to withhold sex completely. I don't know what to do."

Body Oneness

What Is the Answer to Pornography Addiction?

There are generally two approaches to overcoming a pornography addiction. The first is what we call the discipline approach. This approach instructs people to "just say no." For the most part, we find the discipline approach to be ineffective. When we open the Bible to the book of Genesis, we read that in the beginning God told Adam and Eve to eat freely from any tree in the garden. He instructed them to "just say no" to the tree of knowledge of good and evil. As we all know, the "just say no" campaign was a bust. Adam and Eve failed. Certainly discipline helps in victory over addictions, but it takes more than discipline to successfully defeat the power of a pornography addiction.

The second approach is the passion approach. Rather than "just saying no," this approach focuses on healing by passionately embracing God and His truths. Jesus is the Way and the Truth and the Life. We believe the antidote to lust is godly sorrow. Sorrow leads to repentance. Repentance brings the promise and hope of a better way. The Bible says, "The kindness of God leads you to repentance."[12] Even repentance is a God thing.

Pornography is a spiritual battle that requires spiritual weapons. The passion model challenges people to fight lust and pornography with the power and promises of God. It involves believing and stepping into the truths of God instead of the lies of Satan. A person typically does not give something up until they find something else they want more. The passion approach to addiction replaces lies of the enemy with the truths of God.

We offer these steps for people struggling with a pornography addiction. We refer to these as the Ten **R**s:

1.   Repent, ask the Lord to forgive you. "The kindness of God leads you to repentance."[13]

2.   Remove pornography from your life (computer, films, magazines…). "Flee immorality. Every other sin that a man commits is outside the body, but the immoral man sins against his own body."[14]

Body Oneness

3. **Refocus** your attention on something else (renew your mind). "And do not be conformed to this world, but be transformed by the renewing of your mind, so that you may prove what the will of God is, that which is good and acceptable and perfect."[15]

4. **Reveal** your struggle to a trusted friend/counselor. "Therefore, confess your sins to one another, and pray for one another so that you may be healed."[16]

5. **Resist** and **Renounce** the enemy. "Submit therefore to God. Resist the devil and he will flee from you. Draw near to God and He will draw near to you."[17]

6. **Realize** your vulnerability. "Be of sober spirit, be on the alert. Your adversary, the devil, prowls around like a roaring lion, seeking someone to devour."[18]

7. **Reclaim** God's authority in your life. "Greater is He who is in you than he who is in the world."[19]

8. **Relationships** with healthy friends are critical. "Where there is no guidance the people fall, but in abundance of counselors there is victory."[20]

9. **Remember** this is a spiritual battle. "For our struggle is not against flesh and blood, but against the rulers, against the powers, against the world forces of this darkness, against the spiritual forces of wickedness in the heavenly places."[21]

10. **Rejoice** in freedom and victory. "Rejoice always; pray without ceasing."[22]

Pornography often appears to be harmless, but it advances with tornado-like devastation, leaving a path of destroyed lives, marriages, and families. It can only be defeated through passion, purity, and commitment. The enemy wants a person to believe there is no hope. That is a lie. Pornography is **smaller story** "It's all about me" living that leads to death.

The Bible declares, "If God is for us, who can be against us?"[23] God is a God who heals, and He invites you to step into the **Larger Story** and let Him orchestrate your healing. If you are struggling with pornography, talk to someone and get some help. When you accept God as the main character and involve others in the process of repentance, you can experience healing and deliverance from this addiction.

HOW TO BREAK AN UNGODLY BOND OR SOUL TIE

Whether formed through pornography, past sexual encounters, or other images and experiences, ungodly bonds will continue to undermine your efforts at spirit, soul, and body oneness until they are directly confronted and broken.

How do you break these unhealthy soul ties? Once again, there is no specific formula. If you are in relationship with God, talk to Him. Pour out your heart as David did in Psalm 142. Here is a list of some areas to process with the Lord.

1.   If you have been involved in any kind of sexual sin, such as adultery, fornication, or pornography, repent. Tell God you are sorry. Ask Him to forgive you. Receive His forgiveness. *Lord, I am sorry for* _____ . *Will you forgive me?*

2.   Forgive the other person involved. Note: If you are a victim of abuse, you have been sinned against. Ask God for the strength to forgive your abuser. *Lord, I choose to forgive* _____ .

3.   Forgive yourself. This is often one of the hardest steps. *Lord, I forgive myself for being involved in this sin. I receive your forgiveness.* Note: If you are a victim of abuse, you might pray, *Lord I forgive myself for any way that I believed that what happened to me was my fault. I receive your forgiveness.*

4.   Ask God to break any ungodly bonds or soul ties. *In the name of Jesus and in the authority I have as a believer, I break any ungodly bond or soul tie between myself and* _____ .

Body Oneness

5.   Bless and release that person. You no longer want to be connected in unhealthy ways. *Lord, I bless* _____ *and release this person from any ungodly connection with me.*

6.   Give thanks to God as you walk in freedom, with a renewed faith in His transforming power. *Thank You, Lord. You are good, and I believe You are good to me.*

With regard to the steps involving forgiveness, it may be helpful to review the chapter on forgiveness. To forgive and bless someone who has taken advantage of, abused, or traumatized you can be very difficult. Also, forgiving yourself can be difficult, especially if you were the initiator in sinful sexual relationships.

A man once approached us after our seminar saying, "I was in the military. Talk about soul ties. I can't remember the number of women I've had sex with. Getting drunk and having sex was a way of life. It's how I survived. How can I possibly break all these soul ties when I don't even know their names?"

We reassured him that God not only knows their names, He knows every detail of a person's past. We encouraged this man to repent of his sins, ask God to break any ungodly bonds or soul ties, and receive God's freedom.

Today God is looking at your heart. Are you teachable? Are you open to engaging in the battle that is raging for your soul? Remember, a good Father hears His children's humble prayers. You can trust Him to hear yours.

IS THIS FOR REAL?

Ungodly bonds or soul ties are not something that we hear about in church. In fact, in all our years of ministry, we have never heard it taught at any marriage seminar or conference. Yet this problem affects almost every person we meet. A counselor recently called us to share the benefits her clients were experiencing as they broke soul ties. This experience encourages us to continue sharing this practical teaching in order to help men and women find freedom.

Body Oneness

However, we recognize that many people are skeptical or question the existence of ungodly bonds and soul ties — and we understand. As Christ followers, we spent decades reading our Bibles, praying, loving, and serving God. There was a time when we declared, *If it is not in my Bible, I don't believe it!* But we no longer make that declaration.

Not everything that we encounter in our walk with God is mentioned in the Bible. For example, youth ministry is not specifically mentioned in the Bible, yet we have invested in youth ministry for decades and still do. In fact, the word Holy Bible is not in the Bible.

As we continue to be exposed to things we don't always understand, we believe God cannot be kept in a box. As we listen to the Holy Spirit, hear people's stories, and witness the healing and breakthroughs people are experiencing, we are forced to our knees. We have made the decision to trust God and be willing to receive new revelation and insights from the Holy Spirit. Following the direction of the Holy Spirit does not always make total sense and may not be directly connected to a specific Bible verse. However, we know that the Holy Spirit never leads us to do something that contradicts the principles in the Bible. In our ministry and our personal lives we continually ask, "Lord, does anything we are doing go against the collective truths and principles You have placed in the Bible?"

As we watch men and women engage in breaking ungodly bonds and soul ties, we see them experience a depth of freedom, healing, and peace they never imagined. This affirms to us the reality and importance of the principles we are teaching.

If you are a pragmatic person who focuses on results, you may be asking the key questions, *Does it work? What are the results?* We challenge you to talk to God right now. Ask the Holy Spirit to show you if you have any ungodly bonds or soul ties (sexual or non-sexual) that need to be broken. If He invites you to take a step of faith, then pray to break the ungodly bonds and soul ties in your life — and then see what happens.

Body Oneness

HONORING YOUR BODY

Sex is for celebration, procreation, protection, pleasure, and comfort. But the enemy works nonstop trying to mess with sexuality. He wants to destroy intimacy through sexual sin, abuse, lies, and distortions. He wants to connect people with ungodly bonds and soul ties.

If your sexual past feels like something you carry through life like a heavy backpack, we bring *good news*. God is a God of second chances. He is much more powerful than the enemy. You can repent from past sins and mistakes and begin a new chapter in your life and in your sexuality. Every person can choose to take steps to grow in purity and in honoring their body.

The Bible says, "Present your bodies a living and holy sacrifice, acceptable to God, which is your spiritual service of worship."[24] As a follower of Christ, you are the residence of an honored Guest — the Holy Spirit — which means you should think about and treat your body as a place of honor.

Honor is defined as personal dignity. It includes respect, integrity, and strong moral character. Honor adheres to ethical principles. A person's sexual reputation is to be associated with honor. How a person treats their own body and the bodies of others is an honor issue. Husbands and wives must lead by choosing to honor their body and their spouse's body. As spiritual moms and dads we need to model for and teach the emerging generation the meaning and importance of honor in relationships and in maintaining sexual purity. Children from an early age must be taught to honor their bodies. Honor is so important, it needs to be taught in schools and preached from pulpits.

If you have honored your body by maintaining purity, we thank God for the protection it provided you and for the strength for you to obey. We believe your purity is a gift that God has given you to encourage others.

If you have dishonored your body in any way, or if you are currently living in sin, we encourage you to repent, to break ungodly bonds, and to turn away from sinful behavior. Receive God's forgiveness, forgive yourself, and then "go and sin no more."[25]

If you are a victim of sexual abuse, you have been sinned against. Remember, it's not your fault! We have a word of encouragement: God is a God of restoration. He can make all things new. We have personally experienced His transforming power in our lives and have witnessed this in the hearts and lives of others. Seek professional counsel to help you walk in healing and wholeness as you take back what the enemy has stolen from you. Don't settle for less than what God intended for you as His precious child.

Growing in God's grace, understanding, and forgiveness brings healing and helps you advance in intimacy with God and others. No matter where you are right now, ask God to delete any thoughts from your mind that distract you from Him. We pray God leads you into truth and righteousness. We ask God to help you see yourself the way He sees you.

+ Chapter 17

Keeping the Covenant

Standing Firm Against the Tide of Adultery and Divorce

Jewish wedding celebrations are filled with rich tradition. In biblical times weddings often included a reception prior to the actual ceremony. The bride and groom would sit next to each other on chairs, like a king and queen. They ate and drank freely while enjoying music and dancing. Guests would sing songs of celebration and toast the upcoming marriage. Such celebrations often lasted more than a week.

Jesus attended weddings like this. In fact, the celebration of a husband and wife becoming one served as the scene of Jesus' first public miracle. At this particular wedding feast they ran out of wine. In response to the shortage of wine, Jesus called the servants to fill some large ceremonial hand-washing pitchers to the brim with water. He then turned the water into the finest wine…and the band played on.

Rather than week-long feasts of celebration, modern weddings typically consist of a thirty-minute service followed by cake and punch served in the basement of the church. Nevertheless, many traditions containing rich symbolism live on. For example, in one tradition that sometimes takes place at Jewish weddings, the mothers of the bride and groom break a glass plate on the floor. The glass plate represents marriage and the seriousness of the marriage covenant. Like the plate, every couple's relationship is fragile. It must be treated with love, care, and respect so it doesn't break. This tradition is a visual reminder to honor the marriage relationship by taking care of each other. What God joins together is sacred and should not be broken.

At a wedding we attended a few years ago, a glass of wine was poured for the bride and groom. They sipped from a shared glass as the pastor explained the significance to those gathered as witnesses. He said, "The bride and groom are presenting their hearts, lives, and bodies to God and to each other. The sweet wine they drink from the shared glass represents oneness and sexual intimacy. These gifts are from God and are reserved for them within the covenant of marriage."

When the bride and groom finished drinking their wine, the pastor took the empty wine glass and wrapped it in a cloth. He placed it on the floor in front of the couple. The groom joyfully stomped the glass under his foot as it broke into hundreds of pieces. This symbolized their commitment to faithfulness and fidelity. The pastor announced, "No one else will ever drink the wine of sweet love from their marriage. No one else is to ever share in their sexual union." Later that evening the shattered glass was placed in a container and presented to the couple as a tangible reminder of their covenant with God and each other.

AN ATTACK ON THE HEART OF MARRIAGE

There is power in *covenant*. The word covenant is used over three hundred times in the Bible, and it describes something much more serious than commitment. Marital covenant is to be an "until death do us part" arrangement. Dying to self and submitting to God and one's spouse are necessary to walk out covenant.

But some people find that the price for a God-honoring marriage is more than they are willing to spend. The truth is, real life is difficult. Relationships are difficult. Marriage is difficult. The Bible says, "Those who marry will face many troubles in this life."[1] Couples often begin marriage with a false assumption that they are equipped for the job. Many couples long to live out God's design for marriage but do not have the necessary tools to navigate through the obstacles of life. When you stop and think about it, most states have absolutely no marriage requirements. Being a certain age and purchasing a license is about all you need. When it comes to figuring out how to stay married and raise the next generation, couples find themselves pretty much on their own.

What's more, the enemy hates when a husband and wife live out covenant with God and each other. He understands the power and protection in covenant, so he encourages adultery and divorce as the quick-fix solution to the inevitable bumps every marriage will encounter.

These days adultery — defined as a married person engaging in sexual relations with someone other than their spouse — is unashamedly promoted in our culture. For example, television programs that could not have been dreamed about a few decades ago glorify "swinging" — a husband and wife agreeing to engage in sex with others. What God created as a sacred celebration of marriage and covenant is distorted and mocked on primetime television.

Even within our churches it seems the sin of adultery is often swept under the carpet, and divorce has become commonplace. The concept of honoring covenant and working through marital struggles has been replaced by *it's-all-about-me* choices and lifestyles. Current statistics indicate little difference between the divorce rate of churched and unchurched couples. The fallout of this laissez-faire view of the marital covenant negatively affects our entire culture — and leaves marriages vulnerable to the enemy's attack.

A woman called me (Anne) to make an appointment to see us, along with her husband. She explained on the phone that she felt like her life had just exploded and she had no idea where to begin to pick up the pieces.

Through tears she said, "Last week I was going through the bills and noticed some unfamiliar charges on our credit card. When my husband got home and I questioned him, I guess I was surprised at his defensiveness. We began to argue as we usually do, and before I realized what had happened, he confessed that he had met his 'soul mate.' I could not believe he was having an adulterous relationship with another woman. On the other hand, so many pieces to the puzzle began to come together for me."

She began to sob uncontrollably, so she stopped speaking until she could calm down a bit. Then she continued, "I knew we had problems. We have been growing farther and farther apart. Why didn't I see this coming? It's so easy to get caught up with work and the kids that I guess I completely missed the warning signs that have been flashing for years."

Although her husband had little hope for the marriage, he had agreed to come to counseling. When they arrived at the office, the emotional disconnect between them was clear. Just having them together in the same room felt like a nuclear explosion ready to detonate. The mounting tension between them was palpable as we attempted to get a brief history.

We learned that they met after college and had been married over fifteen years. They were raising a growing family, attended a vibrant church, were flourishing in their careers, and owned a beautiful home. In every way that is important in the world's eyes, they appeared to be very successful.

When we asked the husband how we could help him, he wasn't sure how to answer. In a monotone voice he finally said, "I don't even know why I came. This marriage is so over that I can't even imagine what anyone could say to change things." He avoided any eye contact when he spoke. Wanting to end the meeting, he simply declared, "I want a divorce. I don't think I ever really loved my wife. I know that now because I've met my soul mate."

We tried to engage him in conversation about the reality of divorce. Tim asked, "What do you see as some of the effects your decision to divorce will have on your children?"

The husband responded defensively, "My kids will be fine. My dad left my mom when I was growing up, and I turned out okay."

This man saw divorce as the only solution to his pain and problems. He had agreed to counseling only to appease his wife and church friends, but his real desire was to hear someone affirm what he believed in his heart. He wanted to hear someone say that his marriage was beyond repair.

Painful stories like this invite many difficult questions. When did this couple's life-giving relationship begin to die? What could they have done differently? When did their goal become protecting their hearts from more pain? At what point did they begin to use their marriage as a weapon to hurt one another?

By the time couples begin to seriously discuss divorce, many of these questions are being asked too late. So much damage has already been done. So what, if anything, can married couples do to prevent finding themselves in a similarly tragic situation?

GUARD YOUR HEART

First, it's important to understand that adultery is, at its core, a violation of marital oneness and a perversion of God's design for marriage. Certainly, whenever a husband or wife engages in sex with a third party, the exclusivity of their marital and sexual covenant is shattered. However, we believe adultery is not limited to sexual intercourse outside of marriage but can also be defined as emotional intercourse outside of marriage.

Have you ever seen a man and a woman who are not married but are connected emotionally in inappropriate and intimate ways? Whenever a person seeks inappropriate emotional intimacy from someone of the opposite sex other than their spouse, it can lead to sin. Soul oneness in marriage is the intimacy of knowing and being fully known. This deep level of relationship and intimacy is reserved exclusively for marriage. God intended a husband and wife to be one in spirit, soul, and body. Their souls are meant to be united, tied together with cords that cannot be broken. Emotional adultery violates this. It forms an ungodly bond or soul tie between two people that needs to be broken.

Emotional adultery can also be one-sided, taking the form of lustful thoughts about a person other than one's spouse. In His Sermon on the Mount Jesus said, "You have heard that it was said, 'You shall not commit adultery'; but I say to you that everyone who looks at a woman with lust for her has already committed adultery with her in his heart."[2] At the time when Jesus spoke these words, adultery was punishable by death. The punishment of physical death symbolized the spiritual and emotional death of a marriage violated by adultery.

Since physical adultery starts with emotional adultery, we challenge couples to examine their relationships for unhealthy or inappropriate emotional attachments by asking this question: *Would every conversation, interaction, and communication between you and your friend be exactly the same if your spouse was present?*

Many people we talk with defend certain actions and behaviors as "harmless flirtations." We have seen far too often how adultery and divorce can ravage a marriage. To use an old Bible phrase, we say, "He who has ears to hear, let him hear."[3]

If you are a single woman and a married man is flirting with you, "hitting" on you, and/or making any sexual innuendos, we urge you to run away as fast as you can. A married man who is in covenant with his wife but is flirting with you is not worth a second look. You may think this is innocent flirtation, but trust us, this is an invitation for heartache and pain. Any married man trying to get his needs met with someone other than his spouse has many unresolved issues. His behavior is an indication of wounds in his own life or marriage. Remember, wounded people wound people. Entertaining or engaging in an inappropriate emotional or sexual relationship with a married man is an invitation for pain and heartache.

If you are a single man and a married woman is flirting with you, we repeat, "He who has ears to hear, let him hear." Run away from her as fast as you can. A married woman trying to get her needs met with someone other than her spouse is an invitation to disaster.

Likewise, if you are married and an unmarried person of the opposite sex is pursuing you in any way, turn around and run away as fast as you can. Any unmarried person who pursues a relationship with a married person is not someone you want in your life. A person who plays with fire will get burned.

In addition to carefully choosing your relationships, it's important to guard your thought life. Reframe any sexual thoughts about someone other than your spouse with this challenge: *Would I want anyone thinking these thoughts about my spouse?* The Bible gives great wisdom: "Rejoice in the wife of your youth.... Be exhilarated always with her love."[4]

One of the best ways for a husband and wife to protect their marriage from adultery is to understand and live out God's design for marriage. This requires open and honest communication. It is so important for couples to talk through the potential dangers in marriage before they experience negative effects and pitfalls.

Do you and your spouse have a plan to protect your marriage? Have you taken preventative steps to build a wall of protection around your relationship? Remember, no one is free from temptation or sin, but you and your spouse together can build a wall of protection when it comes to opposite-sex relationships.[5] Here are some ways to do so:

+ Build trust with your spouse by creating healthy boundaries in your marriage. Do you both agree on what is appropriate behavior when it comes to relating to the opposite sex? Talk openly about any red flags you may have regarding relationships outside the marriage.

Body Oneness

+ Ask your spouse this question: Do you see any relationships in my life that may appear questionable to you or to others in any way?

+ Know yourself. If you struggle with lust or lustful thoughts, maintain accountability. Getting support in this is extremely beneficial. Give your same-sex accountability partners permission to ask you difficult questions. Do not fall into the trap of keeping your thought life hidden.

+ Make a covenant with your eyes not to look at another person lustfully.[6] Make a conscious choice to look away from a person or image that has potential to become an obstacle for you.

+ Keep the lines of communication open between you and your spouse. Make decisions for integrity. In terms of opposite-sex relationships:

Share your daily schedule with each other. If you have to meet alone with someone of the opposite sex, tell your spouse.

Whenever you are with a member of the opposite sex, whether socially or in a business environment, ask yourself this question: *If my spouse were here, would I respond in the same ways? Would I say the same things?*

Avoid one-on-one meetings with someone of the opposite sex as much as possible. If you have to have a business appointment with a person of the opposite sex, bring another person with you. If that is not possible, meet in an open business area.

Do not allow business meetings to become social meetings. Avoid meals or social settings and consider these meetings strictly business.

Do not meet alone with someone of the opposite sex in a closed office. Choose an office with windows so you are visible to the rest of your coworkers. If you do not have windows in your office, keep the door ajar during meetings or have a third party join you.

Do not drive together in a car. Instead, travel in groups. If it is unavoidable, call your spouse and let them know who you are with, what you are doing, and when you'll be home.

+ Be aware of initial steps of intimacy. (We'll talk more about these in the next chapter.) Be careful that your words and actions do not

Body Oneness

suggest flirtation; it's a recipe for disaster. If you want to flirt, flirt with your spouse.

+ "Copy" or "Blind Copy" your spouse on e-mails that include or allude to any non-business information when communicating with the opposite sex. Men and women whose spouses do this tell us they feel honored and protected.

+ Protect your marriage by enjoying a great sex life together. A healthy sexual relationship within marriage provides a strong bond between a couple. Learn your spouse's sexual love language. Look for new ways to please each other. Communicate your sexual desires to your spouse. Making your sexual relationship a priority can help you avoid temptation. When couples are sexually disconnected, they open the door to temptation and to an unhealthy fantasy life.

+ Christians often feel stuck or trapped with sexual thoughts or temptations. The Bible tells us what happens when we actively resist the enemy. It says, "Submit therefore to God. Resist the devil and he will flee from you. Draw near to God and He will draw near to you."[7]

Obviously, this list of preventative steps for protecting your marriage is not exhaustive. We encourage you to review it prayerfully with your spouse and add to it as you make a plan together. Remember, if you fail to plan, you may as well plan to fail. One of the enemy's most effective strategies is keeping a couple too busy to make a plan.

IS THERE HOPE AFTER ADULTERY?

What about marriages already devastated by the pain of adultery? Is divorce a foregone conclusion?

Obviously, the decision to violate covenant assaults God's design for marital oneness, and the consequences are devastating. In the initial stages of processing adultery, it is extremely painful for the one who was sinned against to come to terms with the reality of betrayal. Often people try to attach blame to one specific person or event. Typically the partner

Body Oneness

who commits adultery is held responsible for the breakdown of the marriage. After all, they are the one who broke the covenant.

Healing begins when both partners are willing to take responsibility for their contribution to the breakdown of the marriage. However, there are more than two sides to every story. There is the husband's side, the wife's side, and a deeper side. The deeper side belongs to God. He is the only One who knows the whole story. Inviting God into the process is the only hope for the kind of deep healing a couple needs to experience true restoration.

In marital crisis, the goal is not to just stay together. The goal is to get to the roots of the problems and identify areas that in most cases have never been dealt with. A person's sexual history and family of origin are key issues to explore when adultery invades a marriage. Tracing the tremors of marital earthquakes can lead to healing of hidden places in both the husband's and wife's hearts.

The enemy delights in eliminating hope for restoration. In the tension of marital crisis, the possibility of restoration often appears to be out of a couple's grasp. But the Bible gives hope. It says, "…as people sinned more and more, God's wonderful grace became more abundant."[8]

Let's return to the married couple we met earlier in this chapter. After the initial fallout, they agreed to continue meeting with us individually and as a couple. The wife was trying desperately to get past the deep sense of rejection she felt from her husband's unfaithfulness. The husband was emotionally intoxicated with his new soul mate. The prognosis for this marriage was grim, but their willingness to include a third party allowed room for a potential intervention.

At each meeting we provided opportunities for each spouse to verbalize their perspective of their marriage. This enabled each to hear the other's viewpoint. Deep issues began to surface as both husband and wife expressed pain, disappointment, and frustration. Having the opportunity to put words to heartache and loss is a part of the healing process. This couple began to see there were more than two sides to their story. Over time they realized that many influencing factors led to the breakdown in their intimacy and oneness.

Body Oneness

Both partners had been raised in families that modeled poor communication. They entered marriage without the tools they needed to effectively express their emotions to each other. In exploring their family histories, we also learned that the wife's family was full of strong women and passive men. Afraid of being left alone to raise her family, she became strong and powerful. Her husband perceived her strength as disrespect. He passively controlled by withdrawing. Their sexual relationship became a bargaining chip rather than a source of mutual celebration, protection, pleasure, and comfort. It became easier for them to deal with the children rather than with each other.

As this couple continued on their journey toward healing, they surrounded themselves with a team of supportive people who were equipped to deal with their pain. Along with professional counselors, this team included a few friends from their faith community who were spiritually mature and able to provide day-to-day accountability. Within this circle of believers were several trustworthy prayer warriors. These spiritually discerning people offered support by getting on their knees for this family. They recognized the couple's marriage breakdown as a spiritual battle and responded with prayer. They stood in the gap with very specific prayer requests. The members of the support team knew the adulterous relationship must end before there could be any hope for restoration, so they began to strategically pray for dissatisfaction between the husband and the woman he was involved with. They asked the Lord to soften the couple's hearts and to protect their children. They prayed that God would reestablish the covenant promise the husband and wife had made to each other. Over time, this couple began to experience answers to these specific prayers.

At one breakthrough session, lights began to turn on in the husband's mind and heart. With his head hung in shame, he looked over at his wife and quietly said, "What have I done?" He told his wife he was sorry and asked her to forgive him.

For a long time, neither of them spoke. They just wept over what had been lost.

When the husband decided to leave the marriage emotionally and sexually, his wife's faith and trust were damaged. When he took responsibility for his sin and asked her to forgive him, something inside her changed. She accepted his apology and chose to forgive him. Her decision to forgive released something in both of them. The wife responded by taking responsibility for her own sins. She confessed to being self-protective and choosing to live in fear. As they clung to God, their eyes continued to open and their hearts continued to soften. Surrounded by counselors, family, and a faith community, they began to step into the **Larger Story**.

The reality is that succeeding in marriage — whether or not your relationship has been impacted by unfaithfulness — involves an invest-ment of time, energy, enthusiasm, and resources. But whatever the cost, we believe with our whole hearts the investment is worthwhile.

God is a God of paradox. He says that in order to live, you must be willing to die. Marriage is an invitation to die to your self, to selfishness, to ungodly desires and personal agendas and experience God in ways that selfishness will never produce.

The good news is that a person willing to trust God and work through marital chaos does not have to face life's difficulties alone. God is in the business of healing and restoring relationships, and He uses intercessors, pastors, small group leaders, family, counselors, and friends as His agents of healing. We see the power of community every time we witness the restoration process operating in a couple's marriage, helping a husband and wife repent of their selfishness and make the choice to live in the **Larger Story**.

CAUSE FOR DIVORCE

The enemy rejoices every time a marriage covenant with God and a spouse is broken. However, the enemy's strategy includes much more than just encouraging adultery and divorce. The enemy's plan of attack is much more sinister; it involves the battle between good and evil in every person's heart.

Every follower of Christ is engaged in a spiritual battle, which means every marriage is part of an ongoing battle. The Bible is clear: "For our struggle is not against flesh and blood, but against the rulers, against the powers, against the world forces of this darkness, against the spiritual forces of wickedness in the heavenly places."[9]

The enemy knows Jesus was speaking truth when He said the underlying cause of divorce is hardness of heart: "Because of your hardness of heart Moses permitted you to divorce your wives; but from the beginning it has not been this way."[10] Therefore, the enemy's strategy is to use whatever means he can — including pain, disappointment, circumstances of life — to harden a person's heart. He knows a hard heart is a selfish heart and a selfish heart is the doorway to living in the **smaller story**. In a marriage, the enemy will strategically introduce lies and deceit to entice couples to selfishly make their relationship *all about me.*

A woman sat across from us, unloading years of marital chaos and confusion. She was willing to take responsibility for her part of the marriage breakdown, but her main reason for meeting with us was to get the answer to one question: *Can I get divorced?* She was looking for someone in authority to tell her that her marriage was *bad enough*. She was looking for permission to break covenant with God and her spouse.

In adultery as well as other painful marital problems, couples often are encouraged to jump to divorce as the solution. However, in our experience, when a couple chooses divorce as the solution to marital problems, this solution almost always becomes their next problem. When covenant and the one-flesh principle are violated, both the husband and wife suffer in spirit, soul, and body. The fallout of divorce always affects more than just a husband and wife.

+ One landmark study revealed that 90 percent of children from divorced homes suffered from an acute sense of shock when the separation occurred, including profound grieving and irrational fears. Fifty percent reported feeling rejected and abandoned, and indeed, half of the fathers never came to see their children three years after the divorce. One-third of the boys and girls feared abandonment by the remaining parent, and 66 percent experienced yearning for the absent parent with an intensity that researchers described as overwhelming. Most significant, 37 percent of the children were even more unhappy and dissatisfied five

Body Oneness

years after the divorce than they had been at 18 months. In other words, time did not heal their wounds.[11]   +

While circumstances vary, at its core divorce is always a spiritual problem. Money, sex, and power may be contributing factors in marital breakdowns, but it is hardness of a person's heart that destroys a marriage.

In marriage, hardness of heart develops when a husband or wife's commitment to self becomes more important than the covenant they made with God and their spouse. This hardness may be revealed in a number of different ways, including emotional or sexual adultery, divorce, and various forms of rebellion. It also plays out in attempts to punish, reject, shame, or control a spouse.

The solution to freeing a marriage from this downward spiral begins with God, with understanding and living out His purposes for marriage. Living out His purposes means living unselfishly for God, a spouse, children, and others. Believing that "marriage is not about me" is a critical step in thwarting the enemy's plans.

Sadly, many Christians have no idea what the Bible says about divorce. Most of their information comes from wrong thinking or from other people's opinions. When they experience marital crisis they often choose to talk to friends instead of calling their pastor or making an appointment with a Christian counselor. They depend on well-meaning but often untrained people to answer complicated questions. Some people quote Scripture and confidently declare "no divorce and no remarriage." Others quote Scripture and say that divorce is permitted under certain circumstances, but remarriage is not allowed. Still others believe that both divorce and remarriage are permitted.

Since the decision of whether or not to divorce dramatically influences the lives of both partners, the lives of their children, and future generations, it's absolutely vital to understand God's view of divorce.

The Bible teaches that divorce is not what God intended. In fact God clearly states, "I hate divorce."[12] Divorce is not Plan A. Yet the book of Jeremiah says that God wrote Israel a certificate of divorce because of adultery.[13] Although this passage is written in figurative language, we believe this opens the door to certain circumstances that make divorce an option in certain cases. One example is when a person's heart becomes so hard that it results in desertion of the marital covenant. This goes directly against God's design and purpose for marriage. Another situation where divorce is permissible is when a spouse behaves in addictive cycles of serial adultery or is involved in an ongoing adulterous relationship. In addition, abuse and violence may warrant a process of separation that may potentially lead to divorce. However, separation is never a solution in itself. The goal of separation is to lead to healing and restoration. If separation is not wisely used in conjunction with a plan for restoration, it often leads to divorce.

In our early thirties we served in the marriage ministry at Willow Creek Community Church, where we were trained to approach the decision for divorce on a case-by-case basis. We believe the wisest thing a person can do when evaluating the future of their marriage is to include God in the process. We encourage people to compare what they sense they hear from the Lord with the Bible and with those trained in marriage counseling.

Although the Lord is the only One who can discern the condition of a person's heart, He places leaders in positions to make righteous judgments. There is an extremely thin line that separates righteous judgment from unrighteousness judgment. That is why each marriage situation has to be prayerfully considered on a case-by-case basis.

A WORD TO DIVORCED CHRISTIANS

A Christian marriage is a sacred covenant between God, a husband, and a wife. God hates divorce and what it does to His children by destroying trust and shattering hearts. However, the Bible makes a clear distinction between how God feels about divorce and how He feels about His children. God is your Father and He loves you perfectly. Nothing, including divorce, can separate you from His love.

However, because we live in an imperfect world, we experience the pain of our own sins and the sins of others. Sadly, some churches and Christians have designated divorce as an unforgivable sin. Some divorced people

Body Oneness

have been shunned, even denied participation in their faith community by church leadership. Wounded by the pain of alienation, many have fallen away from their faith.

Ideally, the church should come alongside people who are dealing with marriage problems, especially selfishness, adultery, and divorce. The church must recognize marital breakdown as spiritual warfare and respond accordingly.

If you have endured unrighteous judgment or prideful rejection from church leadership or fellow believers, on behalf of the church we are truly sorry. We encourage you to remember that, because of God's radical grace, nothing you have ever done or will do can possibly make God love you more, and there is nothing you can do to make Him love you less.

Our counsel to divorced people is:

+   Repent for breaking covenant with God and your spouse. (Note: Even if you were not the spouse who filed for divorce, both the husband and wife need to take full responsibility for any part each may have played in the marriage breakdown, and ask God's forgiveness.)
+   Receive God's forgiveness so you can walk in healing and wholeness.
+   Forgive your former spouse for any ways he or she hurt you or was responsible for the breakdown of the marriage.
+   Bless your former spouse. Release that person to the Lord by refusing to allow any lack of forgiveness to tie you emotionally to him or her.
+   Break any ungodly bonds.
+   Ask God to replace any hardness in your heart with His heart.
+   Walk in righteousness and purity in relationships with the opposite sex.

Remember that healing is a process, not an event. Take the time you need to be restored. Listen to the Lord, and He will direct you. We encourage pastoral or professional counseling. Invite godly people to walk with you. Give them permission to ask you hard questions. Often people will not go where they are not invited.

Exhaust any possibility of restoring your first marriage if your former spouse is not remarried. If that is not possible and if, after a season of healing, you sense God leading you to pursue a new relationship, have your accountability circle pray with you about it. Ask the people closest to you if they affirm the new relationship. Talk to spiritual mentors about the factors involved in remarriage, especially the potential impact on any children. Again, take your time. We have many friends who have lived through the heartbreak of divorce. Their decisions to passionately live for God following this painful experience inspires us. Many of them have tender hearts and now enjoy marriages made in heaven.

A MARRIAGE REFORMATION

Divorce is a key link in the breakdown of the family. Recent studies show that the consequences of divorce are much more severe than previously reported. The fallout of divorce includes absent parents, increased relational and financial stress, increase in poverty, and increase in violence and crime.

Another devastating consequence is that the ease and acceptance of divorce has birthed a fatherless generation. Children of divorce enter marriage without a godly example of parents who understood and lived out God's design for marriage. As a result, they often go into marriage thinking that if things don't work out, they'll just get divorced like their parents did.

Many in the generations that have come of age since the 1970s have become part of the collateral damage of divorce. This has resulted in a generation of young men and women who are searching for truth about God, marriage, intimacy, and sexuality. They are making marriage and family decisions that will have far-reaching consequences.

Our prayer is that the emerging generation will fight the subtle seduction in pluralism, relativism, and secular humanism. We pray they will courageously pursue God's truths.

We believe God is inviting this new generation to birth a movement that will be viewed in history as the launch of a new Marriage Reformation. This will begin as men and women reclaim the sanctity of marriage and

Body Oneness

the importance of living in covenant. We pray the emerging generation's passion and commitment to relevance and relationship extends to marriage and is grounded in God's love and truth.

But we don't envision this change as something limited by age; every husband and wife will have their part to play in this Reformation. This must begin with God as couples live out "it's not about me."

+ Chapter 18

Intimate Understanding

The Exhilaration of Advancing in Physical Intimacy

Riverview Amusement Park was a spectacular Chicago destination for families back in the days before Disneyland and Six Flags of America theme parks sprang up. Reportedly, over two hundred million people walked through its gates on Western and Belmont avenues before it closed in the late 1960s after some six decades of entertainment.

When I (Tim) was growing up, our family loved to go to Riverview. Once we walked through the gates, the girls would go one way while the guys of the family headed off in another direction. Typically, the girls started with the train ride around the entire park. They loved to people-watch and take in all the sights and sounds of the park. They checked out the jazz ballroom, the roller rink, and Aladdin's Castle Fun House. They took in a few shows while enjoying cotton candy and caramel corn. For the girls, a day at Riverview called for a leisurely tour of the entire park. It was a mix of experiences and relationships that impacted all of their senses.

On the other hand, when my dad, brothers, and I entered Riverview, we were on a mission. For us Riverview was all about one thing: the roller coasters. With a clear goal in mind, we raced directly to that area of the park. We rode them one after the other: the *Fireball*, the *Comet*, the *Flying Turns*, the *Whip*, the *Shoot-the-Chutes*, the *Silver Flash*, and the *Wild Mouse*. Each ride lasted only a few minutes but was worth every second.

The most famous ride at Riverview was the *Bobs*, an eleven-car roller coaster with an eighty-five-foot drop. It was billed as the fastest roller coaster in the country. People came from all over just to ride the *Bobs*. While all the roller coasters were fun, this ride was definitely the highlight of the day.

On the drive back home, everyone talked about the events of the day. The highlights of the girls' day centered around the people they had met, the conversations they'd had, the food they'd eaten, and other experiences they remembered from throughout their day. No matter how late we stayed at Riverview, the girls always wished they had more time to "take it all in."

However, the men's entire day at Riverview was about the roller coasters. Our conversation in the car was limited to describing one fast ride after the next. In all those years of going to the park, I can't remember a single discussion among the guys that was focused on meeting someone worth remembering or having a conversation worth repeating. None of us ever cared what the weather was like or what we had for lunch. Nothing had more impact than those short, three-minute roller-coaster rides.

STROLLING TOWARD THE ROLLER COASTER

Both men and woman are made in the image of God. Yet as my family's experience at Riverview illustrates, they are different in many ways. This is particularly true in the way they approach sex.

The average man approaches making love with one clear goal in mind. With his sights set on orgasm, this man-on-a-mission is determined to do whatever it takes to get Riverview *Bobs*-like thrills. To achieve that goal, he focuses most of his attention on two body parts: his penis and his wife's vagina. The time frame for what a man considers actual lovemaking can be very short. It's all about one thing: the roller coaster–like experience.

Whereas a man may describe sex as an event, a woman's experience of sex tends to be a process. Her focus is on experience and relationship rather than just the destination. All of her senses are heightened as she receives messages that are being transcribed in her heart and body. Unlike a man, a woman's time frame for achieving orgasm is much longer. While the climax is deeply satisfying, a woman's sexual enjoyment is about much more than having an orgasm.

In talking about sexual intimacy and body oneness, a man's mind often jumps immediately to intercourse while a woman might think more about touching and talking. In reality physical intimacy is a gradual process involving twelve distinct steps.

We're not talking here about the act of sex itself. The truth is, any person can have sex. However, men and women who understand God's design for body oneness desire more than just the act of sex. They long to *know* their spouse and to sexually satisfy that person within the covenant of marriage for a lifetime. They long to *be known* by their spouse.

The word *know* in the Bible means "intimate understanding." It is often

Body Oneness

used to describe sexual intimacy. The Bible tells us that Abraham *knew* Sarah. Another sexual term in the Bible is the word *lay*, which refers to a much lower level of intimacy. For example, when Amnon raped his sister Tamar, the text says, "he violated her and lay with her."[1] Obviously, this refers not to intimacy but to a terrible violation of God's design for sexual expression.

Remember our definition of intimacy: to *know and be fully known*. Intimacy is all about relationship. We are created as relational beings made in the image of a relational God. We are created with a longing for intimacy.

Intimacy is not only deeply satisfying, it is progressive. It involves order and steps to remind us that advancing in intimacy is a process.[2] Of course, we experience varying levels of intimacy with a variety of people, depending on the type of relationship we share; however, the later steps of intimacy are reserved solely for interactions between a husband and wife.

1.   Eye to body

Imagine walking into a room full of people with an expectation of meeting someone new. The first thing you might do is to take a visual overview of the room. As your eyes scan the crowd, you are able to gather quite a bit of data without ever saying a word to anyone. Eye-to-body contact has the power to carry a clear message. There is a distinguishable difference between a non-sexual glance, an admiring gaze, a judging stare, and inappropriate sexual gawking. The data provided by eye-to-body contact determine how you will proceed with the next step.

2.   Eye to eye

Once a person experiences connection with another person through eye-to-body contact, they may advance to eye-to-eye contact. We have all heard the expression, *the eyes are the window to the soul*. Looking into a person's soul-windows requires an increased level of intimacy.
When our kids were young, I (Tim) remember coming home after a busy shift on duty at the firehouse. I was sitting in my chair reading the sports section of the newspaper. My daughter Colleen jumped on my lap and said, "Daddy, watch me dance." I was so involved in reading the paper that I simply nodded and mumbled, "Okay, I'm watching. Go ahead." She jumped off my lap and began dancing around the living room.

A few minutes passed, and she realized I was not watching her. So she returned to my lap and made additional attempts to get my attention. She worked her way under the newspaper but was still unable to make eye contact with me. By this time I had stopped reading the paper and was just enjoying watching her try to get my attention. Sitting directly in front of me, she placed her little hands on each side of my face. With the determination of a four-year-old, she turned my head toward hers to make eye contact. In a firm voice she said, "Daddy, look at me...will you pleeease watch me dance?"

Eye-to-eye contact communicates varying levels of intimacy. Have you ever responded negatively to your spouse after receiving a parental "look" from him or her? Have you felt the tenderness of your spouse's affection as he or she gazes romantically into your eyes? A variety of powerful messages can be communicated through eye-to-eye contact.

3. Voice to voice

The next step in building intimacy is actually speaking to the person. This may sound basic, but it affirms the progressive nature of intimacy. The necessary steps of intimacy often become more apparent when specific steps are skipped. For example, have you ever had a conversation with someone who didn't give you eye contact? When the other person is looking over your head, looking past you, continually glancing at their watch, or at other people, it's difficult to achieve a voice-to-voice connection.

Steps 1 through 3 reflect the progressive nature of intimacy but also have a place in different types of relationships. For example, eye-to-body contact can be defined as a non-sexual glance or a gaze that is more sexual in nature. Women are quick to discern the difference. When inappropriate steps of intimacy are taken, it can feel like a violation to the other person. Eye-to-eye contact can communicate different levels of love, friendship, and acceptance. Similarly, voice-to-voice contact can communicate a number of different things, depending on whether the tone is friendly, inviting, critical, or sexual.

+   +   +

Body Oneness

On the continuum of intimacy, steps 4 through 7 signal a deeper level of relationship.

4. Hand to hand
Holding hands with another person can be sexual or nonsexual. Certainly, holding hands with a child is different than holding hands with your lover; however, both involve a deeper step in intimacy. You generally would not hold hands with a stranger or even a casual acquaintance, but you might take the hand of another person while praying together at church, signifying your shared relationship as children of God.

5. Hand to shoulder
Steps of intimacy are progressive. Placing your arm around somebody's shoulder and drawing them in to your side is more intimate than holding someone's hand.

6. Hand to waist
Placing your hands around a person's waist is more intimate than holding hands or placing your arm around a person's shoulder. This level of contact generally is reserved for encounters between parent and child or between husband and wife.

7. Hand to hair
Often people don't consider their heads an intimate part of their body. But stop and think for a moment: a person would never walk up to someone they just met and touch their hair! Strokes to the hair or head imply tenderness and a deeper level of intimacy.

When the kids were little, Saturday night was bath night. I (Anne) found that getting four kids ready for church the next morning in a home with one bathtub required a system. Tim and I would fill up the tub. One by one, I would rotate each of our four kids in and out of the bath. I would dry them off, wrap them in a towel, and send them to their bedrooms to put on their pajamas. Once they were dressed, Tim would help dry and comb each one's hair. It was a sweet and intimate part of the ritual.

Recently I observed our daughter Amy cradling her daughter Grace in her lap while gently stroking her head. This kind of touch communicates love and nurture.

Body Oneness

8. Face to face

The Bible says to "greet one another with a holy kiss."[3] Many of our friends and family members regularly kiss one another on the cheek. In certain cultures greeting a person with a kiss is being polite.

In our culture, kissing tends to be viewed as significantly more intimate than a handshake. When we speak to young adults we are often asked if kissing between unmarried couples is a sin. In order to answer that question, we ask a few questions to help them discern the different kinds of kissing. On one end of the continuum, kissing can be a nonsexual peck on the cheek. We ask, "What do you mean by kissing? Are we talking about a peck on the cheek, a closed-mouth kiss, an open-mouth kiss, or a French kiss? Are these short kisses or long passionate kissing sessions? Does kissing stimulate sexual arousal for one or both partners? Does it stimulate fantasy or lust in one or both partners? Does it stimulate an erection for the man? Does kissing lead to deeper stages of intimacy?" These are important questions to explore.

Some premarital couples may be able to enjoy kissing as an expression of intimacy yet be able to maintain healthy boundaries before marriage. Other couples may struggle for a variety of reasons. For some, kissing is an acceptable and enjoyable form of intimacy. For others, it may be a temptation that causes them to progress to deeper steps in intimacy. God commands couples to stay pure before marriage. This requires them to develop healthy boundaries that will enable them to successfully maintain purity and honor the other person.

Married couples often tell us they wish they kissed more. We find that kissing is a step of intimacy that often gets shortchanged or even bypassed as a couple is free to move on to steps of greater intimacy. Therefore, we encourage husbands and wives to effectively communicate specific longings and desires to each other to help advance in intimacy.

+   +   +

On the continuum of intimacy, steps 9 through 12 are advanced steps of intimacy reserved solely for marriage.

Body Oneness

9. Hand to body

God designed a husband and wife to enjoy each other's bodies. The skin serves as the largest erogenous zone on your spouse's body. It is filled with nerve endings that are designed to relax as well as stimulate. Using your hands to gently explore each other's bodies is an advanced form of intimacy that has unlimited potential to communicate nonverbal messages of tenderness, comfort, security, sexual arousal, and delight to your spouse.

10. Mouth to body

Gently exploring your spouse's body with your mouth can also be a deeply satisfying step of intimacy. Mouth-to-body contact can communicate powerful messages of love, joy, and commitment to your spouse.

11. Outercourse

This is a term used to describe various forms of foreplay couples use to stimulate one another to orgasm without penetration. Outercourse is a step of intimacy that invites a couple to learn more about each other's body and discover how your spouse responds to specific forms of touch. Communicating sexually to your soul mate is an advanced step in intimacy that requires time and trust.

12. Intercourse

Sexual intercourse is regarded as the ultimate step of intimacy. This most intimate sexual act becomes the symbol of two becoming one. God designed the male and female body to respond to the progressive stages of intercourse with intensifying phases of excitement leading to orgasm. This moment of climax is often described as intense pleasure followed by a sense of release.

+ + +

We've spent time detailing these twelve steps of intimacy because we believe it is important for men and women to understand intimacy's progressive nature. Recognizing these distinct steps can help a couple in setting boundaries in their relationships outside of marriage and provides an opportunity to openly discuss with each other how to incorporate these steps in ways that both husband and wife find satisfying.

SEX CAN BE AN ACT OF WORSHIP AND WARFARE

The Bible says, "Whatever you do in word or deed, do all in the name of the Lord Jesus."[4] Have you ever thought of sexual intimacy in marriage as an act of worship? When a man and woman choose to become reciprocal servants to each other in the name of the Lord, their sexual expressions become acts of worship. If this is a new concept to you, please remember that we are not worshiping sex; we are worshiping the God who created sex.

A healthy marital sex life is also an act of warfare. The Bible is clear on the sexual duty of a husband and wife. It reminds couples that by fulfilling that duty and meeting each other's sexual needs they will avoid temptation. In a healthy sexual relationship neither spouse will deprive the other sexually; instead each views sex as an act of warfare, defeating the enemy's tactics by living out "It's not about me."

Sadly, married couples often settle for much less than what God intended for them sexually. Some couples focus the majority of their efforts on orgasm and miss out on all that God has intended for body oneness. It is not unusual for us to hear one spouse say, "We have been married for years. Sometimes I just miss passionately kissing, cuddling, or putting our arms around each other. There are times during intercourse we barely talk."

When you stop and think about it, our culture tends to place a low priority on genuine intimacy, as if sex itself is the goal rather than a means of advancing in oneness. As important as orgasms are, a key to an exhilarating sex life involves pursuing a spouse's heart, mind, soul, and body. Rather than focusing on getting individual needs met in their sex lives, God invites married couples to live unselfishly, communicating love and affection as each serves the needs and desires of the other. This provides opportunities to advance in soul oneness as well as body oneness.

Did you know the most important sex organ is a person's mind? Thoughts precede action. Advancing in sexual intimacy begins with how a person thinks. This includes how a person perceives God and His design for sex, themselves, and their spouse. In Romans 12:2 we are instructed, "Do not be conformed to this world, but be transformed by the renewing of your mind, so that you may prove what the will of God is, that which is good and acceptable and perfect."

Body Oneness

Transforming your mind when it comes to sex and intimacy begins with inviting God into your process, studying the Scriptures, and allowing Him to renew your thoughts. God designed marriage to be a safe place where sexuality can be celebrated.

We love to officiate at marriage ceremonies. After a couple states their vows, we invite the groom to kiss his bride. The kiss is an important part of the ceremony as it represents the husband's commitment to lead out in his marriage by breathing life into his wife. It is a symbol that foreshadows the husband and wife sealing the marital covenant. God designed sexual intercourse as a seal between a man and a woman who are in covenant with God and each other.

It makes us wonder…*what if?* What if couples truly understood the power and protection sexual intercourse provides in marriage? What if couples viewed sexual intimacy as acts of worship and warfare? What if couples refused to settle for the world's definition of intimacy and sexuality?

Unfortunately, the sad reality is that too many couples often think the cost for a great sex life is too high. Many believe that working through marital chaos and growing in intimacy and oneness is simply not worth the investment. One husband told us, "I think I just stopped trying. My wife will never change. I just turn on the computer, hit a few porn sites, and meet my needs." This husband just gave up. He abdicated his role as a husband made in the image of God. He is buying into the enemy's lies and deception.

This reminds us of the story of an elderly couple who saved up for years to celebrate their fifty-fifth wedding anniversary by taking a cruise. They had never done anything like this before. They had the time of their lives. As they prepared to leave the ship at the end of the cruise, the captain shook their hands and encouraged them not to wait until their sixtieth wedding anniversary to take another cruise.

The elderly couple politely thanked the captain and started to move on. Suddenly, the wife stopped and turned back to the captain. "We had such a wonderful time," she said. "But throughout our stay we couldn't help noticing all the beautiful banquet tables. They were filled with a variety of

Body Oneness

delicious food and extravagant ice sculptures. There were unlimited choices, and everything was so beautifully prepared."

She hesitated, then asked, "Captain, if we take another cruise, how much more would it cost us to have the meals included? We brought our own food and enjoyed it. We had cheese and crackers in our cabin. We so enjoyed our cruise and can't begin to imagine how wonderful it would have been if we would have been able to eat from the banquet table…"

The captain was shocked. He couldn't believe the couple did not understand that the food was included in the price they had paid for their cruise ticket. He was deeply saddened to learn that this dear couple had missed out on the banquet table that was prepared for them every night.

This elderly couple's cruise experience bears a heartrending resemblance to the sexual area in many marriages. God has prepared a banquet table. He invites every husband and wife to eat, drink, and imbibe deeply in spirit, soul, and body oneness. Yet so many couples settle for cheese and crackers. They do not understand that God has prepared a feast for them.

Growing in any area of life takes commitment. Advancing in the sexual area involves an investment of time, energy, and resources. But for those who refuse to settle for less than the full banquet God intended, the investment is so worth it. Think of a child on Christmas Eve who is barely able to sleep, knowing that Christmas morning means surprise gifts chosen just for them. What if couples renewed their minds by taking this same excitement into the sexual dimension of their marriage? One young wife told us, "Sex is the least expensive thing we can do with each other that gives us the most pleasure."

Couples who advance in living out God's purposes for marriage and sexuality can enjoy both roller-coaster exhilaration *and* a fulfilling multi-sensory experience that brings joy, orgasmic pleasure, and sexual satisfaction.

However, one of the biggest barriers to advancing sexually is the reluctance, particularly within Christian circles, to speak honestly and directly about the questions and problems many married couples have when it comes to the topic of physical intimacy.

Body Oneness

When we joined the marriage ministry team at our local church years ago, we were asked to teach the sexuality section of their premarital seminar. Our nursing and EMT backgrounds seemed to qualify us to cover these topics. In preparation for teaching we read books, took courses, and attended marriage conferences. When we realized that many key areas seemed to be overlooked, we decided to poll our audiences by asking them to write down any questions or topics in the area of sexuality they would like to hear addressed. The issues they raised form the basis for much of our ongoing teaching on body oneness.

A pastor contacted REAL LIFE Ministries to talk to us about hosting a Marriage Advance at his church. We gave him an overview of our seminar and talked through some of the administrative details including dates, times, costs, and follow-up information. Then he asked about how we handle the session on body oneness and sexuality. We told him that we approach this session just like every other — in a biblical and relevant manner. We explained that the body oneness session strategically builds on the spirit and soul oneness sessions. He asked what specific subjects we addressed. We explained that we try to help couples answer real life questions about frequency, locations, timing, positions, and quickies as well as address sensitive sexual topics, including masturbation, lust, pornography, orgasms, oral stimulation, oral sex, anal sex, and other specifics.

There was a L-O-N-G pause. Then the pastor asked, "Do you talk about these things *out loud?*"

Yes, in fact we do. We're convinced that, for the most part, the church has not been effectively addressing sensitive sexual issues, and as a result many couples have a distorted view of God's incredible design for sex.

A number of years ago at one of our marriage seminars, a woman in her late fifties approached me (Anne). She told me she had been married over thirty-three years and wasn't sure if she had ever had an orgasm. She was obviously uncomfortable disclosing this information. We talked for a while, I shared some stories, and she began to relax. As we pressed deeper into conversation, tears ran down her cheeks. "In all the years I have been going to church," she said, "no one ever talked to me about any of these things." For over thirty years this woman had a limited understanding of the gift that God had available for her to enjoy. Not only was she missing the opportunity for pleasure but her husband was missing the joy of bringing her pleasure. As we finished talking, she encouraged me and Tim to press through and continue talking to couples about these sensitive sexual topics.

In the next few chapters we will address some of these areas. We pray that you will find fresh insight for experiencing the full exhilaration and satisfaction of body oneness.

Body Oneness

Body Oneness

+ Chapter 19

We Need to Talk

Clearing the Air About Sexual Expectations

On a recent trip to the west coast, I (Tim) contacted a graphic arts design business that was doing some work for REAL LIFE Ministries. Up to this point our business contact had been limited to e-mails and long-distance telephone conversations, so while I was in Los Angeles, I wanted to personally visit their offices.

I spent almost an entire day with one of their employees, a guy in his late twenties who I'll refer to as Joe. The two of us were discussing the design project he was working on for us when our conversation took a sudden turn. Joe began asking me questions about my job. The name REAL LIFE Ministries caught his interest. He asked, "What exactly do you do?" I explained that my wife and I are ordained pastors who travel around the country encouraging couples by conducting seminars that teach God's design for marriage, intimacy, and sexuality.

He asked, "Why do you call your seminars Marriage Advances?" I explained that marriages are in bad shape and we believe it's time for Christ followers to *advance* instead of retreating in their marriages and families.

I asked Joe if he was married. He responded cautiously, as if he had to think about it for a minute. He said, "No…but maybe someday. I have a great girlfriend right now. We just bought a house."

Since Joe seemed uncomfortable with my questions about his personal life, I switched subjects and asked how he got involved in creative graphic design. I could feel his passion for his job bubbling up as he shared his story. I told Joe I could relate to his love for his career. I grew up always wanting to be a fireman, then spent over twenty years on a busy fire department.

After a few firehouse stories and jokes, Joe seemed to relax. So I asked him to tell me more about his girlfriend. After a long pause, he started describing her as he stared into his computer screen. I was a bit surprised at how eager he was to articulate his girlfriend's attributes. He said, "She's a beautiful woman who comes from a great family and has a pure heart." He stopped for a meaningful moment, then added, "She's the one."

We went back to talking business, but over the course of our time together, I learned a lot about Joe's life just by listening to his stories. At a certain point I looked at Joe and asked, "What makes your girlfriend the one?"

There was a long silence. Part of me wanted to rescue him and go back to talking shop, but I waited. Then for the first time, Joe turned in his chair to look me directly in the eyes. He said, "You probably won't relate to this, but I want to marry a woman who's faithful…a great mom…and is wild in bed." His penetrating stare challenged me to respond.

I could have played it safe and responded to the *faithful* or *great mom* part of Joe's answer. Instead I said, "Yeah, the sex thing in marriage is really important." We then went back and forth on how that played out in real life.

When we finished our work, I gave Joe my card and invited him to bring his girlfriend to one of our REAL LIFE Marriage Advances. He shook my hand and said, "Thanks."

Heading home, I sat in traffic on a southern California freeway thinking about my day. I smiled as I thought about Joe's description of his dream wife. She was a woman who was faithful…a great mom…and wild in bed.

Over the years, Anne and I have spoken to many couples, some who are in relationship with God and some who are not. Regardless of where they are spiritually, many of them want the same things in marriage that Joe articulated. They desire a faithful spouse, someone who has the potential to be a great parent, and a great lover.

GETTING ON THE SAME PAGE

Without a doubt, sex in marriage is extremely important. According to God's design, marriage is the only relationship where a man and woman are to celebrate sex. The Bible says, "In *everything* give thanks…"[1] When couples thankfully celebrate God's design for sexuality, this can be an act of worship. When couples obey the command to sexually satisfy one another, it is an act of warfare. The power of the sexual bond in marriage strengthens and protects a couple.

Body Oneness

So what happens when a married couple has differences in how they express their sexuality? It is rare for two people to get married and magically find themselves on the same page emotionally (Soul Oneness) and sexually (Body Oneness). Since every person is unique, it is normal to enter marriage with different sexual expectations. A sexual expectation is a verbal or nonverbal wish or desire. Many factors help shape sexual expectations, including family of origin, gender, temperament, cultural influences, religious beliefs, sexual histories, sexual imprinting, and a person's life experiences.

In addition, one spouse may feel more sexual freedom than the other. One may be less inhibited, more explorative, and more adventuresome while the other is more reserved and lives life with one foot on the brake. They hear God's invitation to come to the wedding feast, and they understand the freedom they have to imbibe deeply and eat from the banquet table, but they are content to enjoy only a few items.

In marriage, sexual freedom is to be celebrated. However, the book of Galatians gives a warning: "For you were called to freedom, brethren; only do not turn your freedom into an opportunity for the flesh, but through love serve one another."[2]

So how do couples negotiate these differences and still celebrate their sexual freedom?

Following God's example always leads a couple in the right direction, so let's stop and think about how He approaches freedom. Did Jesus ever force Himself or His beliefs on you? He never demands, shames, or condemns. Instead He gives every person time to process as He continues to invite them to enjoy deeper levels of intimacy. He lovingly encourages every man and woman to take steps in faith, to trust, and to risk. In the same way, God desires husbands and wives to develop unselfish and other-centered attitudes in every area of life. This Christlike attitude communicates "It's not about me."

Every man and woman can frame sexual expectations in either the **Larger Story** or the **smaller story**. In terms of body oneness, **smaller story** living is where you are the main character and sexual expectations are all about getting your needs met. Often a spouse may try to convince the other person that God is on their side, perhaps even paraphrasing a few Scriptures as support for their demands: "Your body no longer belongs to you. It now belongs to me, so hand it over!" A person who chooses to "look out for number one" may win a few sexual battles, but they lose out on the true beauty of sex and marital oneness.

Living in the **Larger Story**, by contrast, means Reflecting and Revealing God to your spouse in every area of marriage, including your sex life. To advance in body oneness you must advance in soul oneness, working together toward unity. When it comes to resolving differing expectations about sex, this involves a husband and wife being willing to stand emotionally naked before each other.

As you and your spouse consider your expectations in the following areas, we challenge you to bring your sex life to God. Ask Him for His heart and listen for His response.

FREQUENCY

The topic of sexual frequency is one that affects every married couple. It is not unusual for couples to ask, "How often should we be having sex?"

No specific Bible verse or reference book specifies an optimum number of sexual encounters per week for a healthy marriage. Since every person is different, every couple must decide what works best for them.

Successfully negotiating differences and reaching agreement requires healthy communication skills. This is one reason why a person's understanding of soul oneness is key to body oneness.

Take the example of one spouse who may like to have sex twice a week. This person's spouse also enjoys sex but considers twice a month to be just fine. How does this couple negotiate their differences? The problem is not in having different wants and desires. In fact, it is natural for two people to think and feel differently. Differences become problems when a person or couple is unable to effectively communicate and process their desires and needs with each other. Couples seeing a counselor to work on sexual issues will often spend more time on their communication skills

Body Oneness

than on the sexual issues they originally came to resolve. A counselor will review families of origin. They will ask each person to answer important questions:

How did your parents model communication while you were growing up?

Were your parents able to effectively communicate their needs and desires to you? to each other?

Were other family members able to communicate their needs and desires to you? to each other?

How would you describe the communication between you and your spouse?

How would you describe your ability to communicate in other relationships in your life?

How do you communicate your sexual desires to your spouse?

How does your spouse communicate their sexual desires to you?

It has been our experience that often a couple's differences in the area of frequency are not as far apart as they may think.

We have friends in their midfifties who are now in the empty-nest season of their lives. These friends are a great couple who love marriage, but like every married couple, they have had their share of ups and downs. One issue they have struggled with over the years is in finding agreement on sexual frequency. The husband has a very high sex drive. If it were up to him he would have sex every day. On the other hand, his wife would be happy with sex once a week.

As their thirty-fifth wedding anniversary was approaching, the wife wanted to do something special for her husband. After giving it some thought, she bought a card and placed a handmade coupon inside. It read:

Happy 35th Anniversary!
Let's commemorate this year by having sex every day
for the next 35 days!!!
(I'll even initiate)

Her husband later told us that when he read the card he dropped the TV remote control and almost fell out of his La-Z-Boy! He thought he'd died and gone to heaven.

We asked them how things progressed. The wife began, "Well…the first few days went great." They looked at each other and laughed. She continued, "Day three was just as good as day two! On day four I walked into the bedroom with a new nightgown on, and we enjoyed the evening together. Day five I gave him a backrub."

Looking at each other, they smiled and the husband continued, "By day seven or eight we started getting a little tired — "

"But I'd made a promise," the wife interrupted, "and I really wanted to keep it, so I pushed through."

"Hey, it was great!" the husband said. "I had more sex following our thirty-fifth anniversary than I could have ever dreamed. But in all honesty, by the middle of the second week I was running out of gas. By day nine or ten, she came downstairs and began to initiate sex…again! I took a deep breath, looked her in the eyes, and said, 'Honey, how about we just order a pizza and watch TV?'" He dialed the phone to order the pizza while she jumped into her flannel nightgown.

So you see, sexual satisfaction isn't about finding the perfect frequency. God allows differences in a husband and wife's sexual desire for a reason, and those differences can provide opportunities to advance in intimacy, to know your spouse and be fully known. Instead of an obstacle, try viewing your different expectations as occasions to Reflect and Reveal God to each other.

TIMING

Couples often ask, "What happens when we disagree on when to have sex or the best time for sex?"

Choosing a time that is good for both partners is another area that often requires negotiation. It is important to be aware of your body clock. Some

Body Oneness

people are night owls. They enjoy the peace and solitude of late-night hours. Others are early birds. They find peace and solitude in the early morning. Can you see how these differences can interfere with sexual timing?

I (Tim) remember that we had this problem when we were newly married. Anne loved to stay up very late. That was her favorite time of the day. If she could, she would stay up well past midnight and sleep until 8 a.m. On the other hand, I am an early-morning person. I grew up with my dad leaving for his milkman route at 3 a.m. While I've never wanted to begin my day quite that early, I am usually ready to go before 5 a.m.

These different timetables presented a problem in deciding what times would be best for both of us to enjoy sex. Learning about God's design for marriage helped us realize we had choices to make. We could try to manipulate and control each other so we could have things our way. Or we could choose to live in the **Larger Story** by serving one another instead of "working it" to get our own way. Something changed when we chose God's way. Our focus became serving and satisfying each other instead of ourselves.

Again, healthy communication skills are the first step toward successfully reaching agreement and avoiding potential problems. Creating a calendar that reserves "alone time" on specific days and times may initially seem to lack romance and spontaneity. If you are a romantic idealist who can't imagine scheduling specific times and days, we encourage you to answer these questions:

How often does romantic and spontaneous sex actually happen in your life?

How many times have you had romantic, spontaneous sex in the last six months?

Is that frequency enough for both you and your spouse?

If so, we would say it's working for you. But for most couples, real-life schedules have a way of interfering with spontaneous sex.

ORGASM

You and your spouse were created as sexual beings. God designed our bodies to experience intense sexual pleasure. That means a husband and wife should both be regularly experiencing orgasms when they have intercourse.

Orgasms were God's idea. He created a woman's clitoris with twice as many nerve endings as anywhere else on her entire body. God created a man's penis with more nerve endings than anywhere on his body. Think about it — what on earth feels better than experiencing mutually satisfying orgasms with your spouse?

Clifford and Joyce Penner describe the orgasm experience this way:

+ "Most of the time we let our minds control us. But in the moment of orgasm we are released from that control. Climax is a "total being' experience; everything about us enters into it. Perhaps this is how the sexual experience represents our relationship to God. In this total, intense fusion of body, emotion, and spirit, we are connecting with what it can be like to be totally one with God. This is, indeed, a mystery."[3]   +

Achieving orgasm is different for every person. That is why it is so important for every person to understand how their body functions. Understanding God's design of male and female anatomy helps couples relax and enjoy their sexual journey together.

I (Anne) can't help but think of one Sunday after church when we ran into a young couple who had come to us for their premarital counseling several months earlier. "Bob and Lisa" told us all about their honeymoon, their new apartment, and their puppy.

At some point in the conversation we asked how their sex life was going. Bob quickly replied, "Sex is great." Lisa simply nodded, a less-than-enthusiastic response. Tim asked a more specific question: "Are you both having orgasms?" Again, Bob gave an immediate response, "No problem in that department…" His bride hesitated as if she didn't know how to answer the question. She said, "I think so. I mean…it feels okay, I guess." Bob looked at Lisa with surprise.

Body Oneness

Tim pulled out his Day-Timer and said to Bob, "Let's do lunch this week. How about Wednesday at Chili's? 11:30. You're buying!" Bob agreed.

When they met over lunch, Bob began their conversation by declaring his confusion, "I could not believe how Lisa responded to your question about orgasms! What did she mean when she said she's 'not sure'? I'm pretty sure that if she had an orgasm she would know it. Wouldn't she?"

Bob came from a fatherless home and had very little sexual training or experience. Growing up, everything he heard about sex came from the locker room. We discussed sex during our premarital meetings; however, after he got married he never thought to ask his wife if she was enjoying sex. Bob did not grow up in a family that communicated well or shared their feelings. Talking to Lisa about how she responded sexually or whether she experienced orgasm never occurred to him. He just assumed that sex was as great for Lisa as it was for him.

Tim looked around the restaurant to see if anyone was within earshot of their conversation. Leaning toward Bob, Tim drew a simple sketch of the female genitalia on a paper napkin. Bob stared at the napkin as he listened attentively to every word. He explained about foreplay, direct and indirect pressure, rhythm, and the different phases of orgasm. He encouraged Bob to talk to Lisa and ask her questions. As Bob paid for lunch, he thanked Tim and shook his hand.

Tim looked into this young man's eyes and said, "Bob, when the Bible commands you to fulfill your sexual duty that means it's your job to make your wife's toes curl. So get to work on that!"

A few weeks later, the couple approached us after church. Lisa was glowing. She said, "Ask me if I've been having orgasms." I looked at her and said, "I don't think we have to. It looks like things are going great."

On the way home from church, Tim asked me if I noticed Bob's response when his wife was talking about her sexual success. Tim said, "Bob looked like a peacock at Lincoln Park Zoo. He was proudly displaying his feathers and strutting his stuff as Lisa talked about being sexually satisfied by her man."

We once shared this story at a Marriage Advance. A young man in the audience raised his hand before the session ended to ask, "Hey, Tim, any chance husbands can get a copy of that napkin?"

Since this topic seems to prompt questions with nearly every young couple we meet, let's briefly consider the phases of orgasm. The sex research team of Masters and Johnson broke down the sexual response pattern into four specific phases.[4]

1.   **The Excitement Phase.** This is the initial arousal phase when sexual stimulation causes a man's penis or a woman's nipples to become erect. Your spouse may be visually stimulated by your body or sexually charged by a memory of a romantic time together with you. Many things can distract a person from the excitement phase, and a person's sexual response can be diminished if other areas of their life are out of balance. Some of the issues that can interfere with arousal include stress, illness, hormone imbalance, lack of sleep, poor nutrition or health, depression, and low self-esteem.

2.   **The Plateau Phase.** This is the longest phase of lovemaking as arousal intensifies for the man and the woman. A women's clitoris and a man's penis experience the most dramatic change during this phase. A man's penis swells while a women's vagina becomes lubricated in preparation for penetration. In this phase a husband and wife usually take turns sexually stimulating one another leading up to orgasm.

3.   **The Orgasmic Phase.** This is the shortest and most intense phase, when orgasmic contractions are experienced. Intense sexual stimulation occurs; breathing increases; blood pressure and heart rates rise; muscles contract; a man ejaculates. A man's climax is centered around his genitals, while a woman's climax tends to encompass her entire body.

Couples who enjoy mutual orgasms may be disappointed if their goal is to experience simultaneous release. While reaching orgasm at the same time may happen occasionally, it is the exception rather than the rule. Some couples never achieve orgasm simultaneously, but this should not interfere with their sexual satisfaction. Often a husband brings his wife to orgasm first. When she has climaxed, she can focus on her husband achieving orgasm.

Body Oneness

4. The Resolution Phase. During this final phase, muscles relax and the body returns to pre-stimulated state.

BREAKING DOWN BARRIERS

You may have identified yourself as a person who is not experiencing a satisfying sex life. You may be struggling with achieving regular orgasms or with some other sexual issue.

Please know that most couples will experience some sexual difficulties at some point in their marriage. Yet very few get outside help or counsel. Too many couples settle for less than God's design for sex. They refuse to seek counsel or talk to a physician, pastor, or trusted friend. Some people won't even talk to their spouse. They may feel embarrassed or ashamed to even admit having sexual questions or concerns. As sexual problems arise, couples often simply endure them, hoping the difficulties will resolve themselves over time.

However, in working with couples over the years, our experience shows that without some kind of intervention, problems do not usually disappear or get better on their own. In most cases, things get worse. Often couples believe that sex problems are the main problem, but it is usually only the fruit of the problem. Root issues in a person's life can stay hidden for a long time, then surface in the sexual dimension of a couple's relationship.

Sexual struggles can be red flags trying to get your attention. These may be rooted in a lack of knowledge, a medical issue, or an emotional or relational issue. Whatever it is, do not let these troubles become obstacles. Instead ask the Lord to help you see them as opportunities.

The good news is that we have seen couples in all seasons of marriage experience tremendous healing and breakthroughs in body oneness. Choosing to discuss sensitive sexual topics often demystifies areas that couples keep hidden. We encourage you to begin by first bringing your concerns to God, and then discussing them with your spouse. If you are unable to reach agreement, it is wise to include a third party who may help you get to root issues hidden beneath the surface.

The Bible reminds us, "Without good direction, people lose their way; the more wise counsel you follow, the better your chances."[5] If things surface that need to be addressed, make the decision to get help. You may start by purchasing a Christian book on sexuality and then seek outside counsel, if needed. This will enable you and your spouse to advance in body oneness as you understand and passionately live out the miracle and mystery of what it means for two to become one.

On the other hand, if you are married and enjoy body oneness the way God designed, give thanks to God. Then prayerfully choose one couple you can invest in.

The Bible instructs older women to invest in younger women. Women, take a young wife out for coffee. Pray for an opportunity to talk with her about sex. Push through any uncomfortable barriers that may be present. Young married women desperately need the godly counsel, encouragement, and wisdom that come from mature women.

Men, we challenge you to reach out to one young man and share your experiences. Many young men are longing for spiritual dads. We sincerely believe that as more men and women step into the roles of being spiritual parents, the relational and sexual temperature of many marriages will dramatically increase for the better.

Body Oneness

+ Chapter 20

What's Okay and What's Not?

Dealing with Sensitive Sexual Topics

In the previous chapter we discussed a variety of areas where couples need to be honest about their expectations in order to move toward body oneness. Through our years of working with couples, we've noticed that certain other topics regularly come up as issues that create conflict in the bedroom.

In this chapter we'll discuss some of these sensitive sexual topics, looking to God's Word for wisdom to help you and your spouse advance in soul and body oneness.

LOCATIONS

When we first got married, we lived in an apartment. I (Tim) wanted to make sure Anne was safe when I was on duty for my twenty-four-hour shifts as a fireman, so I installed heavy-duty dead-bolt locks on the door of our second-floor apartment.

One Sunday after church we decided to spend the afternoon in bed. Just as things were beginning to get a little frisky, Anne suddenly slammed on the brakes. "Tim, will you close and lock the bedroom door?"

I said, "Hon, trust me, we are completely alone in this apartment. No one else is home. We are safe and secure. We have double locks on the one and only door to this apartment. We are on the second floor. I put a steel bar in the sliding patio door. I parked the car on the other side of the complex. No one even knows we're home. There has not been a crime reported in this area in who knows how many decades. Trust me: a cat burglar could not get into this place!"

Anne responded, "I know…but…I'd just feel better if the bedroom door was locked."

This was a moment of truth. I could make a big deal out of this, cause a fight, and wreck the moment. Or I could jump out of bed in my birthday suit and lock the stupid door. Over thirty years later, this story seems silly. But at the time it could have easily turned into an argument.

The Bible says, "When a man takes a new wife, he shall not go out with the army nor be charged with any duty; he shall be free at home one year and shall give happiness to his wife whom he has taken."[1] I think this was the right idea. It has taken time to *know* Anne and to learn how to please her emotionally and sexually. After over three decades of marriage, I still don't fully know my bride, but I am committed to never stop trying.

God wants husbands and wives to celebrate the sexual freedom He has given them in marriage. Since we are made in the image of a creative God, we are designed to have that creativity extend into every area of our life, including our sex life.

Having sex in a variety of locations other than the bedroom may be one way for a couple to creatively enjoy sex. Some couples have sex in different rooms in their home, in the car, or outside under the stars. Personally, we believe having sex in a variety of locations is okay with our creative God. But it's important to have a conversation with your spouse about it. Implement the Traffic Light Principle to make sure you both are in agreement.

While experimenting with different safe locations to enjoy sex can be exciting for some husbands and wives, others find the idea scary. One wife realized how many rules and restrictions she had regarding sexual freedom, and she decided to try her husband's idea of enjoying sex in different locations. She said, "I actually imagined reading the morning headlines of our local newspaper: *Mr. and Mrs. Smith, Elders at First Community Church, Arrested by Local Authorities for Having Sex in Their Car in an Open Field!*"

When processing sexual creativity, we encourage implementation of the Traffic Light Principle (see chapter 11). Wait until both partners have a green light. Unity is critical for mutual success and enjoyment.

SEXUAL POSITIONS

If you are looking for creativity, many resources are available. Plenty of books are available that suggest a variety of sexual positions. But we find that most couples, rather than seeking creative sexual positions, are asking for help on how to reach agreement on sexual positions. The

Body Oneness

What's Okay and What's Not?

questions they ask point to a power struggle: "Whose way is the right way? How do I handle it when my spouse keeps insisting on sexual positions that I am not interested in trying? We seem to end up in arguments before we even begin."

Most often, these couples are really dealing with power struggles, demanding spirits, anger, and trust issues. Here again, we encourage couples to focus on questions involving soul oneness. Are you basing your decision on "me" or on "**We**"? How is your communication in other areas of your marriage? Are you in unity? Are you living in the **Larger Story** sexually? Are you praying for each other? In what specific ways are you Reflecting and Revealing the goodness of God to each other?

Sexual intimacy is about friendship and advancing in communication skills. The best solution is to go back to God's plan. Passionately look for new ways to reframe whatever sexual obstacles you are experiencing in the context of "It's not about me."

It is amazing how individuals find their hearts changing when they reframe sexual issues by focusing on God and their spouse.

QUICKIES

At a recent REAL LIFE Marriage Advance, one of the questions submitted was, "What is a quickie?" Before we could respond, the senior pastor jumped up out of his seat and said, "Let me answer this question." We handed him the microphone.

He stood in front of his congregation and invited his wife to stand next to him. He said, "Friends, let me give you a great definition of a quickie." He paused for a moment. "My wife and I enjoy food. A few times a year we like to make reservations at a really nice restaurant. These restaurants promise a fine dining experience. They have white linen tablecloths, silver utensils, and fine china. They offer multiple courses, including appetizers and dessert. Whenever we have a fine dining experience, it lasts for hours."

He paused, "Don't get me wrong; we love fine dining. But on our budget and with our lifestyle we only are able to enjoy it occasionally. Most of time we are so tired and hungry at the end of the day, we just grab something fast. Sometimes we even zip through the drive-thru window. My wife and I like to refer to quickies as drive-thru sex."

This pastor's sheep roared, and the permission this leader gave to his flock was much more valuable than anything we could have said about *quickies*.

MASTURBATION

This controversial topic generates passionate opinions, strong feelings, and much disagreement among Christians. Some firmly believe it violates God's principles. Others consider masturbation to be a natural expression of a person's sexuality. At one Marriage Advance a man commented, "God has given food to enjoy. He has given sex to enjoy. He has given orgasms to enjoy. Why are Christians so hung up on the subject of masturbation?"

In processing this topic, we begin by asking, *Where does it say in the Bible, "Thou shall not masturbate"?* We do not find masturbation specifically addressed in the Bible, and we believe any topic not clearly dealt with in the Bible must be approached with humility and wisdom.

The second question we ask is this: *If masturbation is not in the Bible, what does the Bible say about lust?* Lust is defined as "the strong physical desire to have sex with somebody, usually without associated feelings of love or affection."[2] Lust is addressed throughout the Bible and clearly defined as sin. It is a form of counterfeit intimacy. Whereas godly intimacy is a life-giving and life-affirming component of love and marriage, lust is a self-centered, **smaller story** experience. It reflects an attitude of "I want it all and I want it now."

This leads to our third question: *Can a person masturbate without lusting?* Masturbation usually involves lustful fantasy. Since such fantasizing does not involve relationship with a real person but with a mental image, this type of self-gratification is a counterfeit form of God's design for sexual intimacy.

Body Oneness

People often use pornography as part of their masturbation process. Pornography is a doorway to lust, and leads to progressive and destructive addiction. An orgasm releases powerful chemicals in the brain, which means masturbation — and whatever images or experiences are on the mind at the time of climax — becomes a part of a person's sexual imprinting. We have counseled people, especially those who masturbate compulsively, whose minds are so deeply imprinted with negative sexual distortions that it affects all their relationships.

God designed sex to help married couples advance in oneness, but masturbation is a solitary act that has the potential to undermine intimacy. Look at it this way: A couple opens a joint bank account a few weeks before they get married. They agree to a specific plan of using godly principles to steward their finances. Because it is a joint account, they manage their money together. Every week they agree to both make a direct deposit. If one spouse ever wants to withdraw money from their joint account, they agree to first discuss it. This financial plan provides them a level of accountability and protection from many financial stressors that negatively impact a marriage relationship.

Now what if every couple viewed their sexual relationship the same way? Here's how one husband describes this approach: "When we got married, God opened a joint intimacy and sexual account for us to enjoy. He wants us to make regular deposits in that account so we can strengthen and encourage each other. Every time I show love to my wife, I am making a deposit in our joint intimacy and sexuality account. Every time my wife encourages me, she is making a deposit in our account. Together we manage and monitor our intimacy and sexuality account. When we enjoy intimacy and sex we are withdrawing from the surplus in our account. We would never think of making a sexual withdrawal unless we both agreed."

We believe masturbation can be compared to making a withdrawal from a couple's joint sexual account. Often masturbation lowers a person's sexual desire. If one spouse desires sex, the partner who is masturbating may not be as interested because their sexual needs have already been met. Masturbation also can be a way to avoid intimacy and avoid working through any sexual chaos. We refer to masturbation as "me-sex" because it violates the one-flesh principle.

If you engage in masturbation and don't believe it creates any problems in your relationship, we encourage you to process the following questions:

Does your spouse know that you masturbate?
Do you tell your spouse every time you masturbate?
Do you tell your spouse what you are thinking about while masturbating?
Do you masturbate in front of each other?

Questions like these invite couples to seriously explore deeper aspects involved in masturbation. It has been our experience that married couples who regularly masturbate rate their sexual satisfaction low. Masturbation becomes a way to avoid intimacy as well as a means of self-medicating and avoiding marital problems.

ORAL SEX AND ORAL STIMULATION

We define oral stimulation as one spouse orally stimulating their spouse's genital area, and oral sex as orally stimulating one's spouse to orgasm. Neither of these sexual topics is addressed with detail in the Bible. As with the previous subject, whenever a topic is not clearly and specifically addressed in the Bible, we believe it must be approached with care and considered in light of broader principles given in God's Word. In this case we ask, *Does oral stimulation or oral sex violate any of the principles clearly stated in God's Word?*

The Old Testament book called the Song of Songs explores marital intimacy and sexuality. It is a love story rich in imagery and figurative language. The Song of Songs also speaks graphically about the sensual pleasures in marriage. It refers to specific body parts that visually stimulate and bring pleasure to a spouse. It describes stages of sensual arousal a couple experiences as their passion and love for each other increases.

In chapter 4, the text alludes to the husband being invited into his bride's garden. "May my beloved come into his garden and eat its choice fruits!"[3] Biblically, the garden is symbolic of female genitalia. Here, the wife is inviting the husband into "his" garden to take in all its splendor. Another

Body Oneness

passage says, "In his shade I took great delight and sat down, and his fruit was sweet to my taste."[4]

Men and women generally have strong feelings about oral sex and oral stimulation. These feelings can range from extremely negative to extremely positive. Some married couples have no desire to participate in this form of sexual stimulation. Others tell us that oral stimulation is an important part of their sex life, increasing their pleasure and taking their sexual enjoyment to new levels. An elderly woman who had been married almost fifty years approached us at a Marriage Advance and thanked us for addressing sensitive sexual topics. She then quietly whispered to us that at her and her husband's age oral stimulation was almost a necessity for both of them to experience orgasms.

As with other difficult subjects related to sexual expressions, opinions range all over the map on this subject. Some of the comments we've received from seminar participants include: "We believe oral stimulation is okay, but a man ejaculating in a woman's mouth is not okay. The only place for a husband to place his seed (sperm) should be in his wife's vagina." "Orally satisfying one another is a highlight of our lovemaking!" "Orally satisfying one another is something we are not remotely interested in!"

Various couples have described oral stimulation and oral sex as *fun, gross, joyful, sinful, natural, and unnatural*. With such a wide variety of reactions, it's no surprise that a number of people have told us that these topics cause division and strife in their marriage. When a husband and wife begin to explore each other sexually, one person may feel a measure of freedom to experiment while their partner does not share the same enthusiasm. These kinds of differences often cause conflict. Some feel pressure from their spouse to engage in this form of sexual activity.

One young man approached Tim and said, "My wife wants me to perform oral sex. I have never done that before. I am not opposed to giving it a try, but honestly, I have no clue what I am supposed to do."

Practically speaking, how does a married couple process the idea of oral stimulation and oral sex?

Body Oneness

We strongly caution against pressuring your spouse to do something he or she is not comfortable with. Manipulation and control are not God's idea. Being together as one, loving and respecting each other, and being on the same page is more important than one spouse getting his or her way.

Our practical counsel to couples about intimate sexual areas is for both the husband and wife to implement the Traffic Light Principle. We encourage both the husband and wife to talk openly and then prayerfully bring their requests to the Lord. Be open to listening to God. Read through the Scriptures together. Ask the Lord to give you the freedom to explore and enjoy each other's bodies within the covenant of marriage.

Often disagreements in marriage can lead a couple into deeper levels of intimacy and understanding as together they explore the roots of the problem. It is important for couples to explore any resistance they have and look for ways to open the dialogue. Praying together and getting counsel provides tremendous benefits and breakthroughs. For example, a husband or wife may not want to experiment with oral stimulation because they were raised in a toxic religious environment. Throughout their formative years when the subject of sex came up, they may have observed a lot of fear and negativity. Or if a husband or wife experienced emotional or sexual abuse, they may have wounds that need to be processed with a trained counselor.

Couples who open themselves to growth and commit to a healthy process will reach a healthy outcome. The key is to focus your heart and attitude on God's design for marriage. In marriage any obstacle can become an opportunity to Reflect and Reveal the love and goodness of God.

Some couples tell us that oral sex and oral stimulation are exciting and adventurous parts in their lovemaking. We celebrate the decision they have mutually reached. We talk with other couples who say they've identified these as areas they don't even want to try. We celebrate the decision they have mutually reached. We talk to couples who are on different pages on these topics. One spouse wants to experiment with oral stimulation and oral sex and the other spouse does not. We encourage these couples to humbly live out God's design for marriage, to avoid pressuring one another, to pray, and watch God work.

Body Oneness

What's Okay and What's Not?

ANAL SEX

We realize this may be an uncomfortable subject to raise, but when we speak to married, premarital groups, or students, we regularly get questions about anal sex. We have been approached by women who privately say to us, "My husband really wants to try anal sex. I don't want to be a prude. What should I do?"

Unlike some of the other areas we've discussed, we believe the Bible is clear on this topic: The Bible says anal sex is unnatural and perverted.[5] This leads to the conclusion that anal sex is not God's design.

Unfortunately, even among Christians there is a measure of confusion surrounding anal sex. Some Christian authors state that anal sex is only prohibited between two men. Their position on anal sex between a husband and a wife is that it is permissible if both agree. These authors base their position on the silence of Scripture. In other words, if it is not specifically prohibited in the Bible, they conclude it is permissible between a consenting husband and wife.

We believe that equating the silence of Scriptures to permission to engage in a particular act is a dangerous model of biblical interpretation. Why? Because the Bible is silent on a number of things. For example, sadomasochism is not specifically addressed in the Bible as being forbidden in marriage, yet this behavior violates the principles of love and reciprocal servanthood and therefore is damaging to marital oneness.

We must judge behaviors on whether they Reflect and Reveal the character of God. The Bible specifically identifies anal sex as an unnatural perversion. Whether this act is between two men, between a man and a woman, or with animals, it is not a natural or life-affirming behavior. Therefore, we believe a man sodomizing a man or a man sodomizing a woman are both unnatural and dangerous acts.

A person's rectum is designed for the purpose of eliminating toxic by-products of digestion. It is not designed to receive a male's penis. The anus is not self-lubricating in the same way a women's vagina is. From a medical standpoint, anal sex is potentially dangerous. Penetration can tear the wall of the rectum and cause bleeding that may go undetected.

Body Oneness

Tears in the bowel can lead to infection and other medical problems, including toxic shock, which can result in death.

Hurting a spouse in any way is never a part of God's design. This is one of the most basic and foundational principles in the Bible.

INTIMACY-BUILDING QUESTIONS TO ADVANCE IN BODY ONENESS

As a practical response to this chapter, we encourage you to prayerfully discuss with your spouse the following questions, viewing them as tools to help you advance together in soul and body oneness. Couples we have worked with have experienced remarkable growth as they prayerfully processed these questions together.

1.   Are we doing anything that is prohibited by Scripture?
Jesus said, "If you love Me, you will keep My commandments."[6] God allows tremendous sexual freedom within the bonds of marriage. However, the Bible also sets certain prohibitions that must be obeyed for a marriage to thrive. In their book *Intimate Issues,* authors Linda Dillow and Lorraine Pintus list ten things specifically prohibited by Scripture: fornication, adultery, homosexual acts, impurity, orgies, prostitution, lustful passions, sodomy, obscenity and coarse joking, and incest.[7]

2.   Is there anything I am doing that is hurtful or offensive to you?
The Bible tells us, "Do nothing from selfishness or empty conceit, but with humility of mind regard one another as more important than yourselves; do not merely look out for your own personal interests, but also for the interests of others."[8] Hurting a spouse in any way is a violation of God's design. Your sexual relationship should never involve anything that is harmful or offensive to your spouse.

3.   Is there anything I am doing that you would prefer me not to do?
Remember, " 'Everything is permissible for me,' but not everything is beneficial."[9] Often a husband or wife may feel more sexual freedom or desire for creativity than their spouse. Here's where the Traffic Light Principle can be helpful. If one spouse has a yellow or red light, it requires discussion. We encourage couples to prayerfully process any differences.

Body Oneness

In sex, as well as every area in marriage, marital unity is always more important than one spouse getting his or her way.

4. Is there anything you would like to try or experiment with together?
The Bible clearly indicates God's intent for a married couple to fully enjoy each other's bodies: "I am my beloved's and my beloved is mine."[10] "Eat… drink and imbibe deeply, O lovers."[11]

God designed sex to be enjoyed with freedom and creativity. Initiate discussion with your spouse about the sexual area of your marriage. Look for new and creative ways to please each other. One couple told us they equate sex to food. They both agree that food is something they enjoy every day. They decided to take the same approach to their sex life. Every day they look for some way to nurture their body oneness. It may not include sexual intercourse or mutual orgasms, but they try to do something every day to bless each other in the sexual dimension of their marriage.

+   +   +

After you have processed these questions with your spouse, we encourage you to ask these same questions to the Lord.

+   *Lord, is there anything I am doing that is prohibited in Scripture?*

+   *Lord, is there anything I am doing that is hurtful or offensive to You?*

+   *Lord, is there anything I am doing that You would prefer I not do?*

+   *Lord, is there anything You would like me to try or experiment with?*

+ Chapter 21

Joy in Duty

Finding Pleasure in Meeting Each Other's Sexual Needs

We were counseling a couple who had been married for more than fifteen years. Their life together included many stresses typical for families in their stage of life. They both held full-time jobs outside the home. Their three children were involved in activities that required the family's participation. The wife's elderly mom lived nearby and needed a lot of attention, particularly since she had recently been diagnosed with cancer.

Up until recently, they had been able to juggle their responsibilities, but lately their marriage had been showing the effects of their demanding lives — and their sexual relationship was taking the hardest hit. In making time for everything and everyone else, they had put their sexual needs last. It was always the first thing eliminated from their to-do list when family life got busy...and it was always busy. The enemy was slowly adding ingredients to a recipe for marital disaster.

Whenever the bedroom door closed and the subject of sex came up, they became different people. Sex was often used as a form of manipulation and control. One spouse would withhold sex from the other in attempts to nonverbally communicate disapproval or anger. It became a power play that allowed one or both spouses to get their needs met.

When we first started discussing their sexual relationship, the tension between them was incredibly high. The husband said he felt ignored and accused his wife of being controlling and manipulative. The wife defended herself by saying her sexual satisfaction was almost zero. She had little if any interest in working on an area of their life that seemed to be all about *him*.

Since they found it difficult to listen to each other, we challenged them to listen to what the Lord had to say about their sexual relationship by spending some time praying through 1 Corinthians 7:2-5:

"Each man is to have his own wife, and each woman is to have her own husband. The husband must fulfill his duty to his wife, and likewise also the wife to her husband. The wife does not have authority over her own body, but the husband does; and likewise also the husband does not have authority over his own body, but the wife does. Stop depriving one another, except by agreement for a time, so that you may devote

Body Oneness

yourselves to prayer, and come together again so that Satan will not tempt you because of your lack of self-control."

When they returned a few weeks later, they both confessed to struggling with the idea of sex as a duty they were responsible to fulfill. Even though romance had left their sexual relationship years ago, they felt that sexual duty sounded way too regimented. The husband bluntly said, "Are you kidding me? We are supposed to view sex as a duty to fulfill? That sounds more like a military command!"

The fact is, a husband and wife have a sexual duty to each other. Duty is defined as "something that somebody is obliged to do for moral, legal, or religious reasons."[1] The Corinthians passage specifically instructs a married couple to fulfill their sexual duty to one another.

Fulfilling a duty may not sound very romantic. When I (Tim) was in the fire department, I worked a twenty-four-hour shift every third day. Reporting for duty meant I was required to be at the firehouse, available to work, and ready to engage. I loved being a fireman. Most duty days were filled with lights and sirens, excitement and risk. But there were plenty of days when I did not feel like reporting for duty. I was exhausted from working seventy hours at two different jobs, and things were stressful at home. On those days, reporting for duty seemed more like work than joy.

Likewise, there are times in marriage when sex is fun, exciting, and a lights-and-sirens experience. But there are also times when one spouse, or both, is working long hours or feels tired and stressed. During these times, one spouse may desire sexual intimacy when the other spouse does not. On those days sex can feel more like reporting for duty than celebrating body oneness.

However, the command to fulfill sexual *duty* is not to be viewed as a millstone around a spouse's neck. It is an invitation to celebrate your emotional and relational connection and to protect your marital oneness. It is a duty birthed in obedience and freedom to love and serve a spouse. In freedom, one spouse chooses to serve and bring pleasure and comfort to the other. Your motive and attitude are key to fulfilling your sexual duty as you step into the **Larger Story** and live out "marriage is not about me."

There are times in our marriage when one of us may desire sexual intimacy and may affectionately say to the other, "Hon, would you like to fulfill your duty tonight?"

SEXUAL OBEDIENCE AND SUBMISSION

Let's return to that 1 Corinthians 7 passage for a moment. Verse 4 says, "The wife does not have authority over her own body, but the husband does; and likewise also the husband does not have authority over his own body, but the wife does."

In marriage a husband's and wife's bodies belong to each other. The husband and wife have mutual authority in body oneness, which opens the door to being reciprocal servants to each other.

Unfortunately, this passage is often misrepresented in discussions between spouses. We have actually heard husbands say, "The Bible says my wife's body belongs to me. She needs to meet my sexual needs!" We also have heard women saying, "My husband's body belongs to me. He needs to meet my sexual needs!" Biblically, are they both right?

The text is clear and straightforward. If sex was just a physical act, couples could choose to view this text as the law and take a legalistic approach. One spouse could demand or shame the other into following the letter of the law. However, couples who choose this style of relating miss out on the heart of what God is saying.

At the heart of this command is the idea of focusing on reciprocal servanthood rather than on one spouse's authority or perceived rights. Sexual expression in marriage is an invitation to lovingly process duty, authority, and mutual submission together as a "**We**."

This passage reframes the sexual dimension in marriage, shifting a couple's primary focus away from self and onto God and His plan for sex. Fulfilling your sexual duty within marriage means arranging your priorities so that you are first pleasing God, then serving your spouse, and then having your individual needs met.

The Bible gives only one exception to the command for a husband and wife to fulfill their sexual duty to each other. If a husband and wife decide not to have sex, their decision must meet all of these criteria:

1. except by agreement (by mutual consent)

2. for a time (temporary)

3. to devote themselves to prayer

In other words, it's not okay to withhold sex from each other for any reason except prayer. This command forces a couple to process any differences instead of using sex as a form of manipulation or control.

This passage concludes by reminding a husband and wife to "come together again so that Satan will not tempt you because of your lack of self-control." The enemy realm includes spirits and demons, so we find it interesting that the Bible specifically identifies Satan himself as the tempter for couples who sexually deprive each other. Satan will jump at the chance to attack a couple and wreak havoc in a marriage if they fail to heed this command. That is why understanding and living out God's design for sexuality and body oneness is important in every marriage.

Perhaps you are disturbed by the idea of sex as an issue of obedience and submission. You may think, *My body belongs to me, not to my spouse. I would never totally give my body to my spouse. Maybe he or she can use my body occasionally, but it is mine.* If you are experiencing any of these responses, it may be an indication that you have trust issues or other wounds that need to be addressed. Submitting sexually may stir up issues related to your childhood, past relationships, forgiveness, abuse, or other wounds. We encourage you to bring this passage to the Lord. Talk to Him about any hurt, confusion, resistance, or rebellion. This may be an invitation for you to see a trained Christian counselor, talk to a trusted friend, or meet with someone who specializes in the sexual area in marriage.

Body Oneness

AGREE TO SUCCEED

Let's return to the couple we met at the start of this chapter. You'll remember that amid the chaos of life, their marriage, and particularly their sexual relationship, had been seriously neglected.

This couple's story is a good example of how a presenting problem — *"The only thing wrong in our marriage is our sex life"* — is often a signpost leading to other issues that need to be addressed. People's stories are complex. Problems in one area of marriage are generally related to other areas. Sex problems (Body Oneness) are almost always related to intimacy (Soul Oneness) issues. So we challenged them to review areas of their lives including parenting, finances, relationships, work, and play. We asked them to work together on a plan for how they would manage these areas to advance in intimacy.

When they returned several weeks later, the wife, who had great administrative skills, pulled out a detailed spreadsheet of the different areas in their lives. Together they had put together a plan for parenting that included scheduled family nights. Recognizing that they needed more time alone to dream and have fun, they also had planned bimonthly date nights for the two of them. They had a financial plan that included tithing to their church and saving for retirement. They had a plan for their involvement at church. They even renewed their health club membership and began to work out regularly.

As we reviewed each area of their life, we applauded them for all the healthy choices they had made. The wife commented, "We should have done this years ago. It does take time and discipline, but we are both taking personal responsibility instead of blaming each other." The husband added, "It is a lot of work, but we believe it's worth the effort."

We then asked if they noticed anything missing from their master plan. As they looked over their spreadsheet, the lights suddenly went on. They realized they had not included a plan for their sex life. We said, "Just like every other area of your life, your sex life takes time and discipline. But if you are both willing to take responsibility instead of blaming each other, it will be worth the effort."

Body Oneness

We challenged this couple to make a sexual agreement, a detailed plan to help them to succeed sexually. (We'll explain sexual agreements in detail in the next chapter.) When they returned for their next session, they did not yet have a full plan. They explained that they had argued about sexual frequency and taking turns initiating. As a third party, we helped them process through some of their differences and reach agreement.

They returned three weeks later, and we sensed a change as soon as they walked in. They described their experience with the sexual agreement, "It seemed awkward at first," the husband said. "A little too regimented. But when we looked at it as a way to strategically approach our sex life like every other area of our life, something clicked."

The wife continued, "The sexual agreement just took so much pressure off of us. We now understand that we each have a duty to meet each other's sexual needs. We are both taking responsibility. It's like we have became a team sexually. We don't have to fight about locations, or who should initiate, or other specific sexual preferences. These areas have all been discussed and agreed on together."

Helpful though it can be, a sexual agreement is not a cure-all for sexual problems and frustrations in marriage. As we continued to counsel with this couple, other issues surfaced. We reviewed and processed their families of origin. We dealt with their sexual histories, soul ties, and some childhood wounds. We met individually with each spouse. We talked about how men and women respond differently sexually.

We walked with this couple over the next few seasons, and we were delighted to hear that their sexual intimacy and joy in body oneness increased exponentially as they continued to grow in unity and walk out their sexual agreement. Sometime later, they came in for a checkup and they humbled us with their love for God and each other.

BUT WHAT IF...?

Before moving on, we want to address a difficult subject often raised by both husbands and wives. They say, "I hear you describe how God designed body oneness, and it sounds great. I just wish I viewed sex with

Body Oneness

my spouse the way you describe it. But what if I am not attracted to my spouse the way I used to be? Is there anything I can do?"

We encourage couples struggling in this area to start with God. We challenge them to memorize and live out the Bible passage that reads, "The LORD does not look at the things man looks at. Man looks at the outward appearance, but the LORD looks at the heart."[2]

Remember, sex involves a person's spirit, soul, and body, but our culture indoctrinates people from an early age to focus almost exclusively on the body. Billions of dollars are invested in advertising and marketing to entice men and women to focus on outward appearances. The reality is that after ten, twenty, thirty, forty-plus years, most couples look different than they did on their wedding day. A person's body will inevitably change over time. That is why it is so important to fight against the inordinate significance our culture places on outward appearances.

We challenge every husband and wife to develop a healthy and holistic view of spirit, soul, and body oneness. And for individuals who feel a lack of attraction to their spouse, we urge them to prayerfully focus on what we call soul-sex. Focus on your spouse's heart, on intimacy, friendship, and how you have walked side-by-side together through life. When you ask God to give you His heart for your spouse, we're convinced you will find yourself drawn toward intimacy at every level.

+   +   +

One night the two of us had stayed up late. When we finally went to bed, I (Tim) asked Anne if she wanted me to massage her feet. She asked if the question beneath my question was, *Can I have sex?*

I responded, "Well…sex would be nice!"

There was a long pause. Anne didn't say yes…but she didn't say no. So I decided to proceed with the massage and hope it would lead to sex. I grabbed the lotion and got to work. Soon I noticed that Anne was falling asleep. In a subtle attempt to wake her, I squeezed her feet. Then I paused and thought, *Can I just massage her feet without it leading to sex?* Then I wondered, *Is that even possible?* To which I responded, *I can do this!*

As I continued massaging her feet, I tried to resist any thoughts of *her* foot massage being about *my* having sex.

Determined not to think about sex, I let my mind wander in other directions. I began to reflect on how our feet have walked side by side throughout life. I looked at Anne's feet and thought about how she likes to wear sandals and walk barefoot. I thought about our decades of marriage and how many times I have seen her taking care of her feet. I thought about the tiny pink sponges she puts between her toes when she paints her nails.

As I continued with the massage, I began to remember all the places Anne's feet have taken her. I remembered the two of us walking together down the hallways in junior high school. I remembered her walking toward me down the aisle of the church where we were married. I remembered her bare feet in the hospital when each of our four children was born. I remembered her pushing baby strollers, following Big Wheels, and running behind our kids as they attempted their first bike rides.

Then I began to remember all the times Anne and I stood together side by side. We stood together raising our four children. We stood together at sporting events, concerts, plays, recitals, and church activities, supporting our kids and cheering them on. I remembered standing together at graduations, fire department promotions, and retirement parties. I remembered standing together side by side when we were baptized in an old movie theater.

As I continued massaging Anne's feet, I began to remember difficult seasons in our life. I remembered standing together side by side next to hospice beds in our living room. I remembered Anne standing next to me, practically holding me up, as I spoke at my dad's funeral. And I remembered walking together side by side as we carried parents and loved ones to their graves.

Then I pictured Anne joyfully dancing at our children's wedding receptions. I remembered all three times we walked side by side into hospitals to welcome our grandchildren into the world. I remembered watching her loosen their tightly wrapped newborn baby blankets and tenderly kiss their tiny feet.

Body Oneness

I reviewed how we had journeyed together through so many life changes. Moving away from family, lifelong friends, and a great church in Chicago to serve in a small church in Western Michigan. Moving again just five years later to Pasadena, California, to serve as deans at a new leadership school for twenty-somethings. Moving yet once more to Colorado and then quitting our jobs to step into REAL LIFE Ministries full-time. And with each transition and all the associated ups and downs, by God's grace we walked in faith…together…side by side.

Then I thought about Anne's body connected to the feet I was massaging. I thought about all the celebration, pleasure, comfort, and joy she has given me. I thanked God for her health and for giving her such an awesome heart, soul, mind, and body. I reflected on the amazing fact that, out of six billion people on this planet, this one person, a young girl named Anne O'Shaughnessy Evans, captured my heart! I thought about the Song of Songs verse that says, "I am my beloved's and my beloved is mine." [3]

Then I thought about one of our favorite books, *Windows of the Soul*.[4] The author, Ken Gire, tells how God gives us windows throughout our lifetime. If we take the time to experience these windows, he writes, they can become a source of wonder. As I massaged Anne's feet, I reviewed windows of life we have been in together and thanked God for the wonder, the miracle, and mystery in marriage of *two becoming one*. Wonder is a short stepping stone to worship. I found myself worshiping and thanking God for Anne, for our oneness and marriage. I was not worshiping Anne. I was in awe of the God who created her.

About half an hour had passed and Anne was sound asleep. I finally confessed to myself that, initially, massaging Anne's feet was really all about me. It may have appeared like I was serving her, but my real agenda was to have sex. I told God I was sorry, and with a worshipful heart I thanked God for this window, for Anne, and for allowing us to stand together…side by side throughout life.

I gently kissed her feet and slipped them into her favorite warm socks, crawled in bed beside her, and placed my feet under hers. I wrapped my arms around her and fell asleep. Together again, side by side.

TAKING BODY ONENESS TO A WHOLE NEW LEVEL

Whatever the current state of your sexual relationship, we challenge you to take these Body Oneness Challenges and discover an even deeper level of sexual intimacy with your spouse:

1. View sex as an act of worship

Sex is a gift from God for celebration, procreation, protection, pleasure, and comfort. As a couple passionately lives out sexual intimacy in marriage, their body oneness can become an act of worship, a celebration in thanksgiving of the author of sex. Inviting God into your lovemaking opens the door to worship. Picture God observing your sexual intimacy the same way He did with the married lovers in Song of Songs. Visualize God saying to you and your spouse, "Eat, friends; Drink and imbibe deeply, O lovers."

Life-Giving Challenge: Prayerfully invite God, the author of sex, to lead a time of lovemaking with your spouse. Begin by doing a heart check. Ask the Holy Spirit to identify anything that may be inhibiting or blocking your intimacy and soul oneness. This may include unforgiveness, a past hurt or disappointment, stress, frustrations, bitterness, hardness of heart, or anything else that God brings to mind.

After you have dealt with anything that may have been inhibiting your intimacy, initiate making love with your spouse. Afterward, take note of how your spouse responded to your initiating sex. Record how you felt after inviting God to lead this experiment.

2. View sex as an act of spiritual warfare

God says the only person who should meet a husband or wife's sexual needs is their spouse, but the enemy tries to create division and disunity through temptation. God designed sexual intimacy in marriage as an act of spiritual warfare. When a husband and wife are sexually pleasing each other, this becomes a hedge of protection around their "**We**." Understanding that a healthy sex life helps a couple resist Satan's temptation is a great motivator for mutually living out God's design for body oneness.

Body Oneness

Life-Giving Challenge: Read 1 Corinthians 7:2-5. What does the Bible mean when it says, "Stop depriving one another, except by agreement for a time, so that you may devote yourselves to prayer, and come together again so that Satan will not tempt you"? Do you understand the warfare component to a healthy sex life? Do you or your spouse ever experience sexual temptation? Do you resist temptation by unselfishly serving each other sexually?

Ask the Holy Spirit to guide you in a "heart check," identifying anything that may be inhibiting or blocking your intimacy with your spouse. Pray for a time when you can initiate a discussion about this passage with your spouse and share what the Lord is showing you. Encourage your spouse to share how withholding or controlling sex might impact your oneness and open the door to temptation.

3. Review yourself as a sexual partner

This challenge is not about how you think your spouse feels about you in the sexual area of your marriage; this is about how you rate *yourself* as a lover of your spouse. Begin by listing all the positive aspects you bring to your marriage sexually. Do you understand God's design for sex? Do you know the importance of your sexual role? Is sex exciting and enjoyable for you in these ways? Would you say you are sexually creative and playful? Do you initiate? Are you sexually adventuresome, uninhibited, expressive, and responsive? Is sex a high priority in your life? Why or why not?

Or maybe when you take an honest look at yourself as a lover, you realize that your sex life is routine, monotonous, or boring. Do you need to put the "play" back in foreplay? Do you have any hurt, anger, or frustration in this area in your life and marriage? Do you ever use sex as a bargaining chip with your spouse? Do you withhold, control, or punish your spouse or yourself in the area of sex? Is sex a low priority in your life? If so, why? We know these can be difficult questions. But by identifying obstacles in this area of marriage, you can ask God to turn them into windows of opportunity.

Life-Giving Challenge: Set aside some time to be with the Lord and pray about your part of the "**We**" relationship. Take responsibility for the ways you may have failed to be the sexual partner God designed. If necessary, repent. Then set up a time to discuss your sex life with your spouse. After processing the above questions with the Lord, talk with your spouse about how you rated yourself sexually. Ask for honest input about the issues you raise. Together work out and agree on a plan to advance in the sexual area of your life.

4. Review body oneness in your marriage

At different stages of your marriage, you will experience differing degrees of body oneness. The goal is not to achieve some ideal level of perfection but to continually seek ways to deepen your intimacy.

If your sexual life is in a good place right now, thank God. We challenge you to encourage and invest in other couples who may be struggling.

If you and your spouse have hit a wall sexually and can't seem to work past it, we encourage you to talk with a pastor, a counselor, or trusted same-sex friend who can help you take the necessary steps to move forward.

Maybe your sex life is okay, but you feel it's time to look for new ways to fan the flames, rekindle, or even restart the sexual fire in your marriage. Remember, starting a fire is not accomplished by placing large logs together and lighting a match. Starting a fire begins by first igniting kindling, then adding small pieces of wood on top of the kindling. As the fire gets going, larger pieces of wood can be added. Before long you will be enjoying a blazing fire.

As you explore new ways to advance in body oneness, filter any potential activity through these four questions:

+ Is it prohibited by the principles in the Bible?
+ Does it involve anyone other than my spouse?
+ Will it increase our intimacy and help us advance in Spirit, Soul, and Body Oneness?
+ Have we reached agreement in unity? (do we both have a green-light?)

Let's pause here for a word to wives: I (Tim) have worked with men for decades. I was raised in a home with four men and served over twenty years on a fire department with 150 men. I am comfortable with and enjoy

Body Oneness

hanging out with men. Whenever I'm teaching men on marriage and the subject turns to sex, I ask them this question: "When do you feel most like a man sexually?" Their response is so predictable. After the typical macho responses subside, I press them for a genuine response. Usually an older (wiser) man will say, "I feel most like a man sexually when my wife is sexually satisfied." This response opens doors for all kinds of honest dialogue on intimacy and sexuality.

Wives, please hear me on this: Men try to appear to have it all together sexually. But we don't. Every man longs to be his bride's knight in shining armor. A husband longs to sexually satisfy his bride. Bring this information to your prayer closet and ask the Holy Spirit to speak to you about how this may play into the ways you live out body oneness in your marriage.

Life-Giving Challenge: Schedule time with your spouse to discuss your sex life and these advanced life-giving challenges. Ask for honest input on what you share and discuss practical ways the two of you can increase your sexual intimacy.

+ Chapter 22

Let's Give It a Try

Putting a Sexual Agreement to Work in Your Marriage

As you've probably figured out by now, God is pro-sex! Sex is a precious gift that God created for a husband and wife to celebrate in covenant with Himself and each other. Sex provides unlimited opportunities to live in the **Larger Story** and to Reflect and Reveal the love and goodness of God.

We believe sex is both an art and a science. A successful two-point plan to advance sexually includes the science of understanding and living out God's design for sex and the art of not taking yourself too seriously. Looking back over thirty-plus years of marriage, we realize that key components of our advancing together have included extending much grace to each other and focusing on keeping our sense of humor. Over the years we have probably laughed more in the bedroom than in any room in our home.

Unfortunately, many individuals approach their sex life in only one way — *their* way. Their way is not open to discussion and healthy process. A person's way is often connected to family of origin issues, sexual imprinting, sexual histories, and life experiences.

By contrast Jesus said, "I am *the way*, and the truth, and the life…"[1] And the Bible says, "There is a *way* which seems right to a man, but its end is the way of death."[2] God has designed marriage to work a certain way. That way involves a husband and wife becoming one in spirit, soul, and body.

With this in mind, we encourage each spouse to set aside their own ways and be open to exploring different ways to approach body oneness. We believe the heart of sex is much more about an attitude and environment than an act. God is a passionate and creative being. Are you willing to explore creative ways to sexually please your spouse?

Remember, God is pro-sex. Although He has set certain sexual prohibitions, He gives married couples great freedom to celebrate sex in creative ways. His design for body oneness includes celebration, procreation, protection, pleasure, and comfort. As a husband and wife look for new ways to serve each other, they fulfill God's design for marriage. They will joyfully advance in friendship, intimacy, and mutual sexual satisfaction.

Body Oneness

NEW WAYS, NEW DISCOVERIES

I (Tim) am a loyal Chicago Cubs fan. In fact the entire Evans clan are Cubs fans. I can still recite from memory the lineup of the 1969 Cubs. The truth is, at over fifty years old I still haven't healed from the 1969 Cubs late-season crash when those rotten New York Mets passed my beloved Cubbies and went on to win the World Series.

My dad, brothers, and I always attended Cubs games. This was male bonding at its best. However, going to "The Friendly Confines of Wrigley Field" to experience a Cubs game had to be done in a certain way. My dad taught me and my brothers The Way, and when I became a father I couldn't wait to take my son Timmy to Wrigley Field and make certain the DNA was passed on to the next generation.

The Cubs Way included a number of important components: arriving at the ballpark early to watch batting practice, packing a lunch and bringing your baseball glove to catch balls, purchasing a scorecard and tracking every batter, bringing pencils (not pens) from home to keep score, buying a chocolate malt cup after singing *Take Me Out to the Ball Game* in the seventh inning.

The Way had worked for generations of Evanses. It was tried and true, and Timmy and I enjoyed every bit of it.

One day we came home from a game and my three young daughters asked, "Daddy, will you take us to see the Cubs play?"

I gently said, "It's more fun to watch the Cubs on television."

They said, "No, we want to go to a Cubs game!"

I told them that this was a father-son tradition. I explained that when I was growing up, Poppy (their grandpa) took his four sons to Wrigley Field. I added that the game went on for hours and they would be bored.

I looked to Anne to support my not-so-subtle male chauvinistic Cubs Way. She smiled and said, "I think the girls would love to see the Cubs play."

Body Oneness

Let's Give It a Try

The girls chimed in, "Daddy, pleeease can we go?" They persisted, and with four women on a mission, I didn't have a chance. I agreed to take the girls to Wrigley Field to see the Cubs vs. the Pirates.

We got to the ballpark early in full accordance with The Way. But the girls soon tired of watching batting practice. Finally the game started. And so did the questions. Colleen spotted the souvenir stores in the ballpark and asked, "Daddy, can we go shopping?"

I said, "Shopping? No, we're here to see the Cubs." I had my scorecard ready and had purchased scorecards for the girls. I passed out pencils, wrote down the starting lineup, and started to explain to the girls how to keep score.

Amy asked, "Daddy, why are we spending so much time writing this stuff down? We're gonna miss the game." Cate-the-Great kept sitting backwards in her seat. I told her to turn around and face the field, but she was more interested in the funny faces the fan behind her was making. Amy looked at the famous Cubs scoreboard and asked, "Daddy, what if that man falls out of the scoreboard?"

How I longed for Timmy to be sitting next to me. He knew The Way.

The game went on and the questions continued. I pointed out a star Pirates player named Barry Bonds. After staring at him for a while, Cate asked, "Daddy, why does Barry Bonds wear his pants down to his ankles and the other players have their pants just below their knees?" Amy asked, "Daddy, why do some players flip their sunglasses up and down?" Colleen asked, "Daddy, is the ivy on the outfield wall Boston Ivy or English Ivy?"

I tried to explain The Cubs Way, but the girls just didn't get it. They wanted the promised chocolate malt cups in the third inning, even though that was a seventh-inning experience. Amy wanted to go to the upper deck and see Lake Michigan, Colleen wanted to start a cheer, and Cate wanted to walk around and talk to the Andy Frain ushers.

Here were my three precious daughters and not one of them was interested in learning The Cubs Way. I was exasperated!

Another inning brought only another series of nonstop questions. Out of sheer frustration and as a relatively new Christian, I asked God for help. I sensed a question bubble up in my mind: *Tim, who is this day about?* I thought, *Who is this day about? It's about training three girls in The Cubs Way!*

As I sat there, it was like a veil suddenly fell away. I realized that the girls were not my dad, my brothers, Timmy, or me. They were excited just to be with their daddy at their first Cubs game at Wrigley Field. They were experiencing the Cubs and Wrigley Field with eyes that I would never see through in a thousand ballgames.

I thought about that question, *Tim, who is this day about?* The truthful answer was it was all about me. It was about my plan and my way of doing a Cubs game. To me the girls were just an obstacle to what I wanted. My new revelation was interrupted as the girls asked if they could buy some crayons to color the pictures they were drawing on their scorecards.

I made one last valiant attempt to get them involved in the game by asking the score and which team was up to bat. In unison they responded, "Daddy...*who cares?!*"

It was a moment of truth. I said to myself, *Okay, this is the girls' first Cubs game; it should be about them, not me.*

I took a deep breath and asked, "Who wants to go shopping?" Three girls screamed, *"I do!"*

I asked, "Who wants to get a chocolate malt cup...now?" Three girls screamed, *"I do!"*

I asked, "Who wants to check out Wrigley Field?" Three girls screamed, *"I do!"*

We attacked Wrigley Field. We went shopping and had malt cups. We went to the upper deck to the far right field grandstands and looked at the boats on Lake Michigan. We went to the upper deck to the far left field grandstands and looked down on the firehouse of Engine Co. 78. The girls stopped and talked to every vendor and Andy Frain usher.

Body Oneness

Let's Give It a Try

The highlight of the day was when we went to the upper deck patio behind home plate. We folded our scorecards into shapes of airplanes. The girls giggled as one by one they launched their scorecards and watched them sail all the way down to the intersection of Irving Park and Addison Streets.

Experiencing Wrigley Field with three precious, passionate, unpredictable girls was so life-giving. I saw through their eyes things I had never experienced doing it The Cubs Way. As all this occurred, something in me changed. We even left before the game ended (a total violation of The Way) because the girls were tired. Cate-the-Great was so exhausted that I had to carry her to the car.

We drove home and pulled into the driveway. Before I got out of the car, one of my girls said, "Daddy, this was one of the best days of my life." The other girls chimed in: "Thanks, Daddy! When can we go to another Cubs game?"

Anne and Timmy greeted us. Timmy asked, "Did you see Barry jack that homer out of the park? How about that double play in the eighth inning?" I just looked at him. He said, "Dad...wait...you didn't leave before the game was over, did you? Let me see the scorecard!"

Amy said, "Timmy, a bus ran over our scorecards." Colleen was showing her mom her Cubs souvenir, and said, "Mom, it was on sale." Cate looked at her brother and asked, "Timmy, did the Cubs win?" My poor son looked frantic.

I said, "Timmy, I didn't see a lot of the game...but I did see things I've never seen before." The truth is, I had a great day at Wrigley Field with my three girls. Whenever possible, we still go to Cubs games together. And although they still don't do it The Cubs Way, I've learned new ways to enjoy the Cubs and Wrigley Field.

The defining moment for me that day was recognizing the truth that now serves as our REAL LIFE slogan: *It's not about me.* This truth is not only for marriage; it is true in every relationship. As I look back on that experience, it makes me wonder, *In what other areas of life do I insist on my way? And what am I missing out on because of it?*

Body Oneness

REAL LIFE **MARRIAGE**

MOVING TOGETHER IN A NEW WAY

Every person has certain ways they like to do things. They have their own way of relating to others, handling conflict, and stewarding their finances. People have different ways of living out their faith, raising their children, enjoying holidays and vacations. In marriage, each spouse has a preferred way of living out body oneness.

Obviously, when a husband or wife insists on doing things "*my way*," it creates conflict and disunity. But as we've seen, when each spouse gives up their way and steps into the **Larger Story** together, a couple advances in intimacy.

We find it interesting that, in almost every area *except* body oneness, most couples are willing to discuss their differences and negotiate their way to agreement. For example, if they face financial troubles they'll sign up for a seminar that provides teaching and encourages accountability. Couples are more than willing to develop a budget, track their spending, and agree on purchases. In striving for financial success most couples willingly submit themselves and their ways to a third party. They give this person permission to speak into their lives, point out areas of weakness, and encourage areas of strength. Their mutually agreed-upon process protects them and keeps them accountable.

However, in our experience, most married couples do not discuss their sex lives in the same healthy way and with the same resolve that they discuss other areas of their lives. Some hold on to the romantic idea that sexual success and satisfaction happens magically. Other couples approach their sex life selfishly, where sex becomes "all about me."

To help couples move beyond roadblocks in their journey to body oneness, we suggest sexual agreements as a practical tool for negotiating this dimension of marriage.[3] Couples who have implemented sexual agreements say doing so has increased their sexual satisfaction and has provided new ways to advance in intimacy and sexuality.

In the remainder of this chapter, we'll walk you through the details of a sexual agreement. As you and your spouse work through the process of negotiating this agreement, we encourage you to be open to considering

Body Oneness

different ways than the ones you've grown accustomed to. If struggles arise surrounding the choices open to you as a couple, consider your differences as invitations to Reflect and Reveal the goodness of God to your spouse.

OUR SEXUAL AGREEMENT

"Do two walk together unless they have agreed to do so?"[4]

It is our desire to walk together in body oneness. We understand we have differences. Therefore, we agree to:

+ walk together in unity in the sexual dimension of our marriage
+ be open-minded to each other's sexual needs and desires
+ take an honest look at our sexual histories and sexual patterns
+ take responsibility for our sexual needs by intentionally communicating with each other

Husband's initials _____   Wife's initials _____

Comments: Knowing the power of sex, the enemy looks for ways to bring sexual disunity to a marriage. He tries to divide men and women in ways that weaken the one-flesh relationship. Married couples who commit to accountability discover a new level of motivation that enhances their understanding of God's design. Accountability not only helps a couple advance in intimacy with God and with each other but also provides a marriage with greater strength and protection.

This next section of the sexual agreement lays the foundation for advancing sexually by helping a couple put words to specific ways a couple agrees to walk together in unity.

Frequency: We agree to sexual intercourse _____ times

☐ per week   ☐ per month

Comments: It is not unusual for a husband and wife to have different desires for sexual frequency. But the truth is, they are often a lot closer to agreement than they realize. Negotiating frequency gives a couple opportunities to prayerfully process as they compromise on a number that satisfies both of them.

Specific days of the week: _____

Comments: One couple agreed to have sex every Friday night (T.G.I.F.) Making a simple decision to choose a specific day of the week allowed them to advance in sexual intimacy. They realized that being able to count on a specific day of the week eliminated the sexual frustration and tension that was created by not knowing when they would next have sex.

Specific times of the week: _____

Comments: Some people are night owls while others are early birds. Differences like these can create disunity in marriage. If you and your spouse have different body clocks, you may want to consider alternating the times of the day you have sex in an attempt to accommodate each other. One couple who agreed to enjoy sex one afternoon a month told us they both experienced a childlike anticipation of their monthly afternoon rendezvous.

Husband agrees to initiate: _____

Wife agrees to initiate: _____

Comments: Couples often complain that one spouse initiates sex more often than the other. One practical way to avoid misunderstanding and to increase creativity is for both husband and wife to take responsibility for their sexual relationship. This includes taking turns initiating sex. By specifying in your agreement who will initiate intercourse and how often, you can prevent this from becoming an area of disunity.

Body Oneness

We agree to the following sexual acts, positions, locations: **Only if I initiate:**

_____   _____

_____   _____

_____   _____

_____   _____

Comments: This section is an invitation for a couple to participate in an open discussion about specific sexual acts, positions, and locations. Putting this in a written sexual agreement eliminates potential for repeated arguments over a specific topic.

For example, one woman wanted her husband to perform oral sex on her. The husband was reluctant but agreed to participate in this sexual activity only when he initiated. This allowed him a measure of control in an area where he felt less comfortable than she did. Once he realized he had the freedom to initiate the activity, it eliminated much of his resistance.

Another example is a husband who wanted to have sex outdoors with his wife, but she had issues with privacy and felt threatened by a strange environment. The husband gave her several suggestions for providing the privacy she needed. He expressed his desire but agreed to wait for her to initiate. Wanting to meet his sexual desire, she agreed and initiated. This process allowed her a measure of control over a situation that felt risky for her. Knowing that her husband was not demanding a specific sexual experience left her feeling honored rather than pressured.

God wants a husband and wife to enjoy the freedom He intended for them to celebrate. You are made in His image. You are free to be sexually creative. Remember, God is pro-sex!

Body Oneness

We believe the following activities are against Scripture:

_____

_____

_____

_____

_____

_____

_____

_____

Comments: God gives a husband and a wife freedom to enjoy sex. However, the Bible clearly lists some specific prohibitions. These include fornication, adultery, homosexual acts, impurity, orgies, prostitution, sodomy, obscenity, lustful passions, incest, bestiality.

Since some individuals may interpret certain passages as prohibiting other behaviors as well, it is important for couples to search the Scriptures and engage in a discussion with each other about what they read in God's Word. Sexual agreement helps couples clarify their personal beliefs and convictions and communicate them to their spouse. It also prepares them to share God's design for sex with their children in biblically accurate ways.

Self-imposed consequences for breaking this agreement:

(Husband) If I do not fulfill my sexual agreement with my wife, I agree to:

_____

_____

_____

(Wife) If I do not fulfill my sexual agreement with my husband, I agree to:

_____

_____

_____

Comments: This section is not to be approached in a punitive manner. Instead each spouse determines their own consequences in the event they do not fulfill their part of the sexual agreement. One woman agreed to

Body Oneness

wash and vacuum her husband's car if she did not fulfill her parts in the sexual agreement. One husband agreed to crosscut the lawn and turn over the dirt in the yard if he did not fulfill his part in the sexual agreement. They chose tasks that would bless their partner.

Self-imposed consequences are intended to motivate each person to take responsibility for their sex life. One husband had set washing dishes as his consequence for failing to fulfill his agreement. After a few nights of kitchen duty he commented, "This will never happen again!"

As with other aspects of marriage, this section of the agreement should be approached with love and an attitude of reciprocal servanthood rather than legalistic enforcement. We know of one wife who failed to fulfill her sexual agreement, which meant accepting her self-imposed consequence of cleaning out the garage. She woke up early Saturday morning, reluctantly got out of bed, and headed for the garage. When she opened the door, she realized her husband had already secretly cleaned and scrubbed the garage for her. She ran back to bed to thank him. Let's just say he was more than happy to serve his wife!

Remember to keep your sense of humor. With the right attitude, this section can provide fun for both parties.

Time limit: We agree to keep our commitment to this sexual agreement

until _____ . On this date we will review, amend, or make

changes. We agree that _____ will initiate this discussion.

Comments: Review and follow-up are vital to the success of the sexual agreement, but it is important for a husband and wife to give the agreement a reasonable amount of time to work before evaluating the results and making adjustments. We suggest at least three months. Designate which partner will be responsible to initiate the discussion on the agreed-upon date.

If we reach an impasse, we agree to seek professional Christian counsel if we are not successful in our attempts to live out this sexual agreement as we walk together in unity. The pastor/counselor we have chosen to contact is _____ .

We agree _____ will call to schedule our meeting.

Comments: Entering a sexual agreement may bring to the surface issues that require the help of a third party. Choosing someone both spouses trust allows a couple to explore underlying issues that may be blocking what God has intended for them to enjoy. Agreeing on a specific person and a specific date increases accountability. Reaching agreement beforehand on a specific course of action eliminates disunity.

Please note: When either spouse has a sexual history that includes abuse, pornography, sexual addictions, or major distortions of God's design, we advise them to seek professional counsel. Receiving healing is essential to step into the freedom God intends for every husband and wife.

Miscellaneous comments or additions to the agreement:

_____

_____

_____

_____

_____

Comments: Is there anything else you and your spouse would like to include in your sexual agreement? If so, you may add it to this section. You may want to develop your own sexual language. For example, one couple incorporates playful terms to communicate sexually with one another. When the husband asks, "Is the store open tonight?" he is not talking about the grocery store. Another couple agreed to read one book on sex per year and together review what they learned. Others have agreed to take turns scheduling a yearly weekend getaway devoted to advancing in their sexual intimacy. We encourage couples to prayerfully personalize their sexual agreement.

Body Oneness

Sign and date:

X _____ Date: _____
Husband's Signature

X _____ Date: _____
Wife's Signature

Comments: Signing and dating the sexual agreement adds an element of formality that affirms your commitment. Also, since accountability between a husband and wife can be difficult, including another person in your process can help create a positive atmosphere of support, encouragement, and accountability.

X _____ Date: _____
Signature of husband's same-sex accountability partner

X _____ Date: _____
Signature of wife's same-sex accountability partner

A TOOL AND A TEST

Filling out and agreeing to a sexual agreement can be risky. It may involve dying to old ways and being open to new ways. A sexual agreement is both a tool and a test. As a tool, it can assist married couples in making a sexual plan. However, advancing in body oneness requires much more than frequency, positions, timing, locations, etc. True sexual intimacy is a matter of the heart. In that sense, the agreement is a test of both partners, an opportunity for self-evaluation.

When we teach on sexual agreements people often ask, "Who should lead out when there is sexual disagreement?" It is our experience that the person who is more mature in the Lord is often the person God invites to initiate conflict resolution. The more mature spouse can choose to trust God and sexually serve their spouse.

The key question each spouse can ask themselves is, *Who is the main character in my sexual story?* If the main character in your story is you, you are living in the **smaller story**. If the main character in your story is God, you are living in the **Larger Story**.

Note: REAL LIFE *Companion Journal* contains a copy of the Sexual Agreement for husbands and wives to fill out.

REVIEW PART 3

In Part 1 we examined the basics of **Spirit Oneness** as we looked at God's original Plan A design for marriage. We saw that marriage was designed to Reflect and Reveal the plurality of God. To accomplish this purpose, a husband and wife must be in covenant with God and each other.

In Part 2 we considered what it means for a couple to enjoy **Soul Oneness**. We saw how Rulership was lost in the Garden but later reclaimed by Jesus, freeing couples to live out God's Plan A design for marriage, in which Rulership, dominion, and authority are given to both the husband and wife. The key to successfully walking this out by choosing to live together in unity. This involves **Larger Story** living where "marriage is not about me."

The heart of **Soul Oneness** is genuine intimacy — to know and be fully known. Advancing in intimacy means focusing on the "**We**" of marriage. This includes learning how to delight in each other's differences — in spiritual gifts, styles of relating, temperaments, families of origin, and more. We looked at implementing the Traffic Light Principle as a practical way of making decisions in unity. We concluded Part 2 by challenging couples to demonstrate *inexhaustible forgiveness* to one another.

In Part 3 we focused on **Body Oneness** as we addressed steps of intimacy, sensitive sexual topics, and intimacy-building questions to ask each other. We said that God's purposes for sex include celebration, procreation, protection, pleasure, and comfort. We challenged couples to consider sex as an act of worship and warfare. We concluded by walking through the details of implementing a sexual agreement.

Now is a great time to review the advanced Body Oneness Challenges from chapter 21 with your spouse:

+ View sex as an act of worship.
+ View sex as an act of spiritual warfare.
+ Review yourself as a sexual partner.
+ Review body oneness in your marriage.

REAL LIFE *Companion Journal* is available for study questions and personal applications for each chapter.

Body Oneness

"Follow me..."

— *Jesus of Nazareth, Matthew 4:19*

+ Epilogue

Where Do We Go From Here?

In chapter 1, we described our first attempt to climb Pikes Peak. As beginners we envisioned ourselves conquering the mountain and standing on the summit doing the happy dance. However, as you may recall, the day that began with such hope and excitement ended in frustration and disappointment. That experience was a painful illustration of the truth, *Where you start determines where you end.*

Although our first attempt to reach the summit failed, we learned some important lessons and determined not to give up on our dream. The following month we gave it another try. Once again, we arrived at the trailhead before dawn — this time we made sure it was the *correct* trailhead. Although we were excited, we were less confident than before. Our assurance grew as we hit every checkpoint on our way up the trail.

Throughout our hike we noticed small rock piles at regular intervals along the trail. These piles of stones are called *cairns.* Traditionally, as hikers continue along the trail they add a stone to the growing pile of rocks. These small rock formations are like visual road maps that help other hikers stay on course and successfully reach their destination. Cairns also are used to commemorate important events. They are built on battlefields as memorials, on graves to honor the dead, and as standing stones after encounters with God.

Cairns are found on every continent of the world. Some of these mini-monuments are stacked so creatively, they would humble the most gifted designers and engineers. Each one tells a story and points the way.

Everything was going as planned on our second attempt to climb Pikes Peak. It was a beautiful day and the trail was clearly marked. We reached the tree line and came to a clearing where we could see the summit. Our excitement increased as we continued hiking the switchbacks. A few more hours passed, then suddenly our well-defined trail came to an abrupt end. We found ourselves standing before a massive pile of boulders that had to be twenty stories high.

Looking up, our first thought was, *There is no way we will ever be able to make it to the top.* About that time, we noticed two hikers descending from the summit. Tim shouted out to them, "What's the best way to the top?"

Pointing to a distant cairn stacked on top of a huge boulder, they shouted back, "Head toward that cairn. Then look for the next one. They will lead you to the top of the mountain."

Following their advice, we began our scramble up the rocks. We traversed back and forth up the mountain from one cairn to the next. But at some point all the rocks seemed to blend together. We found ourselves standing side by side on a huge boulder at almost fourteen thousand feet above sea level. We looked around in every direction, but there were no cairns in sight. Although we were not sure of our next steps, we were certain of two things: First, we knew there had to be a way. Second, we knew other hikers had gone before us and successfully made it to the summit. Their success gave us the confidence to keep going.

Standing on that massive boulder, we had a decision to make. Together we agreed on which way to go and we stepped out in unity and faith. To our amazement, within a few steps, a cairn came into view. It was a spiritual experience for us. Every time we stepped out in faith, God revealed the next cairn. Before long we reach the 14,110-foot summit. Standing on the top of Pikes Peak, we celebrated our accomplishment by doing the happy dance.

A DIFFICULT BUT REWARDING CLIMB

Marriage is a lot like climbing a mountain. Couples begin their journey with great hope and excitement, looking forward to the exhilarating vistas ahead. However, over time the stress of life takes a toll. Some couples get tired, discouraged, and lose their passion. Others feel distant, as if they are traveling two separate paths. Some couples regret they even started. Others reach a point where they want to give up, retreat, or turn back.

After thirty-plus years of marriage we can say with confidence, it's true — marriage is difficult. The Bible says, "Those who marry will face many troubles in this life."[1] Every marriage will experience hope and heartache, joys and sorrows.

An old firehouse saying is *What a difference a day makes*. Whenever I (Tim) was on duty and the fire alarm went off, everything changed in a moment.

This firehouse slogan is also true in life. The phone rings, and in a heartbeat everything changes. Recently, friends of ours received one of those calls. After performing a dance routine at school, their healthy eighteen-year-old daughter collapsed and died. She had a rare heart defect that they were unaware of.

When this tragedy occurred, we were flying out of Colorado to join our family for the birth of our first granddaughter. Her delivery was scheduled the day before the funeral. For us, that entire weekend was a visual picture of the reality of life. On Friday morning we were at a hospital in Michigan, standing with family and friends to celebrate the arrival our little Grace Elizabeth. Wanting to hold onto this miraculous moment, we thanked God for her life.

Saturday morning, we drove to a funeral home in Chicago and stood with dear friends as they mourned the tragic and unexplainable death of their only daughter. Wanting to hold on to these last moments with their little girl, we watched as they said their final good-byes. Together, with family and friends we thanked God for her life.

Marriage is filled with joy and sorrow, celebration and loss, life and death. But God designed marriage to be lived out in relationship, just like the Trinity. When a couple enters covenant with God, He invites them to journey together with Him in love and servanthood. When the journey begins, there is no guarantee of what twists and turns your path together may take. As we said in the prologue, "this book is not a fairy-tale fantasy about a never-ending honeymoon." The process of two becoming one is never easy, and doing life God's way will cost you something. But we believe the experience of reaching the summits of marriage will bring heights of joy beyond description.

We don't know where you are on your marital journey right now. You may be just starting out on the trail, or you may be above the tree line and beginning to feel the effects of high altitude. Perhaps you are lost, having started from the wrong place or finding that the shortcut you chose led in the wrong direction. Maybe you and your spouse are facing some giant boulders, unsure of your next steps but choosing to move forward in faith. Or maybe you're both doing the happy dance on a marital summit.

No matter where you are in your journey together, whether you are at the trailhead or the summit, we are certain of two things. First, we know God has designed a way for marriage. Second, we know others have gone before you. Couples have traveled the path you are on right now. Their marriage is telling a story that will point the way.

Looking back over our years of marriage, we see that we have been blessed by others who have gone before us. Many godly couples have placed life-giving cairns on the trail to point the way for us. These men and women encouraged us to build our marriage on biblical truths, including…

+ God is God, you are not.
+ God has created a Plan A for marriage.
+ God is not only good, He is good to *you*.
+ The heart of marriage is love and relationship with God and your spouse.
+ God's purposes for marriage are to be lived out in the **Larger Story** where "marriage is not about me."

We pray that, much as God used these couples to guide us, He has used this book to guide you on your marital journey. It is our prayer that you will base your life and marriage on these and other biblical principles, seeing them as cairns that provide strength, encouragement, and guidance toward marital summits.

LET YOUR MARRIAGE POINT THE WAY

Passing on a godly marital legacy to our children and grandchildren is a primary desire of our hearts. One of our favorite Scriptures is, "I have no greater joy than to hear that my children are walking in the truth."[2] As grandparents we have a deeper understanding of God's generational design, and the power He has given marriage to impact future generations. This encourages us to choose to live in the **Larger Story**, walking out the truth that "marriage is not about me."
We live in exciting times. Our country is at a crossroads where different worldviews converge and lead toward the realities of good and evil. In the

foreword to this book Dr. Gilbert Bilezikian noted that marriage is "the most fundamental of all relationships entrusted to humankind." We wholeheartedly agree. And as fundamental as the marital relationship is, God designed marriage with much more God-glorifying potential than any one man and woman.

Throughout this book we have shared stories from our experience, from the Bible, and from the people we've counseled. We've chosen to do this because life is about story. And when we choose to live in the **Larger Story** of our creative God — the Author of story — life takes on a whole new dimension of meaning.

One key chapter in God's **Larger Story** involves the impending marriage of Jesus Christ. The Bible says Jesus will one day return for His bride, the Church. Not any particular local church or denomination, but the "Big-C" Church that consists of all followers of Christ. Sadly, the bride of Christ is currently fractured and fragmented, but God's plan is for His bride, the Church, to ready herself for the return of the Bridegroom. Jesus will soon be coming for a bride that "has made herself ready."[3]

One of the ways we believe God is readying the Church is through marriage, inviting husbands and wives to experience the miracle and mystery of oneness in this unique life-giving relationship.

Meditate on this fact; God began humankind by creating a married couple. He established marriage — one man and one woman — as the most basic building block of societies. Marriage affects men and women of every race, color, and creed. God did not begin humankind with a family, church, village, culture, or country. He began the human race with a marriage and declared it "very good." God created marriage with unlimited life-giving potential.

The truth is, every marriage tells a story. *What do others think about God and marriage when they look at you, at your marriage and story?* The sad reality is many marriages die while the husband and wife are still breathing. But the good news is God is in the business of redeeming hurting marriages, and strengthening strong ones. We challenge you to ask the Lord to breathe His life into your marriage so your story becomes a cairn pointing others toward Him.

WHAT IF...?

Proverbs 29:18 declares, "Where there is no vision [revelation], the people perish."[4] We have a vision for marriages to advance by returning to God's original Plan A. We believe we are on the verge of a powerful move of God, which makes us wonder...what if?

What if...
people with open hearts and minds pursue God as they humbly answer the question Jesus asked thousands of years ago and He asks still today: "Who do you say that I am?"[5] We are not talking about any specific religion. One of our spiritual fathers says: "Is there truth in other religions? Yes. Is there beauty? Absolutely. Is there salvation — eternal life? The Bible states, 'There is no other Name in heaven or on earth by which you can be saved.' "[6]

What if...
God is allowing the cultural craziness, the attempts to redefine marriage, and the attacks on Christians to invite us to focus on being salt and light in much darkness? This will ignite the synergistic power in love and truth as we model unity and community. Our encouragement to followers of Christ is this: focus on what you are *for* rather than spending too much time and energy focusing on what you are *against*. On a practical level, this begins by focusing on God and what He is *for*. God is pro-marriage, pro-intimacy, and pro-sex.

What if...
when Jesus told His followers about the "greater things" they would do,[7] He was not referring to healings, demonic deliverance, and raising people from the dead? What if Jesus was describing a time when His followers would reclaim and restore God's Plan A for marriage?

What if...
God's original Plan A for marriage is passionately reclaimed and humbly restored? We sincerely believe marriage is the most untapped positive change agent in the world. We envision couples stepping into their identity in Christ, living in covenant, Reflecting and Revealing the

goodness of God and in unity reclaiming the Rulership and dominion God has designed for them in marriage.

WE HAVE A DREAM FOR MARRIAGE

On August 28, 1963, Dr. Martin Luther King stood at the Lincoln Memorial and delivered what is considered one of the greatest speeches in all of history. This speech has become known as the "I have a dream" speech. Every time we hear those four words — *I have a dream* — it stirs something in us. Hearing Dr. King describe what he envisioned but could not yet experience inspires us to dream for more than we can see right now.

When it comes to God and marriage, we have a dream. With a measure of holy anticipation we envision the next chapters in the unfolding REAL LIFE story.

We have a dream…
of husbands and wives living in the **Larger Story** in spirit, soul, and body oneness. As couples walk out the miracle and mystery of marriage, it will open doors to walk out the four Rs: Reflecting, Revealing, Ruling, and Reproducing.

We have a dream…
of God using marriage and the power of story to engage our culture. We are not talking about a story centered on religious terminology or to-do lists. We are not referring to a story that focuses on unrighteous judgment. We are talking about God using marriage to tell a story that draws people to Him.

We have a dream…
that followers of Christ will come together in unity and step into their call to be the light of the world. In our culture as the pendulum continues to swing away from God's design and purposes for marriage, this will create opportunities for the Church to shine. Remember the Church is the prototype that is supposed to foreshadow the kingdom of God. We see God inviting His Church, the Bride of Christ, to step into its finest hour.

We have a dream...

that the love and commitment married couples model will speak volumes to a fatherless generation. We envision the Holy Spirit restoring "the hearts of the fathers to their children and the hearts of the children to their fathers."[8] We envision the emerging generation embracing God's original Plan A design for marriage and becoming passionate leaders in the Reformation of marriage.

We have a dream...

of God inviting ordinary men and women to be the kindling that will ignite a Marriage Reformation — a Reformation that begins in the hearts of people who recognize their selfishness, repent of their sins, and turn toward God. We envision the entire world watching as this radical shift in marriage occurs.

We have a dream...

We believe the ignition point for the Reformation of marriage will be husbands and wives passionately pursuing God and humbly living out "REAL LIFE marriage — it's not about me."

+   +   +

We began this book with a prayer. We asked God to give you an open heart and mind as you revisited His story. We prayed that you would encounter God and invite Him to be the main character as you stepped into the **Larger Story**. We prayed that God would give every husband and wife the desire and supernatural power to live out "REAL LIFE marriage — it's not about me."

As we finish writing this book, it is the desire of our hearts that God answered our prayer.

OUR REQUEST OF YOU

In this book we've explained God's original Plan A for marriage and have challenged couples to live out the four **R**s of marriage: **Reflect** and **Reveal**, **Rule**, and **Reproduce**.

We would love to hear your REAL LIFE stories of living out the four **R**s. We're particularly eager to hear about times when you and your spouse faced a decision and exercised unity by implementing the Traffic Light Principle as you stepped into Rulership together. We will gather these stories for use in a future book.

When you send us your story, please include answers to the following questions:

+ What was the specific challenge or decision you faced?

+ How did you implement the Traffic Light Principle in your process?

+ Did you reach unity? Explain your answer.

+ What were the positive and negative results of making decisions in unity?

To e-mail us your story, visit our Web site at www.RealLife.us.com

Thank you,

tim + anne

ACKNOWLEDGMENTS

Life is about story, and writing this book has been a story filled with friends and family. Our experience is that anything successful in life involves a team. God built an amazing team for this project. The reality is there are too many people to list. However, we want to extend our heartfelt thanks to the following people:

+   To our Prayer Shield Team. These are the nameless and faceless who were on the sidelines praying for us and this project. Their strategic frontline position goes before us and opens the door for God's truth to penetrate hearts. We want to acknowledge one of our key intercessors, Jill Youngquist, who went home to be with the Lord before this project was completed.

+   To our parents Bill and Jeanne Evans and Jack and Pat O'Shaughnessy, for laying a strong foundation that continues to be built on.

+   To our children: Tim, Amy + Curt, Colleen + Johnny, and Cate. A long time ago, God invited us to join Him on a journey. He wanted to tell a story through our lives. As a family we all agreed to take a leap of faith, believing the net would appear. Every chapter of our story has been a mix of adventure and challenge. As your parents we want to thank you for being willing to follow God even when it cost you something. Thank you for choosing the **Larger Story** and learning earlier than most kids do that "It's not about me."

+   To our grandchildren: Joel, Trey, Gracie, and future grandkids. Our thanks flows out of who you are, rather than anything you've done. Your sheer existence brings us joy!

+   To our spiritual parents. Dick and Alice Swetman, you introduced us to Jesus and imparted to us a passion for God and His Word. Thank you for loving and praying for our clan. To Gilbert Bilezikian, our *Schmeekah Rabbi*. In the spring of 1987 we took your course at Wheaton College where we were introduced to many of the principles in this book. Gil, your course was life-changing for us. Thank you for encouraging us to passionately pursue oneness. In addition, thank you to *all* the mentors and spiritual parents God has blessed us with over the years; the list is too long to type.

+   To key co-laborers in writing this book: TJ and Deb Bratt, Jim and Kathy Kubik, Keith and Robyn Brodie, Steve and Pam DeBoer, Bruce and Sue Osterink, and John Tekautz. It is because of you that our vision for this book has become a reality.

+   A special thank you to those who read our manuscript and provided their endorsement: Dr. Che and Sue Ahn, Brady and Pam Boyd, Dr. Gilbert Bilezikian, Dr. Timothy and Nancy Brown, Don Cousins, Dr. Dick and Dee Eastman, Lou and Therese Engle, Dr. Chester and Betsy Kylstra, Josh and Dottie McDowell, Ben and Lauretta Patterson, Dr. C. Peter and Doris Wagner, and Willy and Joan Wooten.

+   To Stephanie Elhart Frankhouse (aka *Yoda*), our exterior and interior book designer extraordinaire, and the entire fuel D "home" team: Jay, Sammi, Abby. You gave us more than your gifts; you brought such joy and creativity to this project.

+   To our editors, Laura Barker and Tara VanDyke. You were God's gifts sent in His perfect time. Your professionalism and attention to detail formed more than a business relationship. You became friends who partnered with us through this project. To Rose Yancik for her advice on book production, and to Elisabeth Hendricks for proofing the final copy. Thank you to Jim Clemons and the Versa Press team.

+   To all the godly men and women who added to our vision for the book: Ken Gire, who read our first rough draft, took us to breakfast, and with the love of a spiritual father gave us two insightful words of wisdom: "Start over!" Dan Hathaway and Sam Beumeir, who encouraged us to reach the emerging generation. Our thanks to Brad Herman for sharing your wisdom and passion for books, to John and Kem Stickl and Tom and Jan Murray for being a fresh set of eyes at the beginning of this book, and to Noriko Mosher for feedback as we neared completion.

+   Where you write often impacts how you write. Thanks to Steve and Pam DeBoer for providing refuge in the Colorado Mountains. And to Marty Anderson and Mark Garlick for making room for us at William Carey International University in Pasadena, California. Thank you to Kirk and Deanna Moore for providing a laptop computer, and to Legacy Photography for the image on the back cover.

+ While writing this book, we were blessed at critical times to be on the receiving end of encouraging words that cheered us on to press in and keep going. A special thanks to: Kathy and Jim Kubik, Jim and Sharon VanDyke, Linda Laird, Craig and Kristina Davis, Dan and Angela Gieck, Mary Jo Pierce, John and Caryl O'Shaughnessy, Tom and Marilyn Bratt, Ben and Lauretta Patterson, Dan and Jane Evans, Jean Blount, Jack and Becky Sytsema, Jack and Lynn Hinds, Adam Taylor, Paul and Barb Osburn, Marty O'Connor, Tom and Julie Vroon, George and Melodee Cook, Gabe Ahn, Chester and Betsy Kylstra, Brent and Lauri Smith, Troy and Kate DeWys, Mike and Mary Banas, Mark and Raquel Soto, Charles and Judy Cash, Carl and Vera Lenz, John and Arlene Morrison, Steve Wells, Bob and Deb Busscher, Bill and Barb Vroon, Steve Slaight, Andy Nguyen, Mike and Anne Risher, Alan and Ruth Breuker, Denny and Scoob Ellens, Chuck and Bev Osterink, and so many others. Thanks for responding to the Holy Spirit. Your calls, notes, and gestures of kindness arrived at just the right time.

+ A special thank you to the men and women who are represented through the REAL LIFE stories in this book; your lives tell a story that points us to God. Thank you for having the courage to share the struggles of your journey with other travelers. Seeing you *advance* with God and your spouse inspires us to stay on the trail.

+ Lastly, we thank God for creating marriage, intimacy, and sexuality. It is our prayer that Your original Plan A design for marriage is reclaimed and restored.

ENDNOTES

PROLOGUE
1.   The concept of Larger Story/smaller story living is adapted from the teaching and writing of Dr. Dan B. Allender.

CHAPTER 1
1.   Genesis 1:1-3, emphasis added.
2.   Genesis 1:2, NKJV.
3.   John 1:1-2, emphasis added.
4.   John 1:14, emphasis added.
5.   Genesis 1:26, NIV, emphasis added.
6.   John 14:10-11, NIV.
7.   Genesis 1:27-28.
8.   A quote from Dr. Gilbert Bilezikian's book *Beyond Sex Roles* 3rd ed. (Grand Rapids: Baker, 1995, 2006); Matthew 19:10-12 and 1 Corinthians 7:25-35.
9.   Genesis 1:31.
10.   Matthew 19:4-6.

CHAPTER 2
1.   Genesis 2:7.
2.   Genesis 2:18.
3.   Genesis 2:21-22.
4.   Genesis 1:31.
5.   Luke 19:10.
6.   1 John 4:19.
7.   Romans 3:23.
8.   Romans 2:4.
9.   Matthew 10:16.
10.   Matthew 10:32-33.
11.   Matthew 16:15.
12.   Luke 22:70.
13.   *Sharing Your Faith and Telling Your Story* by Anne Evans. Available through www.RealLife.us.com.
14.   Luke 15:10.
15.   James 4:2.

CHAPTER 3
1.   Dan Kimball, *They Like Jesus but Not the Church* (Grand Rapids: Zondervan, 2007), 237.
2.   1 Corinthians 7:28, NIV.
3.   James 1:2.

CHAPTER 4

1. Richard J. Foster, *Prayer: Finding the Heart's True Home* (New York: HarperCollins, 1992), as quoted on the dustjacket.
2. Luke 18:1.
3. Philippians 4:6.
4. Jack Hayford, *Prayer Is Invading the Impossible* (Gainesville, FL: 2002), 71.
5. C. Peter Wagner, *Praying with Power* (Shippensburg, PA: Destiny Image, 1997), 37-38.
6. 1 Thessalonians 5:16-18.
7. Phillip Yancey, *Prayer: Does It Make Any Difference?* (Grand Rapids: Zondervan, 2006), 53.
8. Brother Lawrence, *The Practice of the Presence of God* (New York: Image/Doubleday, 1977).
9. Phillip Yancey, *Prayer, 191-192.*
10. Matthew 7:7.
11. Proverbs 3:5-6, TLB.
12. 2 Chronicles 7:14, NKJV.
13. Proverbs 29:18.
14. C. Peter Wagner, *Prayer Shield* from The Prayer Warrior Series (Ventura, CA: Regal, 1992).
15. Exodus 17:12.

CHAPTER 5

1. Luke 22:42.
2. John 10:10.
3. Genesis 2:16-17.
4. Gilbert Bilezikian, *Beyond Sex Roles*, 3rd ed. (Grand Rapids: Baker, 1995, 2006), 29.
5. Genesis 3:1, emphasis added.
6. Genesis 3:3, emphasis added.
7. Genesis 3:4-5.
8. Genesis 3:6.
9. Genesis 3:9.
10. Genesis 3:10.
11. Chester and Betsy Kylstra, *Restoring the Foundations* (Hendersonville, NC: Proclaiming His Word, 2001), 352.
12. Sandra D. Wilson, *Released from Shame* (Westmont, IL: InterVarsity, 2002), 9-10 as quoted in Chester and Betsy Kylstra, *Restoring the Foundations* (Hendersonville, NC: Proclaiming His Word, 2001), 353.
13. Chester Kylstra, *Transforming Your Business* (Hendersonville, NC: Proclaiming His Word, 2006), 196.
14. Genesis 3:11-13.
15. Merriam-Webster Online, s.v. "enmity," http://www.merriam-webster.com/dictionary/enmity (accessed October 2, 2008).
16. Genesis 3:15.
17. Genesis 3:16.

18. Carol Caster Howard as quoted in Gilbert Bilezikian, *Beyond Sex Roles*, 217.
19. Merriam-Webster Online, s.v. "domination," http://www.merriam-webster.com/dictionary/domination (accessed October 2, 2008).
20. Genesis 3:17-19.
21. Gilbert Bilezikian, *Beyond Sex Roles*, 42.
22. Genesis 3:12.
23. Genesis 3:6.
24. Genesis 6:5-6, NIV.

CHAPTER 6

1. Genesis 1:31.
2. Merriam-Webster Online, s.v. "mutual," http://www.merriam-webster.com/dictionary/mutual (accessed October 2, 2008).
3. Merriam-Webster Online, s.v. "equality," http://www.merriam-webster.com/dictionary/equality (accessed October 2, 2008).
4. Encarta Dictionary Online, s.v. "egalitarian," http://encarta.msn.com/dictionary_/egalitarian.html (accessed October 2, 2008).
5. Encarta Dictionary Online, s.v. "feminism," http://encarta.msn.com/dictionary_/feminism.html (accessed October 2, 2008).
6. Matthew 3:17.
7. Matthew 4:3, NIV.
8. Matthew 4:4, NIV.
9. Mathew 4:6, NIV.
10. Mathew 4:7, NIV.
11. Comments posted on the Biblocality web site under Christian Forums, "Man's First Sin," http://biblocality.com/forums/showthread.php?t=2207 (accessed October 23, 2008).
12. Matthew 4:9, NIV.
13. Matthew 4:10, NIV.
14. Luke 4:13.
15. Romans 6:14, NKJV.
16. James 4:7-8.
17. 1 John 4:4.
18. Hebrews 9:16.
19. Ecclesiastes 4:12, NIV.
20. Genesis 3:16.
21. Genesis 3:16.
22. Matthew 19:4-6.
23. Gilbert Bilezikian, *Beyond Sex Roles*, 3rd ed. (Grand Rapids: Baker, 1995, 2006), 126.
24. Gilbert Bilezikian, *Beyond Sex Roles*, 127.
25. Ephesians 5:22-23.
26. Ephesians 5:29.
27. Ephesians 5:28-29, emphasis added.
28. Genesis 3:16.
29. Gilbert Bilezikian, *Beyond Sex Roles*, 209.

30.   R. Paul Stevens, *Marriage Spirituality* (Vancouver, BC, Canada: Regent College, 1997), 127.

31.   Romans 6:14, NKJV.

CHAPTER 7

1.   Dr. Gilbert Bilezikian, "Marriage & Family in the New Testament" course, Wheaton College, 1987 spring semester.

2.   Genesis 2:25.

3.   Genesis 3:10.

4.   Genesis 3:11

5.   Erwin Raphael McManus, *Soul Cravings* (Nashville: Thomas Nelson, 2006), 8.

6.   Hebrews 12:25.

7.   Psalm 119:97, NIV.

8.   Richard J. Foster, *Celebration of Discipline* (New York: HarperCollins, 1978).

CHAPTER 8

1.   Dan B. Allender and Tremper Longman III, *Intimate Allies* (Carol Stream, IL: Tyndale, 1995), 144.

2.   Matthew 22:37-40.

3.   1 Timothy 4:16.

4.   Ecclesiastes 4:12, NIV.

5.   Ephesians 5:33, NIV.

6.   Titus 2:4, NLT.

7.   Emerson Eggerichs, *Love and Respect* (Nashville: Thomas Nelson, 2004), 6.

8.   Hebrews 11:1, NKJV.

CHAPTER 9

1.   Genesis 1:27-28, emphasis added.

2.   C. Peter Wagner, *Your Spiritual Gifts Can Help Your Church Grow* (Ventura, CA: Regal, 1979), 44.

3.   For more information visit http://www.onlinediscprofile.com/.

4.   For more information visit http://www.tjta.com/abouttjta.htm.

5.   Gary Chapman, *The Five Love Languages* (Chicago: Northfield, 1992).

6.   John 13:34-35.

CHAPTER 10

1.   Encarta Dictionary Online, s.v. "legacy," http://encarta.msn.com/dictionary_/legacy.html (accessed October 13, 2008).

2.   Exodus 20:4-6, NIV.

CHAPTER 11

1.   James 1:5

CHAPTER 12

1. Ronald Murray, "Two Families United in Tragedy," interview by James Dobson, *Focus on the Family*, February 28-29, 2008.
2. David Works, "Two Families United in Tragedy," interview by James Dobson, *Focus on the Family*, February 28-29, 2008.
3. Merriam-Webster Online, s.v. "inexhaustible," http://www.merriam-webster.com/dictionary/inexhaustible (accessed October 13, 2008).
4. Proverbs 3:4-6, TLB.
5. Matthew 6:14-15.
6. Jeremiah 31:34, NIV.
7. James 1:20.
8. Deuteronomy 5:16.
9. Proverbs 14:12, NIV.
10. Luke 23:34, NIV.

CHAPTER 13

1. Genesis 2:25.
2. Genesis 2:24.
3. Genesis 1:27.
4. Genesis 1:22.
5. 1 Corinthians 7:5.
6. Song of Songs 5:1.
7. 2 Samuel 12:24.
8. Rob Bell, *Sex God* (Grand Rapids: Zondervan, 2007), 123.

CHAPTER 14

1. Genesis 38:8-10, NIV.
2. Merriam-Webster Online, s.v. "stewardship," http://www.merriam-webster.com/dictionary/stewardship (accessed October 13, 2008).
3. James 1:5.
4. "The Fertility Race: Statistics" as found at http://americanradioworks.publicradio.org/features/fertility_race/common/stats.shtml (accessed October 13, 2008).
5. 3 John 4.
6. Psalm 127:3-5.

CHAPTER 15

1. Job 12:13, NLT.
2. Dr. Larry Crabb, *Counseling by Encouragement* tape series.
3. Proverbs 4:23.
4. 1 Samuel 16:7.

CHAPTER 16

1. 1 Samuel 18:1.
2. Ephesians 4:15-16.

3. Rape, Abuse, and Incest National Network (RAINN), "Effects of Rape," Who Are the Victims? http://www.rainn.org/get-information/statistics/sexual-assault-victims (accessed October 14, 2008).

4. Dan B. Allender, *The Wounded Heart*, rev. ed. (Colorado Springs: NavPress, 2008), 13.

5. Dan B. Allender, *The Wounded Heart*, 20.

6. John 8:1-11; John 4:1-30; Luke 7:36-50.

7. John 8:7.

8. John 8:11.

9. 1 Corinthians 6:16-18.

10. Psalm 107:2.

11. 1 Samuel 16:7.

12. Romans 2:4.

13. Romans 2:4.

14. 1 Corinthians 6:18.

15. Romans 12:2.

16. James 5:16.

17. James 4:7-8.

18. 1 Peter 5:8.

19. 1 John 4:4.

20. Proverbs 11:14.

21. Ephesians 6:12.

22. 1 Thessalonians 5:16-17.

23. Romans 8:31, NIV.

24. Romans 12:1.

25. John 8:11, NKJV.

CHAPTER 17

1. 1 Corinthians 7:28, NIV.

2. Matthew 5:27-28.

3. Matthew 11:15.

4. Proverbs 5:18-19.

5. For more on building a wall of protection around your marriage, we recommend Jerry B. Jenkins, Hedges: *Loving Your Marriage Enough to Protect It* (Wheaton, IL: Crossway, 2005).

6. Job 31:1, NIV.

7. James 4:7-8.

8. Romans 5:20, NLT.

9. Ephesians 6:12.

10. Matthew 19:8.

11. Focus on the Family, "What Does Research Say About the Impact of Divorce on Kids?" http://family.custhelp.com/cgi-bin/family.cfg/php/enduser/std_adp.php?p_faqid=1161&p_created=1044651946 (accessed October 14, 2008), citing data from Judith S. Wallerstein and Joan B. Kelly, *Surviving the Breakup* (New York: Basic Books, 1980), 33, 48, 236, 46, 211.

12.   Malachi 2:16, NIV.

13.   Jeremiah 3:8.

CHAPTER 18

1.   2 Samuel 13:14.

2.   Desmond Morris, *Intimate Behavior* (New York: Kodansha America, 1971).

3.   Romans 16:16.

4.   Colossians 3:17.

CHAPTER 19

1.   1 Thessalonians 5:18, emphasis added.

2.   Galatians 5:13.

3.   Clifford and Joyce Penner, *The Gift of Sex: A Guide to Sexual Fulfillment* (Nashville: Thomas Nelson, 2003), 26.

4.   Clifford and Joyce Penner, *The Gift of Sex*, 70-85 as adapted from Masters and Johnson, *Human Sexual Response* (Boston: Brown, Little & Co., 1966).

5.   Proverbs 11:14, MSG.

CHAPTER 20

1.   Deuteronomy 24:5.

2.   Encarta Dictionary Online, s.v. "lust," http://encarta.msn.com/dictionary_/lust. html (accessed October 14, 2008).

3.   Song of Songs 4:16.

4.   Song of Songs 2:3.

5.   Leviticus 18:22: "You shall not lie with a male as one lies with a female; it is an abomination."

6.   John 14:15.

7.   Linda Dillow and Lorraine Pintus, *Intimate Issues* (Colorado Springs: WaterBrook, 1999), 199-201.

8.   Philippians 2:3-4.

9.   1 Corinthians 6:12, NIV.

10.   Song of Songs 6:3.

11.   Song of Songs 5:1.

CHAPTER 21

1.   Encarta Dictionary Online, s.v. "duty," http://encarta.msn.com/dictionary_/duty. html (accessed October 14, 2008).

2.   1 Samuel 16:7, NIV.

3.   Song of Songs 6:3.

4.   Ken Gire, *Windows of the Soul* (Grand Rapids: Zondervan, 1996).

CHAPTER 22

1.   John 14:6, emphasis added.

2.   Proverbs 14:12, emphasis added.

3. We first heard about sexual agreements from Dr. Douglas Weiss's book *Sex, Men, and God* (Lake Mary, FL: Strang, 2002).
4. Amos 3:3, NIV.

EPILOGUE

1. 1 Corinthians 7:28, NIV.
2. 3 John 4, NIV.
3. Revelation 19:7.
4. Proverbs 29:18, KJV.
5. Mark 8:29.
6. Ben Patterson, "The Spirit Says Arise" (chapel message, Hope College Dimnent Chapel, Holland, MI, 1996-1997), referring to Acts 4:12.
7. John 14:12: "Truly, truly, I say to you, he who believes in Me, the works that I do, he will do also; and greater works than these he will do; because I go to the Father."
8. Malachi 4:6.

NOTES

+

+

+

+

+

+

+

+

+

+

+

+

+

+

+

+

+

+

it's not about me

NOTES

+

+

+

+

+

+

+

+

+

+

+

+

+

+

+

+

+

+

+